Gay and Lesbian Cops

GAY AND
LESBIAN
COPS

Diversity and Effective Policing

Roddrick A. Colvin

LYNNE
RIENNER
PUBLISHERS

BOULDER
LONDON

Published in the United States of America in 2012 by
Lynne Rienner Publishers, Inc.
1800 30th Street, Boulder, Colorado 80301
www.rienner.com

and in the United Kingdom by
Lynne Rienner Publishers, Inc.
3 Henrietta Street, Covent Garden, London WC2E 8LU

Library of Congress Cataloging-in-Publication Data
Colvin, Roddrick A.
 Gay and lesbian cops : diversity and effective policing /
Roddrick A. Colvin.
     p. cm.
 Includes bibliographical references and index.
 ISBN 978-1-58826-837-2 (hc : alk. paper)
 1. Gay police officers—United States. 2. Gay police officers—
Great Britain. 3. Lesbian police officers—United States.
4. Lesbian police officers—Great Britain. 5. Discrimination in law enforcement
—United States. 6. Discrimination in law enforcement—Great Britain. I. Title.
 HV8024.C65 2012
 363.2086'64—dc23
                                                              2011041077

British Cataloguing in Publication Data
A Cataloguing in Publication record for this book
is available from the British Library.

Printed and bound in the United States of America

The paper used in this publication meets the requirements
of the American National Standard for Permanence of
Paper for Printed Library Materials Z39.48-1992.

5 4 3 2 1

Contents

Tables and Figures

Tables

Figures

Acknowledgments

I would like to thank all the people in law enforcement who made this book possible, especially the officers from the Metropolitan Police Department in Washington, D.C., and the Hampshire and Wiltshire constabularies in the United Kingdom. Officers from these three organizations met with me on their own time to offer insights and perspectives on policing. Without them, this book would not have been possible.

I would also like to thank several colleagues who offered substantive comments on several of the themes in this book: Maria D'Agostino, Jeanne-Maria Col, Catherine Horiuchi, Russ Lidman, Peter Mameli, Eric Martin, David Schleifer, and Brad Wright.

Support for this book was generously provided by the Professional Staff Congress–City University of New York, the City University of New York Diversity Projects Development Fund, and the Academy for Critical Incident Analysis.

1

Lesbian and Gay
Police Officers

On September 28, 2000, nineteen-year-old freshman Eric
Franklin Plunkett was found dead in his dorm room at Gallaudet
University, the world-renowned school for the deaf and hard-of-hearing
in Washington, D.C. Plunkett had been beaten to death in an environment that considered itself as much a family as a university. With just
over 2,000 students, Gallaudet is a close-knit community, with strong
ties to the deaf and hard-of-hearing around the world. The university has
many safety protocols in place specifically designed with its community
in mind, including a security force trained in sign language, a strict visi-
tation policy, and restricted barcode access to residents' dormitories. In
such a community, crime is low and death—not to mention murder—is
rare. Plunkett's murder represented only the third violent death in the
university's history.[1]

On Friday, September 29, Washington's Metropolitan Police
Department (MPD) dispatched fifteen detectives to the university to
investigate Plunkett's murder. The detectives, with the assistance of
interpreters, interviewed students and other campus community members. The initial investigation yielded little information and incomplete
data. The MPD detectives were able to surmise that Plunkett was gay,
and that he had had an altercation with a friend prior to his death. This
information led officers to focus their investigation on a fellow student,
Thomas Minch. On October 3, under internal pressure as well as pressure from the university community, the MPD accused Minch of
Plunkett's murder. Minch was questioned for six hours, and charged
with second-degree murder based on his violent behavior and inconsistent responses during the interrogation: Minch repeatedly slammed his

1

fists on the table during questioning, and lied about having had a sexual encounter with Plunkett. However, due to lack of evidence, within twenty-four hours charges against Minch were dropped and he was released from custody. In a public statement, the MPD noted that Minch was being released without prejudice, but was still considered a suspect. Based on that information, the university barred Minch from the campus pending the resolution of the Plunkett murder investigation. Although Minch had a confirmed alibi (witnesses had seen him at a theater on the night of the murder), the detectives focused their efforts on gathering additional evidence against him.

Despite interviews with the campus community and pursuit of anonymous tips, the investigation stalled after Minch was released. As the months dragged on, the campus community, the larger deaf and hard-of-hearing community, and the lesbian and gay community began to express concerns about their safety, accusing the MPD of ignoring them and not taking the murder investigation seriously. In particular, lesbian and gay students expressed concerns about antigay incidents that were reported to police but not investigated. Additionally, many in the campus community were offended that the police chief cited "communications problems" as the main reason that the murder investigation was progressing so slowly. Many students, faculty, and other community members highlighted the fact that the campus community was filled with people who interacted with the hearing community on a daily basis. These community members use spoken language, read lips, or use interpreters to communicate. The president of Gallaudet's student council noted that such an excuse would not be tolerated in non-English-speaking communities in D.C., and thus was not acceptable for the deaf and hard-of-hearing community.

Given the lack of progress by the MPD and the investigating officers, it is easy to imagine that Plunkett's murder might have gone unsolved. Because Plunkett was gay, some people thought that his murder might have been hate-motivated. It was this suspicion that led two lesbian police officers to return to Gallaudet to interview members of the gay community, specifically members of the university's lesbian, gay, and straight student group, the Lambda Society, of which Plunkett was the secretary. Based on their in-depth interviews, the officers were convinced that the focus of the investigation should be shifted to obtaining forensics data from Plunkett's dorm room and personal computer, which might yield better information about the murder and which the MPD detectives had failed to do as part of their initial investigation. The efforts of these officers eventually proved fruitful, but not for this case and not before another student was also murdered on campus.

On February 3, over four months after Plunkett had been beaten to death, Benjamin Scott Varner was stabbed to death in the same dorm building. Like Plunkett, Varner was also nineteen years old and a freshman at Gallaudet. Because the primary suspect in the Plunkett case, Minch, had been barred from campus, and because security had been tightened since the previous murder, Varner's death was even more surprising and upsetting. Campus members were unsettled by the fact that the killer was most likely among them and mostly likely a member of the community.

The MPD and the investigating detectives got a lucky break when Joseph Mesa was recorded on video cashing a check drawn from Benjamin Varner's account. The police immediately focused on Mesa as their primary suspect. During the interrogation, Mesa voluntarily confessed to having murdered not only Varner but also Plunkett. Despite the fact that Mesa had a history of violence and that he had used Plunkett's credit card to buy clothing online and divert it to his own address, investigators had missed him as a suspect. In both murders, Mesa's motive appeared to have been greed. With Mesa's confession and charge, Minch was officially exonerated.

Two students dead, one student falsely arrested, and a community in shambles, all because the police department did not have the capacity or cultural competency to work with the communities directly affected by these crimes.

Why This Case Matters

Though it is impossible to know for sure whether this case could have been handled more efficiently and effectively had the lesbian officers been involved from the beginning, clearly their personal experiences and professional skills improved their understanding of the situation and gave them unique insights into certain elements of the case. The officers knew whom to speak with about the incident, understood the social and cultural norms of the community, and had credibility among those interviewed. Had these officers been consulted or included at the beginning of the case, it is possible that the MPD would have better understood the exchanges that occurred during Minch's six-hour interrogation. For example, they might have been better informed and prepared for the reaction they received when detectives accused him of being gay. It is also possible that the MPD would not have wasted almost five months trying to build a case against the wrong suspect. Earlier involvement by the lesbian officers would also have been valuable in maintaining positive community relations as the investigation progressed. At a minimum, lesbian and gay students and community members would have felt safer and more at home in the larger community if the MPD had deployed these officers to investigate previously reported hate incidents.

This case highlights the importance of diversity among officers for community policing. It also highlights the importance of having officers who are culturally competent. The primary investigators missed important elements of the case due to incompetence, homophobia, and ignorance. In this context, good policing requires officers who are committed to serving and knowledgeable about their communities. Good policing—policing that is effective, efficient, and, from a community perspective, equitable—requires officers to bring their unique perspectives, histories, experiences, and identities to the job.

Though the Plunkett and Varner murders resulted in the MPD redoubling its efforts to increase diversity on the force, including diversity in regard to sexual orientation, and to hire and train culturally competent lesbian and gay community liaison officers, such efforts have not been the norm for the majority of police agencies and officers around the world. Among the police agencies that have embraced lesbian and gay officers among their ranks in the pursuit of work force diversity are those in Western European countries such as Sweden, the United Kingdom, the Netherlands, Spain, and Germany. Several other nations around the world have also been leaders in this area, including Canada, Australia, New Zealand, and Iceland. The efforts of the United States have been more nuanced and less uniform. The local nature of policing in the United States means that communities vary greatly depending on location, size, socioeconomic status, history, and leadership. These variations have resulted in the welcoming of gay and lesbian liaison officers in unexpected places, such as Fargo, North Dakota, and San Antonio, Texas. They have also produced resistance in unexpected places, such as Atlanta, Georgia, and Boston, Massachusetts.

This book examines and discusses the work lives of lesbian and gay police officers, and attempts to assess their impact on policing today. Past research on this group has been limited to narrative discussions of small pools of officers operating in hostile work environments. For example, in 1993, two seminal books were published about lesbian and gay police officers: Stephen Leinen's *Gay Cops* and Marc Burke's *Coming Out of the Blue*. Leinen provided valuable insights into the work and personal lives of forty-one lesbian and gay police officers in New York City, highlighting the discrimination and harassment that officers expected, perceived, and experienced. Burke's book, focusing on officers in the United Kingdom, chronicled the daily lives of lesbian and gay officers and how they managed their sexual identities in what was often a hostile work environment.

While this research was instrumental in helping to improve the law enforcement environment for lesbian and gay people in policing, it no longer represents the situation in which many lesbian and gay police officers serve. Today, many lesbian and gay officers serve in communities that have nondiscrimination laws, equal benefits ordinances, and, in some cases, legal same-sex marriage. In the United States, 27 states and over 200 local jurisdictions expressly prohibit public employment discrimination on the basis of sexual orientation (Human Rights Campaign, 2010). In the United Kingdom, police agencies are now among the most gay-friendly employers in the country (Stonewall, 2010). Openly lesbian and gay officers now serve at all levels of law enforcement, including the highest levels of management and leadership. They often work as liaisons to the broader lesbian and gay community, and aid in training and sensitizing law enforcement about the unique needs of this community. Also, many officers find support from other officers through gay law enforcement associations. These associations have become the primary advocates of change for lesbian and gay people in police service. In short, the experiences and work lives of lesbian and gay officers— and others in law enforcement—are richer, fuller, and more complex than previous research suggests. Furthermore, their open participation in policing, corrections, and courts has had a direct impact on criminal justice and law enforcement in both the United States and the United Kingdom.

In this book I explore both the barriers that openly lesbian and gay officers face and the opportunities they encounter. I also explore how police agencies have evolved to become more professional regarding— if not outwardly friendly toward—the idea of police agency diversity as well as more responsive to the needs of the many communities they serve, including the lesbian and gay community.

To tell this more complex story about the lives of lesbian and gay officers, I use both qualitative and quantitative data. Like previous scholars in this area, I conducted interviews with openly lesbian and gay officers—in my case, with members of the Metropolitan Police Department in Washington, D.C., and with members of the Wiltshire and Hampshire constabularies in the United Kingdom. These qualitative interviews are the basis for this book's in-depth stories describing the lives of lesbian and gay officers. The information gathered from these valuable conversations is intermingled throughout the narrative with material drawn from archival documents and other sources relating to the communities in which the officers serve. I also attempt to connect the issues raised in my conversations with lesbian and gay officers to contemporary issues in policing, lesbian and gay studies, and human resource management and theory.

For quantitative data, this book relies on original survey data from lesbian and gay officers. I conducted these surveys in the summer of 2007 at the International Conference of Gay and Lesbian Criminal Justice Professionals, held in Providence, Rhode Island, and in the fall of 2009 in the United Kingdom through online distribution. The data resulting from these surveys were valuable in understanding the aggregate experiences of the officers. Additionally, these data were used to articulate perceptions of their personal and work lives that many lesbian and gay officers share and that are therefore more generalizable than qualitative stories. By integrating the unique narratives with aggregated, quantitative data, this book provides a comprehensive, contemporary view of the lives and shared experiences of lesbian and gay police officers.

I believe that the experiences of these officers together represent a unique and important contribution to our understanding of policing and to our ideas about experiences in the workplace. While law enforcement careers were, for the most part, opened to racial minorities and women via legal mandates, this has not been the case for openly lesbian and gay people in law enforcement. And, while the racial and gender integration of policing has influenced and informed the lesbian and gay experience, the experiences of lesbian and gay people in policing are different. For example, while policies exist in both the United States and the United Kingdom to prevent employment discrimination based on sexual orientation, neither country has adopted explicit positive or affirmative action plans to increase the proportion of lesbian and gay people in law enforcement. To date, efforts to target and recruit lesbian and gay people into policing have been local and voluntary in nature.

Similarities Between the US and UK Experiences

Policing history, customs, and practices in the United States and the United Kingdom are not identical, but the similarities are much more plentiful than the differences, and each country has much to teach us about policing in modern Western societies. One similarity is that both countries have moved toward the community model as a strategy for better policing. Diffusion of innovation between the two countries about policing has no doubt contributed to their similar evolution. The efforts of lesbian and gay officers to achieve equality represents another similarity, in that professional associations for lesbian and gay officers emerged in both the United States and the United Kingdom at nearly the same time, with similar missions, goals, and agendas.

With the exception of the quantitative chapters and the case studies on the Washington, D.C., Metropolitan Police and the Wiltshire Constabulary, I consider the experiences of lesbian and gay officers in both countries together. Where similarities are apparent, I attempt to make comparisons, and where differences are apparent, I try to draw distinctions. The qualitative and quantitative data, as well as the literature, suggest this is an appropriate approach (Boin, 2001). Except where there are specific differences of policing practice, I have approached the experiences of US and British lesbian and gay police officers as being very similar. The shared occupational similarities are more prominent than the geographic differences.

Overview of the Book

Each of the chapters that follow focuses on a specific aspect of policing in relation to lesbian and gay people. Chapter 2 introduces readers to multiple strands of the relevant literature, including background information on discrimination in public employment against lesbian and gay people, the ways in which sexual minorities manage disclosure in the workplace, the recent history of lesbian and gay people in policing, and the development of shared perceptions about the work environment. Chapter 2 also shows how organizational effectiveness can be compromised when police agencies resist diversification, but improved when agencies embrace planned change.

Chapter 3 discusses the emergence and evolution of community policing. Community policing is a philosophy that promotes police and community strategies that support the systematic use of partnerships and problem-solving techniques to proactively address community and law enforcement issues, concerns, or problems. Community policing has been one of several factors that helps to explain why many police agencies have actively attempted to diversify their ranks. The joint community and law enforcement nature of community policing has encouraged agencies to collaborate with a number of communities, including the lesbian and gay community, to improve the efficiency, effectiveness, and equity of law enforcement.

Chapter 4 explores the experiences and shared perceptions of lesbian and gay officers in the United States and the United Kingdom. This chapter presents quantitative information about the officers, including demographic information, experiences in policing, special work opportunities and barriers for openly lesbian and gay officers, and changes in work climate over time. The chapter also offers analysis of the variations between the agencies in the two countries.

Chapter 5 discusses the various ways in which lesbian and gay people have uniquely served in law enforcement. Sometimes, openly lesbian or gay officers serve as informal sources of information for an agency and its staff. In other cases, their work includes diversity training and other human resource–related functions, such as recruitment. In their most highly integrated role, lesbian and gay officers are engaged in investigative work that includes service to all communities, including the lesbian and gay community.

Chapter 6 consists of two case studies: one in the United States and one in the United Kingdom. The US case study highlights the experiences of the Gay and Lesbian Liaison Unit in Washington, D.C. It explains the emergence and evolution of the unit and its work in the Metropolitan Police Department. The UK case study explores the history and functions of lesbian and gay liaison officers (GLOs, also known as LAGLOs) in the Wiltshire Constabulary. It highlights the successes and challenges faced by liaison officers in the United Kingdom. This perspective is unusual in that it focuses on issues relating to lesbian and gay officers living and working in a rural community, including the services they offer to a largely invisible lesbian and gay community.

Chapter 7 explores the role of professional police associations in helping to diversify police agencies. As lesbian and gay officers began to form networks, professional associations emerged to support these officers. These associations, modeled after other minority associations, helped to organize and mobilize lesbian and gay officers as a visible minority within policing. These associations have been among the most important catalysts in diversifying police agencies, by acting as both supportive and antagonistic actors within them.

Chapter 8 identifies organizational, human resource, and administrative efforts to improve recruitment and retention of lesbian and gay police officers. This chapter also articulates some scholarly based best practices and recommendations that can guide other police agencies and other public service organizations as they embrace more diverse work forces.

Chapter 9 offers some empirical best practices based on the data and information drawn from the interviews, focus groups, and surveys conducted in writing this book. These best practices act as a roadmap for the future of law enforcement and for the profession's efforts to create more diverse and inclusive workplaces.

Finally, I have dispersed throughout the book several profiles of lesbian and gay police officers. These profiles are an opportunity for officers to speak, in their own voices, about important issues such as the experience of being a liaison officer, the experience of being openly lesbian or gay, both on the force and in the community, and the experience of handling issues of specific interest to lesbian and gay people, including hate crimes.

* * *

A few notes about the terms: First, I generally use the term *police agency,* even though this is uncommon in both the United States and the United Kingdom, where *police department, police organization, police service,* and *constabulary* are more frequently used. Although any of these terms might serve, *police agency* strikes me as the most inclusive; it simply denotes the local law enforcement organization responsible for protecting life and property in a community. This is usually accomplished through patrol, requests for assistance, and collaborative prevention efforts. Second, in most cases I refer to *lesbian and gay* officers rather than *lesbian, gay, bisexual, and transgender* (LGBT) officers. Since my qualitative data capture information about lesbian and gay officers only, and my quantitative data secure only minimal information about bisexual and transgender officers, my findings are not generalizable to the latter. Based on my previous work on transgender issues in the workplace (Colvin, 2007, 2008), I believe that the experiences of transgender police officers and community members are substantially different from those of lesbian and gay people. While beyond the scope of this book, transgender policing is certainly a worthy topic for further exploration.

Though this book offers a mostly positive perspective on the work of lesbian and gay officers, this is not to suggest that the struggle to make police agencies more responsive and diverse has been easy, nor does it suggest that the process is complete. As the survey data from both the United States and the United Kingdom indicate, lesbian and gay officers still face harassment and discrimination in the workplace. Some openly lesbian and gay officers are routinely subject to verbal abuse, and some conceal their sexuality to avoid persecution in their agencies. However, praiseworthy gains have indeed been made. In 1993, when Leinen's *Gay Cops* and Burke's *Coming Out of the Blue* were published, few would have imagined that lesbian and gay officers would soon serve openly in rural communities like those of Wiltshire or North Dakota, attain the rank of chief of police, and even run for elected office. Few would have imagined liaisons and units designed to protect, serve, and collaborate with local lesbian and gay communities. While much improvement is still needed in the majority of police agencies, I hope this book will serve as a blueprint and an inspiration for police agencies and other public service workplaces to become more efficient, effective, and equitable through inclusion and diversity.

Note

1. In 1980, a nineteen-year-old student was stabbed and pushed out of an eighth-story window at Benson Hall. In 1990, a forty-one-year-old former student collapsed after a dispute with an instructor and a struggle with campus security (Fernandez and Leonnig, 2000).

2
Old Issues, New Realities

In many ways the struggle of lesbian and gay police officers in law enforcement parallels both the struggles of other minorities in law enforcement and the broader struggle of lesbian and gay people in society. In this chapter I review several bodies of literature that place the experiences of lesbian and gay police officers within the broader context of discrimination and harassment, police culture, and shared values in the workplace. Within this context I also attempt to explain the effects of not creating or pursuing an inclusive and diverse police environment. The main effect of failure to create an inclusive and diverse force is an inability to effectively, efficiently, or equitably conduct police work. Finally, I begin to lay the groundwork for the idea of planned change as an approach for managing the transition from traditional policing agencies to community-involved, inclusive, and diverse policing agencies.

Employment Discrimination Based on Sexual Orientation

In the United States, nondiscrimination laws have been most prolific at the local level of government. This has been helpful to lesbian and gay people wanting to enter policing, as most police agencies are governed at the local level in most jurisdictions. Local adoption of such laws, however, has created a patchwork of regulations with varying degrees of implementation and effectiveness. Even though a police agency might fall under the jurisdiction of local nondiscrimination laws, the agency might still resist enforcement of those laws. Reported cases of continuing discrimination are not uncommon. Even in a city known for progressive and strong nondiscrimination ordinances, such as New York, discrimination can be a challenge for lesbian and gay officers. In 2007, New York was sued by openly gay police officer Michael Harrington, who had experienced a laundry list of problems and issues during his employment at the New York City Police Department (NYPD). These included being called a "faggot" by numerous officers, being snubbed while attending the annual department Christmas party with his partner, being subjected to innuendos about his treatment of certain suspects, receiving a death threat, and being transferred to a West Village precinct to "be with his people" (Hartocollis, 2007).

Research on employment discrimination suggests that actual or perceived discrimination based on sexual orientation may negatively affect hiring, firing, and promotion. This research reports wide variations in the level of discrimination experienced by lesbian and gay people (Badgett, 2007). The most commonly cited research indicates that between 25 and 66 percent of gay men, lesbians, and bisexuals experience employment discrimination (Alderson, 2003). Reports of witnessed discrimination are much higher than those of experienced discrimination based on the personal/group discrepancy (Ruggiero et al., 2000; Taylor et al., 1990). This personal/group discrepancy occurs because witnessed discrimination is subject to a multiplier effect: when several people witness a single act of discrimination, they may all report the same act. By contrast, an act of discrimination experienced by one person but not witnessed by others will be reported only by the person experiencing the discrimination.

Most research on employment of gay and lesbian people focuses on discrimination in hiring, firing, and promotion based on sexual orientation (Button, 2001; Colvin and Riccucci, 2002), although some research also deals with inequities in wages, benefits, and other work-related issues (Anastas, 2001; Chung, 2001; Riccucci and Gossett, 1996). Most recent studies have focused on costs to lesbian and gay employees in terms of physical and mental health and costs to institutions in terms of productivity, turnover, and organizational cohesion through shared values (Van Hoye and Lievens, 2003). Finally, several US Government Accountability Office studies (1997, 2000, and 2002) have considered the potential impact of a national nondiscrimination law to protect lesbian and gay people by assessing outcomes of state nondiscrimination efforts.

This research builds on efforts to better understand shared perceptions in the workplace and the effects of shared perceptions on both individual employees as well as whole organizations. Studies collecting this data over time will help us to better understand the capacity of organizations to deter discrimination, and how organizational efforts affect individual employees.

Managing Disclosure

Because the work environment, even in communities where nondiscrimination laws have been enacted, may remain hostile to lesbian and gay workers, individuals must decide whether and when to reveal themselves as lesbian or gay. Heterosexuals typically do not have to decide whether to explicitly reveal their sexuality, because heterosexuality is usually assumed. Members of other groups that suffer discrimination, like women and people of color, typically cannot hide their gender or race. But homosexuality is different, and homophobic discrimination is therefore different. Disclosure of sexual orientation is a delicate matter for lesbian and gay police officers (Button 2001; Chrobot-Mason and Quiñones, 2001; Chung, 2001). In other workplaces, there are sometimes compelling reasons for withholding information about one's sexual orientation. These considerations include the legal protection one has in the jurisdiction, the possible reactions of coworkers and superiors, and the disclosure's impact on police-partner bonding and on advancement opportunities. The unique nature of police agencies and policing makes the disclosure question particularly interesting. Although lesbian and gay people have a long history in policing, it is only recently that we have been able to study openly lesbian and gay police. In the nearly twenty years that have elapsed since the first major works on this subject emerged, the social, political, demographic, and professional environments have all changed extensively.

Unlike gender and race, sexual orientation is not an observable characteristic. Because it is not observable, lesbians and gay men must decide whether, when, and to what degree to disclose their sexual orientation (Van Hoye and Lievens, 2003; Chojnacki and Gelberg, 1994). Thus, in the workplace, employees have to disclose their sexual orientation before its influence on earnings or other work-related matters can be studied. Without such disclosure, we have little evidence to assume correlations between an employee's sexual orientation and employment-related actions by employers. Of course, the kind and degree of impact that workplace disclosure can have may be influenced by a number of other factors, including career choice, length of time in career, future career options, socioeconomic status, industry, and overall workplace climate. Because they have the option to disclose sexual orientation or not, workers may be able to better manage and mitigate discriminatory actions.

Of course, the decision not to disclose one's sexual orientation does not come without costs. As Julie Gedro (2009) suggested, workplace-disclosure decisions for lesbian and gay people are often influenced by internalized beliefs about gender roles and heterosexuality. As lesbian and gay people develop and maintain their careers, the decisions that they continually face about identity management represent their greatest challenge. To operate effectively in many work environments, they often have to make decisions that compromise their personal integrity, including maintaining a false heterosexual identity or avoiding issues of sexuality, family, or home life altogether.

There are scenarios, however, in which lesbian and gay people are able to reveal their sexual orientation explicitly and integrate it into the work context. Using the "work adjustment" theory, Suzanne Degges-White and Marie Shoffner (2002) noted that lesbian and gay people who disclose their sexual orientation explicitly at work are more likely to form better relationships at work, are better able to adapt to the environment or culture, and are better able to fulfill psychological needs. Degges-White and Shoffner noted that, taken together, the benefits derived from being open about one's sexual orientation may supersede any negative consequences of disclosure, in that employee satisfaction, social support, and mental well-being are optimized. Of course, employees who are more satisfied and have better work relationships are believed to contribute more to the organization and its efforts to meet its mission and goals.

Lesbians and Gay Men in Policing

During the past two decades, researchers have approached the topic of lesbian and gay people in law enforcement from a number of different angles. Earlier research focused on the idea that being homosexual and being a police officer represented dual—often conflicting—identities. Scholars attempted to understand how officers reconciled a "deviant" behavior with their law enforcement role as regulators of deviance (Leinen, 1993; Burke, 1994). These studies—based on interviews—spawned interesting research about the mental health, productivity, ability to cope, and self-acceptance of lesbian and gay police officers (Herek, 2003).

The issue of disclosure of sexual orientation in the workplace is related to the idea of dual identity, and a number of studies have considered the factors that affect when or if police officers reveal their sexual orientation on the job (Burke, 1993; Leinen, 1993; Miller, Forest, and Jurik, 2003). The idea of dual identity originated in the psychology literature and suggests that people split their identity as a coping mechanism to operate in different environments. In this understanding, officers split their "gay" identity from their "police" identity.

The general consensus is that lesbians and gay men in law enforcement are under tremendous pressure to conform to prevailing law enforcement gender stereotypes, and that each lesbian and gay officer must determine the costs and benefits of revealing their sexual orientation at work. An individual's decision might include personal considerations such as physical safety, organizational considerations such as social isolation, or institutional considerations such as evaluation, promotion, and assignments. When the benefits exceed the costs, lesbians and gay men are more likely to disclose their sexual orientation. Of course, officers do not always have the option of managing disclosure at work. In many situations, officers—regardless of sexual orientation—are "outed" at work as lesbian or gay. When the person is lesbian or gay, this situation requires the person to reevaluate the costs and benefits and act accordingly. How an officer responds might include exhibiting homophobic actions, dating an opposite-sex partner, or revealing their sexual orientation as lesbian or gay.

Employees of the same organization often view the world from similar angles, and these shared perceptions can have a positive or negative influence on the workplace. For example, if a group of employees all share a negative perception about management, these employees might be less committed to the organization, and this attitude might affect the organization's efficiency and effectiveness. Conversely, when employees have positive shared perceptions, their commitment and motivation will be greater, which can translate into improved efficiency and effectiveness for the organization.

David Sklansky (2006) noted that police agencies have made great strides in diversification to include women and people of color. However, relatively little data exist about efforts to diversify in terms of sexual orientation. Furthermore, few studies have focused on the shared perceptions of lesbians and gay people in law enforcement. Given the unique culture of police agencies, their history of exclusion, and our evolving societal values and norms concerning sexual orientation, it is appropriate to consider the shared perceptions of lesbian and gay police officers (Colvin, 2009).

Recent research has focused on the shared perceptions of target populations in the workplace. The idea of shared perceptions builds on the notion that individual perceptions are often communicated to other people both inside and outside the organization. The individual's perceptions and experiences are also shaped by his or her membership in a specific group (Bolton, 2003). Such experiences and perceptions of the law enforcement workplace have been considered for a number of specific groups, including racial minorities (Alex, 1969; Bolton, 2003; Essed, 1991; Leinen, 1984; McCluskey, 2004), race and gender (Holder, Nee, and Ellis, 1999; Martin, 1994), and sexual orientation (Colvin, 2009). More recent works have examined the shared perceptions and work experiences of officers with multiple group memberships and their interactive effects. Kimberly Hassell and Steven Brandl (2009) explore the roles of race, sex, and sexual orientation and their effects on workplace stress.

Among the explorations of the work experiences of officers with minority status, scholarship around gender and policing remains among the most active and most relevant for this research. The role and experiences of women in policing have a direct connection to police agencies' emphasis on various policing strategies, including professionalism, community policing, and victim-centered policing. The work experiences, shared perceptions, barriers, and opportunities that women have experienced inform our understanding of the "outsider" status of nonmale, nonwhite, and assumed "straight" officers (Hassell and Brandl, 2009; Martin and Jurik, 2007; Myers, Forest, and Miller, 2004).

Perceptions about a workplace can have important implications for an organization. These perceptions can be viewed as either barriers or access points, creating either negative or positive disparities among employees (Bolton, 2003). From a human-resource perspective, perceptions, if shared, can have a dramatic effect on the culture, mission, operations, and productivity of an organization. For example, if there is a shared perception within an organization that men are promoted at a faster rate than equally qualified women, then women in that organization may be less motivated to perform at their highest level. In such a scenario, an inability to retain qualified women might become a residual effect of this shared perception. Conversely, we might consider the role of positive perceptions in an organization. If, for example, an agency has a history of being fair to women and of promoting them on merit, and if the employees share this perception, then women in the organization may be more motivated to perform at their highest level. In such a scenario, the organization with the reputation of being fair to women may well increase the number of qualified women in its work force.

Finally, valuable research has been conducted that considers the effects of lesbian and gay inclusion in the law enforcement environment (Belkin and McNichol, 2002; Miller, Forest, and Jurik, 2003; Myers, Forest, and Miller, 2004). Research on the attitudes and beliefs of heterosexual officers about their homosexual counterparts continues to grow (Bernstein and Kostelac, 2002; Lyons, DeValve, and Garner, 2008). Existing literature on attitudes and beliefs about lesbian and gay people suggests that familiarity with lesbian and gay people is highly correlated with positive perceptions of lesbian and gay people (Lewis, 2006). That is to say, knowing gay and lesbian people reduces animus toward them. Some of the most comprehensive research on inclusion and familiarity has been conducted in the context of integrating lesbians and gay men into the military. Although not perfectly analogous to police forces, the armed forces are also highly cohesive, formerly segregated, single-sex organizations and thus offer a good perspective on the potential challenges inherent in developing more inclusive police agencies (Belkin and McNichol, 2002; Koegel, 1996).

Despite its disparate themes and numerous threads, the existing literature on lesbian and gay people in policing highlights the interconnections between work life and private life. It confirms that people are more complex, both as individuals and as members of an organization, than might be assumed. This is, in fact, a positive evolution for the study of lesbian and gay police officers. No longer do we view police or other public servants as neutral bureaucrats who separate work from other parts of their lives. Instead, we accept them as people with integrated lives and values who, like other people, mesh work and private life. It is this diversity—I argue—that leads to better officers who are committed to the organization and its mission. Officers are less concerned about hiding their sexual orientation through irrational acts of aggression or use of force. They perceive themselves as valued members of the community and of the policing agencies, and work hard to make sure that the organization is able to meet its mission.

Police Agencies and Failure

Although many police agencies have made important strides in diversifying their work forces, challenges remain. Efforts by police agencies, like those of other organizations, are subject to failure. When an organization fails to give value to diversity and incorporate diversity into its culture, the organization will struggle in today's working environment (Noe, 2011). Diversity allows an organization to take advantage of the

Voices from the Field

Name: Karen Norris
Police agency: Metropolitan Police Department (Washington, D.C.)
Rank: Police officer
Length of service: Six years

On the visibility of lesbian and gay liaison officers in the community:

"In most cases, having been on the street, . . . I do not have to separate people where they're insinuating that maybe hate-bias has something to do with it, especially when it's in the gay community. We will go up to the situation and try to calm things down because they'll talk to us alone, whereas they won't talk to a big, burly sergeant . . . or officer so-and-so because they can sense right away that they don't want to be talking to them. A lot of things, probably, are not only under-reported but they're going to pick and choose who they talk to. And that's something that, honestly, when they want GLLU [Gay and Lesbian Liaison Unit] there . . . they come out, it does make a difference to the citizens, and you can see how it makes a difference. They really do care."

On whether or not lesbian and gay officers are better at working with gay suspects, victims, and witnesses:

"I think the same way that an African American officer can come into a domestic scene where it's two Caucasian gay males and be effective by using his head and having some training. . . . Just walking in there and being a human being, he can be just as effective. There are cases where you're not going to be as effective. Sometimes people do need to see that familiar face or someone that's like them that maybe they feel like they can have this understanding with. But me being a lesbian doesn't make me more effective with lesbians. . . . Well, here's the bottom line: police officers are police officers. You go to your job, and you work with some shitheads, and same thing here.

. . . Sometimes you can turn around and you know that there are certain officers that I would trust hands down with any scene, and I know they would do a good job because they are good human beings, because they genuinely go out every day to try to make a difference, and they care. Every scene, while they don't take it home, you know, I don't go home and cry about certain scenes, but when I'm there, it is personal. I want people to feel that I am per-

continues

Voices from the Field continued

sonally involved with them. Whether it's an act or not, I want them to know I genuinely care about what they're saying, and that I'm actively participating in something. And you don't get that with every officer, and that's with any job. It doesn't make me more effective because I'm gay. How am I more effective with narcotics or other issues?"

---

many ideas, experiences, cultures, and perspectives that employees bring to the workplace. Contemporary diversity focuses on a comprehensive range of qualities and backgrounds that are beyond just race and gender. A diverse working environment can create the context for developing effective working relationships with internal and external individuals from varied backgrounds. This is especially important for police agencies, particularly those engaged in community policing, which is built on the ideal that police agencies will communicate and work with the community to maintain order, decide policing priorities, and solve crimes. This philosophy recognizes that every individual has unique qualities to bring to the organization.

Police agencies that fail to diversify and to integrate minority officers, including lesbian and gay officers, risk compromising their ability to meet their missions. Because of the unique nature of police work, any employee who is not integrated into the force may become a "weak link" in the organization. As a weak link, an employee is more susceptible to corruption, which can involve compromising safety, disrupting training, and reducing cohesion among rank-and-file members.

Many different organizational factors help to explain why an organization might fail at integrating a group of police officers or fail to meet other critical aspects of its mission (O'Hara, 2005). Some common organizational factors that might affect the work lives of lesbian and gay officers include structural failure, oversight failure, cultural deviation, and institutionalization.

Structural Failure

Police agencies typically have well-defined systems of hierarchy and task division. These organizational characteristics are designed to provide direction and help the agency achieve its mission. Hierarchy can cause conflict and dysfunction, and this is especially true in paramilitary environments where authoritative personalities and the drive for success can hamper operational efficacy. Task division can also cause problems when specialized units perceive themselves as more important or capable than their counterparts in other divisions or agencies. Although almost every law enforcement agency has a formal hierarchy, informal and sometimes haphazard systems of decisionmaking and communication prevail. Thus, structural failures occur when the design of the organization, by way of standard operating procedures, processes, or policies, leads to malaise and dysfunction. These structural failures may be the result of planned change or evolve from unanticipated events that place pressure on the organization. Organizational "shadow structures" such as fraternal associations or unions can also influence progress and even prevent police management or leadership from recognizing areas that need reform. Unions and associations act to aggregate the voices of members, and to provide cultural, political, and social space for them. They can also be instrumental in helping to create alternative shared perceptions about other officers, their employers, and the missions of the organizations.

Oversight Failure

Oversight failure is a species of structural failure. Oversight failures emerge when accountability measures fail to detect deviations in the organization. These accountability measures could include external boards, internal auditors, and quality-control units (O'Hara, 2005). Moreover, these oversight entities, which are also organizations, are themselves prone to failure. Oversight units are often small and poorly funded, and may be co-opted either by management or by those they are assigned to oversee. For example, when a police officer fails to meet performance expectations, line officers, supervisors, or administrators may identify too closely with the offending coworker. Peer pressure not to report another officer for transgressions committed even while on duty may allow personal misbehavior to spiral out of control. Because of this, oversight units must be staffed by officers or members of the policing community who are above reproach. Any appearance of noncompliance by oversight personnel or of the unequal application of discipline will diminish the authority of agency policies or of the oversight entity itself.

Cultural Deviation

Police training, both in the academy and in the field, inculcates new officers into policing culture, which defines how police officers view the world and their respective role in society. Shift-work and the mind-set adopted by police officers can cause social isolation from those outside law enforcement. Cultural deviations are elements that arise and operate within a larger organization. Large organizations may contain cultural networks that are based on shared characteristics or beliefs and whose members are bound together through symbols or principles. Information can be controlled by such cultural networks, protecting deviant actors from detection or sanction. For example, peer privilege may allow for rule-violating behavior to be excused, ignored, or marginalized by the work-group culture. Line officers and even supervisors may be reluctant to expose mistakes or report unacceptable behavior to superiors because of what they perceive as capricious disciplinary practices. Such deviations can counter the mission or values of the police agency, often resulting in cultural clashes. A recent example of this failure is the scandal involving the New York Police Department fixing tickets, which was exposed in April 2011. Fixing tickets is the general practice of tearing up paperwork on traffic citations before it reaches court as a favor to officers' friends, family, and others. In this case at least forty officers were identified as engaging in this illegal practice, at the behest of the police union. Of course, fixing tickets extends beyond these officers and is practiced frequently in the NYPD. Officers are indoctrinated early in their careers to become team players and to help fellow officers whenever and wherever possible.

Institutionalization

Institutionalization occurs when the needs and preferences of employees supersede the needs and preferences of clients or customers. Institutionalization can also occur when employee needs override goals and objectives articulated in the mission of the organization. Over time, employees can begin to feel as if they "own" their organization and know what is best for it. In law enforcement, police officers may resist the fuller integration of minority groups out of a desire to save or protect the organization. Police agencies tend to face little external pressure to change their operations or structure, given law enforcement's monopoly of police function and because of the public's desire for safety. Organizational successes may lead to an uncritical environment in which superior performance is not aggressively pursued and employees feel comfortable yielding only marginal performance. Such institutionalized agencies may undergo declines, unrecognized by outsiders until a prominent failure exposes the problem. As Patrick O'Hara (2005) noted, institutionalization may be cured through a number of means, including transparency, competition, benchmarking, and external oversight.

* * *

There are many perspectives from which to understand organizational failure. In most situations, the structural, oversight, cultural, and institutional elements are intertwined and mutually reinforcing. Scholars often equate law enforcement failures with failures in police strategy or tactics. But according to my analysis, such failures are associated with compromising the mission of the law enforcement agency. The ability to carry out the mission of an organization can be severely hampered if employees do not share its values or support its goals.

Planned Change to Address Organizational Failure

One of the most commonly accepted approaches to reforming police agencies and responding to organizational failure is the practice of planned change, which is designed to alter individuals, groups, and organizational structures and processes (Jiao and Kocher, 2000). Planned change is specific and limited in scope, directed at improving the quality of life of an organization's clients; it includes a role for consumers and is guided by a change agent. Planned change often stems from declining resources, increased demand for accountability, and expansion of knowledge and technology. Planned change can also be the result of a critical incident, social or political change, or change in leadership. However, although well-documented planned change efforts have been undertaken in numerous law enforcement environments, none so far have focused on the inclusion of lesbian and gay people. But by learning the fundamentals of planned change, we can imagine applying its principles and practices to such a scenario. While the specific issues may vary, the core elements of planned change are universal in application.

Allan Jiao and Charles Kocher (2000) argued that police auditing can be one such effective method of bringing about planned change. Police auditing assesses the value of police services in terms of the amount of taxes and resources the public provides to the police. Police audits are conducted when the police are performing below their capacity; when there is potential for identifying improvements in management, organizational structure, and operating procedures; and when the police have experienced some controversy concerning their compliance with laws and regulations and need updated objective information for management. Essentially, auditing provides a full report of the state of the police agency, which becomes the basis for planned organizational change.

The police auditing process involves an input and an output. The input is the auditing team, which consists of the police agency being audited, the community affected, and any other group with a stake in the audit; the output is what happens as a result of the audit. Between the input and the output is a transformation process, which is a way of converting resources from the input into police activities. This process also involves the application of some key concepts in planned change. Jiao and Kocher (2000) use results from research conducted on the impact of a 1995 audit of the Camden Police Department requested by the state of New Jersey to illustrate the utility of effecting police change and reform.

The 1995 audit of the Camden Police Department was a systematic examination to identify problems that were damaging police effectiveness and efficiency and to suggest methods for addressing them. The seventy-five recommendations that were made can be broken down into four general categories:

1. *Organizational structure.* These recommendations concerned expanding the patrol program, increasing accountability, ensuring compliance with policies, avoiding fragmentation, and saving financial and human resources. Recommendations included a reorganization of the agency and dissolution of the department's special operations units.

2. *Police patrol.* These recommendations involved increasing the number of patrol officers, accomplishing workload proportionality, and increasing patrol-officer hiring and training and patrol-fleet maintenance.

3. *Police problems.* These recommendations included addressing false alarms, domestic violence incidents, and drug-related incidents more effectively so that officers could devote more time to crime prevention and deterrent patrol.

4. *Administrative support.* These recommendations included increasing police supervision, tightening discipline for excessive sick leave, reducing overtime, formalizing police procedures, increasing civilian staff functions, and raising qualifications for all staff.

Researchers Jiao and Kocher conducted both the process and the impact evaluations of the Camden Police Department. The evaluations focused on how the recommendations were developed, how police responded, and what effects the audit had on the police and on the city of Camden. Qualitative methods, including participant observations, personal interviews, and documentary research, were used to collect the data.

Implementation of an audit's recommendations is constrained by local conditions. With regard to the 1995 Camden Police Department audit, it is important to note that Camden has suffered from serious economic, social, and crime problems over the past three decades. It is the poorest city in New Jersey and the fifth poorest in the United States. The implementation team consisted of investigators from both inside and outside the Camden Police Department, in order to neutralize the partisan, race, and class problems, real or perceived, that could have arisen if one or the other side had taken control of the implementation process. The team divided the seventy-five recommendations into three types:

1. *Those requiring financial assistance.* These recommendations, which included the hiring of new officers, job promotions to match the organizational structure, and better management of overtime assignments for officers, were for the most part not implemented.

2. *Those not requiring financial assistance.* These recommendations, which were implemented quickly given their lack of expense, included redistributing the use of captains within a command, increasing the number of police patrols, computerizing records, instituting disciplinary processes for abuse of sick time, expanding training, establishing new internal-affairs policies, and increasing the number of officers assigned to the agency's domestic violence and vice units.

3. *Those compatible with the goals and objectives of the agency's mission.* Except for those related to program elimination and organizational rearrangement, these recommendations were all implemented. The primary obstacles to their implementation were the unions and some officers in specialized units who saw assignment to patrol duty as a demotion. (Some changes, such as the transferring of traffic duties related to fatal accidents to the agency's investigative division, were rejected by department administration.)

Ninety percent of recommendations were implemented within two years following the audit's completion. Generally speaking, the Camden Police Department audit resulted in better police performance (measurable by reduced cost), increased police accountability, strengthened patrol manpower, improved workload distribution, reduced sick calls, intensified problem-oriented police activities, and higher arrest rates. In conclusion, Jiao and Kocher found that auditing can be an effective method of bringing about planned change in a police agency.

Eight Essential Elements
of the Model of Planned Change

Jiao and Kocher (2000) identified eight essential elements for the model of planned change. The first is the presence of external and internal forces and pressures for change. In Camden, such pressure came from the high demand for police services and declining resources to meet these demands. These pressures were related to a high crime rate, the city's depleted tax base, and the lack of patrol officers on the street. Conflict arose between the state government, the Camden Police Department, and the local community, which ultimately transformed the agency's problems into a political issue and led to a general consensus that change was necessary.

The second essential element is the existence of organizational dysfunction due to performance gaps and other problems. For example, that Camden's former chief of police requested the audit highlighted his awareness of an organizational disequilibrium within the agency. The Camden Police Department was unable to meet service demands and lacked technological training, which inhibited effective communication and reporting. Productivity and morale were low. Policies, procedures, and training were unclear.

The third is the systematic examination and collection of relevant data by police auditors. This involves rigorous research and should provide a complete analysis of the agency and an objective description of the current conditions of the police as related to crime problems, police organizational structure, and operations. One of the researchers involved in the audit (Jiao) was on the oversight board for implementation, and the other (Kocher) was a senior member of the Camden Police Department. Because the auditing team was composed of internal and external members, it was in a strategic position to influence change.

The fourth is the presence of innovative, rational decisionmaking by police change agents. Thus, police leaders must consider the various issues an agency faces from a comprehensive perspective and devise an empirically based and creative plan to confront them. It was because of this element that the Camden Police Department was able to restructure its patrol operations and to substantially increase the number of officers on patrol.

The fifth essential element for the model of planned change is a commitment to develop solutions by setting goals and objectives and to search for workable alternatives. It is important to link recommendations with goals to avoid a sterile, purely rationalist approach to the problems and to increase the probability that the final outcomes will resemble what is desired or expected. The Camden Police Department developed a team to identify immediate, short-term, and long-term goals.

The sixth essential element is the requirement that change be implemented through activities that control sources of resistance while simultaneously developing the organization. The Camden Police Department intensified education and training of police officers and modified certain organizational practices, procedures, and policies. Moreover, audit implementation is not an isolated process: police leaders should seize this opportunity to give shape and direction to the agency's culture through a clearly articulated vision of what the organization stands for—a vision that embodies core values and purposes.

The seventh essential element is the maintenance and monitoring of planned change. Commitment is needed to keep officers from resorting to old practices. In the Camden Police Department, two management teams to oversee the progress of change were implemented: one was a department team created specifically to monitor planned change, and the other was responsible for training police personnel in activities related to change.

The eighth and final element is feedback or outcome evaluation of police efficiency and effectiveness. To accomplish this, evaluations of efficiency and effectiveness must be conducted after police have completed implementation of the recommendations. If the desired outcomes have not been achieved, a reconsideration of the recommendations may be necessary. Of course, there are difficulties with outcome evaluations and planned change efforts with regard to police audits. As Jiao and Kocher noted, many of the benefits of evaluation and audits are intangible or qualitative in nature. Audits do not always lend themselves to saving technical, human, or financial resources for police agencies. Moreover, audits are susceptible to statistical fallacy when police agencies increase their clearance rates (numbers of cases solved) by changing recording procedures or the types of cases to be included in an audit.

Implications of Successful Planned Change

Successful planned change efforts can have a dramatic impact on the way police agencies operate and on the communities they serve. In terms of the lesbian and gay community, a police agency that has successfully transformed from a traditional policing model to a community policing model will be better able to address issues, problems, and concerns within the lesbian and gay community. These issues include hate crimes, same-sex intimate-partner violence, public sex, school bullying and suicide, transgender service provision, and suspect harassment and violence. In most police agencies and constabularies, with a few excep-tions, either too little attention is paid to these issues or the responsibili-ty falls to known lesbian and gay officers who may or may not be prop-erly trained to handle them. As we will see in subsequent chapters, these officers usually end up taking on these issues in addition to their regular responsibilities. With the exception of hate crimes or other high-profile incidents, many police agencies—in their current form—are reticent to commit limited financial, human, and other resources to initiate change in these areas or to commit to full models of planned change.

Why This Case Matters

The Camden planned change process gives us perspective in terms of what is really needed to successfully reform a police agency. In attempt-ing to address organizational failures, the Camden Police Department engaged issues and problems on several different fronts. Additionally, the efforts of the agency had to be measured and evaluated in order to understand the nature of the changes being promoted. All eight of the elements of the Camden approach could be applicable to an organization interested in community policing or in becoming inclusive of lesbian and gay officers. This approach can be used to address organizational failures that are causing inefficiency, ineffectiveness, and inequality within the agency. Thus the Camden case study provides a realistic roadmap for change, and for identifying what will be required of police agencies that decide to embark on such efforts.

Conclusion

The major streams of literature suggest three main points regarding the relationship between work, sexual orientation, organizational failure, and recovery: employment discrimination exists, people who are dis-criminated against attempt to compensate for this reality, and planned change can help an organization move toward addressing discrimination through inclusion and diversity.

   Discrimination against lesbian and gay people is real and continues to be a problem. They are exposed to discrimination in all parts of socie-ty, including discrimination in employment. For example, employment discrimination can affect work assignments, performance and evalua-tion, and training sessions. If these effects are negative, then this means negative consequences for the employee and the organization. For this reason, many lesbian and gay people attempt to hide or obscure their sexual orientation at work. In effect, they manage this aspect of their lives through a cost-benefit analysis of the effects of revealing their sexuality. When the perceived costs exceed the benefits, a person might decide to stay "hidden" or lie about her or his sexuality. As the literature suggests, this is not an ideal situation in any workplace, but especially in a police agency. Individual officers, no matter how well qualified, must expend significant energy maintaining a lie and managing their false history in order to fit into the dominant police culture.

Like all police officers, lesbian and gay officers are not immune from the pressure to conform to agency culture, which is often overtly masculine and sometimes authoritarian. Officers in these situations can spend years with a patrol partner without discussing the most mundane aspects of private life for fear of exposure. Officers can become more concerned with concealment than with meeting the basic mission of the police agency: protecting the citizens of the community. When this happens, the police agency—at its most fundamental level—has failed. Since it is not meeting its basic responsibilities (whether due to structural, oversight, cultural, or institutionalization factors), organizational equity, efficiency, and effectiveness all become jeopardized.

One way to prepare for or recover from organizational failure is through planned change. As revealed in our examination of the efforts of the Camden Police Department, there are eight essential elements for the model of planned change: (1) understand external and internal forces and pressures for change; (2) identify organizational dysfunction due to performance gaps and other problems; (3) systematically collect and examine relevant data through auditing; (4) make room for innovative, rational decisionmaking; (5) commit to the development of solutions through goal-setting and a search for workable alternatives; (6) require that change be implemented through activities that control sources of resistance while simultaneously developing the organization; (7) maintain and monitor the planned change effort; and (8) ensure feedback or outcome evaluation.

Police agencies that engage in planned change increase their capacity to effectively and efficiently meet the needs of employees (primarily police officers) as well as community members, including lesbian and gay people. Planned change is also one of the best tools for developing more community-centered, public-minded policing. Although the old issues of employment discrimination and antigay bias still exist, the new realities of community policing and planned change can help promote greater diversity and inclusiveness in the field of law enforcement.

3

Law Enforcement's Move Toward Diversity

In order to understand law enforcement's modern embrace of diversity as an essential component of effective policing, we must understand the historical roots of policing in both the United States and the United Kingdom. With an appreciation of the foundations of policing, we can better understand the contextual factors that have made diversity efforts the norm in both countries. In addition, by exploring these historical roots, we will be better able to understand the modern context for both positive and negative outcomes that have resulted from changes in the field of law enforcement in these countries, particularly in regard to the inclusion of women, people of color, and sexual minorities. Finally, armed with history and context, we will be better able to articulate policy efforts to help other law enforcement agencies improve diversity within their organizations.

Early Policing in the United Kingdom

In the 1800s in the United Kingdom, migration from the rural countryside and towns to the urban center concentrated social ills, including systematic crime, unchecked immigration, poverty, alcoholism, and unsupervised youth (Paterson, 2010). These social ills emerged in the context of little public infrastructure or support, and required more formalized responses. Modern law enforcement, as the world now knows it, began around this time; in the case of the United Kingdom, it began with the formation of the London Metropolitan Police Force (Met) in 1829.

The Met's first chief of police, Sir Robert Peel, built the police agency based on four basic principles: (1) the use of crime rates to determine the effectiveness of the police agency; (2) centrally located and publicly accessible police offices; (3) proper recruitment, selection, and training for police officers; and (4), perhaps most important, the establishment of regular patrol areas, known as "beats."

Before 1829 the police responded only after a crime had been reported (Paterson, 2010). Peel instead assigned officers to specific geographic zones (based on crime rates, location, and selection) and held them responsible for preventing and suppressing crime within the boundaries of their zones (Gash, 1984). He believed that officers would become known to the public, and that citizens with information about criminal activity would be more likely to tell a familiar figure than a stranger. Furthermore, the officers would become familiar with people and places in the area and thus become better able to recognize suspicious persons or criminal activity. In essence, the police officers would become highly visible at their posts, and their presence would have the intended effect of deterring criminals from committing crimes in the vicinity (Paterson, 2010).

To implement the beat concept, Peel instituted a paramilitary command structure. While Peel believed overall civilian control to be essential, he also believed that military discipline would ensure that constables actually walked their beats and enforced the law. The beat patrol officer was forbidden to talk to other officers with adjoining beats, unless about a necessary matter of duty. Officers were also not allowed to enter pubs, smoke on duty, or take unnecessary refreshment breaks (Metropolitan Police, 2011).

Since the protection of individual liberties was highly emphasized in the United Kingdom, police agencies placed explicit controls on policing, particularly in the form of local police authorities. These authorities became responsible for the management of policing, including budget priorities. Composed of elected and appointed members of the local community, police authorities became one leg of the tripartite structure for governing policing in the United Kingdom today. The other two legs are the Home Secretary, who is responsible for national planning and financing, and the Chief Constable, who is responsible for all operational matters (Metropolitan Police, 2011). This philosophy—of limited power within a decentralized, fragmented, paramilitary structure—was the core of traditional policing in the United Kingdom (as well as in the United States).

But despite Peel's original efforts, police work in the United Kingdom during the nineteenth century was hopelessly inefficient, due to officers' reliance on foot patrol with no effective communication system and little direct supervision. Given the lack of official oversight, officers often evaded work. Furthermore, citizens had difficulty contacting the police because the officers could not be located while they were walking their beats (Metropolitan Police, 2011).

Early Policing in the United States

The first police agency in the United States was the Boston Police Department, established in 1838. The first modern police agencies in the United States borrowed heavily from their counterparts in the United Kingdom. In particular, US law enforcement agencies adopted Peel's mission of crime prevention and control, strategy of preventive patrols, and paramilitary organizational design for the London Met (Travis and Langworthy, 2007).

But despite common ancestry and similar founding philosophies, there were many differences between the US and UK systems of law enforcement, one of the most significant of which concerned political influence. While police administrators in the United Kingdom were protected from political influence, their counterparts in the United States were not. This heavy political influence in the United States, among other factors, resulted in a police system characterized as inefficient, ineffective, lacking professionalism, and highly corrupt (Walker, 1999).

In the early 1900s, a broad social and political movement, Progressivism, brought attention to and demanded reform across a broad spectrum of social problems in the United States. Progressives believed it was the government's responsibility to improve the living conditions of citizens. They called for the regulation of big business, an end to corrupt local politics, worker-friendly changes to labor laws, and improvements across social welfare services (Monkkonen, 2004).

Included in the Progressive reform effort was professionalization of police agencies. Unable to enforce the law, the inefficient and corrupt police agencies that had developed during the nineteenth century were totally restructured, and the role of police was redefined (Monkkonen, 2004). Progressive reformers sought to eliminate political influence, hire qualified leaders, and raise personnel standards for officers. In addition, the police reform agenda called for a mission of nonpartisan public service. From a perspective of efficiency and effectiveness, the movement embraced the principles of scientific management popularized by Frederick Taylor (1911), which promoted the scientific study of tasks to identify the "one best way" to perform each task. In terms of policing, this included studying the routine of policing and determining the optimal approach to all of its major components.

Several prominent police reforms had a significant influence on policing during this era. Richard Sylvester, superintendent of the Washington, D.C., Police Department from 1898 to 1915, became the national voice for police reform (Monkkonen, 2004). He served as president of the International Association of Chiefs of Police (IACP) and had a significant impact on acceptance of the reform agenda in numerous police agencies across the United States. Similarly, August Vollmer, police chief in Berkeley, California, from 1905 to 1932, advocated the hiring of college graduates and offered the first collegiate course in police science, at the University of California (Monkkonen, 2004). Vollmer is also famous for development of the principles of modern police administration, emphasizing efficiency. These efforts translated into centralization of authority within police forces and rationalization of procedures of command control (Walker, 1977).

Though this trend of policing reform in the United States has continued through to the present—with continual innovation and reinvention allowing police to respond to changing communities and law enforcement needs—during the first part of the twentieth century it was slow to develop, and in some cities progress was nonexistent. Although considerable gains were made in police agencies in Washington, D.C., and Berkeley, for example, reform efforts were largely ineffective in other agencies, such as those in Los Angeles and Chicago (Monkkonen, 2004). Efforts to professionalize the police increased after the 1931 report by the National Commission on Law Observance and Enforcement (known as the Wickersham Commission, after its lead investigator, former attorney general George W. Wickersham), which contained vivid descriptions of police misconduct and misuse of force. The Wickersham report was the first national study of the criminal justice system in the United States and had a significant impact on the efforts of the reform movement.

The professionalization of US police agencies continued under the direction of Orlando W. Wilson, a former chief of police and former professor of criminology at the University of California. Wilson had a significant impact on organizational changes within police agencies, largely through his textbook *Police Administration* (1950). Utilizing scientific principles of management promoted by Frederick Taylor, Wilson emphasized workload distributions based on calls for service and efficient management of personnel through bureaucratic design. Wilson also encouraged agencies to gauge their success through measurable outcomes (for example, numbers of arrests and citations) and rapid response to calls for service.

According to Samuel Walker (1999), new technologies had a significant influence on policing in the early to middle twentieth century. Three technologies in particular revolutionized policing: the two-way radio, the patrol car, and the telephone. With the introduction of the two-way radio, police officers could be notified about calls for service and police supervisors could contact their officers directly. This change in technology had a significant impact on the provision of services to the public and the supervision of police personnel. Likewise, the use of patrol cars greatly enhanced the mobility of police officers and significantly reduced their response time. Finally, telephones allowed citizens to have direct contact with police agencies. Citizens were encouraged to call the police for any type of assistance, and the police promised a rapid response.

These new technologies also had unintended consequences on policing, the effects of which would not be fully understood until much later (Walker, 1999). For example, the patrol car served to isolate officers from the community. Previously, when officers patrolled on foot, they had greater opportunity to engage citizens in conversation and had greater familiarity with the neighborhoods they were patrolling. But when officers began driving through neighborhoods with their windows rolled up, citizens began to perceive them as outsiders in their communities.

In addition, encouraging citizens to call the police for assistance and promising a rapid response dramatically increased and altered the workload of officers. The ease of contact and rapid response made it easy for residents to call police—even for minor problems and issues. Police officers were called to handle private matters that they had not been responsible for in the past. The interactions between citizens and police took on a more personal nature as police responded to citizens at their homes rather than simply patrolling and engaging citizens on the street. Prior to the introduction of these technologies, a patrolling officer could deter crime simply through his or her presence and knowledge of the community and its members. But after, that same officer, though still in a position to deter crime, now spent much more of his or her time responding to crime.

Despite its unintended consequences, this 1950s-style policing still dominates law enforcement in the United States. Many communities expect officers to patrol by car, settling disputes and responding to emergency calls involving everything from robberies, to domestic violence situations, to automobile accidents, to suspected terrorist activities. These officers are not viewed as members of the local community, but instead as official representatives of the state. This role has been promoted and codified by other institutions—for example, through the use of police reports as official documentation for insurance claims or as evidence in court proceedings.

The civil unrest of the 1960s brought further changes to policing in the United States. In response to citizens' increasing dissatisfaction with social and political conditions, particularly with the treatment of black Americans, the US Supreme Court decided a series of landmark cases that limited the investigative techniques used by police officers. For example, in 1961 the Court decided in *Mapp v. Ohio* that evidence obtained during a search and seizure that violated citizens' Fourth Amendment rights could not be used against them in a court of law. This ruling became known as the exclusionary rule, and it guaranteed that the fruits of an unconstitutional search could not be used during prosecution. In 1966 the Court ruled in *Miranda v. Arizona* that suspects must be advised of their right against self-incrimination (protected by the Fifth Amendment) and right to council (protected by the Sixth Amendment) before police could interrogate them. Any admission of guilt obtained prior to advisement of rights could not be used against a suspect during prosecution. The requirement to "Mirandize" a suspect is now one of the most widely recognized legal rights in the United States (Leo, 1998).

Meanwhile, as the mostly nonviolent black civil rights movement gained momentum in its demands for economic and social justice, a more militant offshoot began to emerge. This was the "Black Power" movement, whose mostly black followers protested against racial discrimination and injustice within the criminal justice system. White male police officers—as representatives of the state—became the symbol of all political and social ills in American society. In response, police officers across the country cracked down on civil rights protests with physical brutality. This excessive force served only to increase the tension between protesters and the police, acting as a catalyst for riots and civil disobedience in black communities throughout the United States.

In addition to the federal judicial response to civil unrest, the executive branch was also actively responding to citizens' demands for social change. One response came through a series of presidential commissions. The most famous of these, the National Advisory Commission on Civil Disorders (also known as the Kerner Commission, after its chair, Otto Kerner, governor of Illinois), investigated the causes of the nearly

200 riots and other civil disorders that had taken place in 1967. The Kerner Commission reported that there was deep hostility and distrust between black Americans and the police, and recommended that more minority officers be hired and that police practices (in terms of law enforcement) be changed significantly. Interestingly, the commission reported that those agencies that were believed to be the most "professional" were in fact located where the most serious disturbances and civil unrest had occurred. The conclusions of the Kerner Commission challenged the central assumption of the professionalism movement— that professionalism, in itself, is enough to ensure accountability and public-mindfulness in policing (Walker, 1999). Under the guise of professionalism, officers had enforced segregation laws, mistreated suspects, turned a blind eye to crimes against women and people of color, and used violence against civil protesters.

This period ushered in the era of identity politics and social movements in the United States. In addition to black Americans pushing for broader civil rights recognition, so too were women, environmentalists, Native Americans, sexual minorities, and others. While each movement had its own agenda, the desire for equal treatment, or "equality before the law," was a common thread. From black Americans fighting for fairer employment, education, housing, and public accommodation, to women fighting for equal pay and equal employment opportunities, to Native Americans fighting for enforcement of treaties and restoration of governance autonomy, to lesbian and gay people fighting for destigmatization of homosexuality, these sweeping efforts acted as catalysts for change in society and, by default, in policing. For lesbian and gay liberation, the most famous and perhaps most important catalyst was the Stonewall riots.

Stonewall: The Birth of the Lesbian and Gay Rights Movement

The first night of rioting began on Friday, June 27, 1969, when police raided the Stonewall Inn, a gay bar in Greenwich Village in New York City. Over the course of six days, lesbian, gay, and transgender people, together with their allies, gathered to protest the unfair treatment of sexual minorities.

At the time, it was not uncommon for the police to raid such establishments and to collect bribes from owners in some cases (D'Emilio, 1991). Police would enter a bar and use any number of "offenses" to justify arrests on indecency charges, including kissing, holding hands, wearing clothing of the opposite gender, or even just being present in the bar during the raid (Duberman, 1994).

Police raids on gay bars were usually met with only passive resistance from patrons and staff. In most cases, patrons attempted to slip away from the scene unnoticed. The Stonewall riots (also know as the Stonewall rebellion, the Stonewall uprising, and the Stonewall incident) represented a shift in patrons' response to the police raids and harassment. On the first night, in an unplanned and uncoordinated effort, patrons of Stonewall, its staff, and onlookers in the community grew more and more defiant as patrons were arrested and loaded into police vans. Onlookers began to shout and taunt the arresting officers. Eventually, onlookers took to pelting the officers with bricks, bottles, and pennies. As the crowd grew, the arresting officers retreated into the bar and called for backup. Empowered and outnumbering the officers, the crowd initiated a violent "melee"—setting trash cans on fire, tossing debris, and damaging property. Reports also indicate that a parking meter was ripped from the ground and used as a battering ram to break down the door to the bar, behind which the police officers had barricaded themselves. Once police reinforcement arrived, the incident was quickly subdued and the crowd was dispersed. The police estimated that about 400 people were involved in the rioting that night; thirteen people were arrested, and four police officers were injured ("Stonewall Rebellion," 2009).

The next day, community activists were quick to seize on the nature of these events; they spread word about the first riot and staged a second for the following night in Sheridan Square in front the Stonewall Inn. In this second, more organized round of civil disobedience, rioters shouted "gay power" and "we want freedom," phrases co-opted from other social movements of the day, namely the "Black Power" movement and the women's equal rights movement (D'Emilio, 1991). In typical and expected form for the New York Police Department of this time, tactical police officers were dispatched and cleared the area for a second night.

As word spread about the riots and resistance, more lesbian, gay, and transgender people, and more allies, returned each night to Sheridan Square to protest police treatment, and to make a claim for equal rights. By July 3, 1969, a coordinated effort to create a gay rights movement was under way. At least one new organization was formed as a result of the Stonewall riots: the Gay Liberation Front (GLF).

The establishment of this organization represented the transformation of the lesbian, gay, and transgender community from the passive homophile movement of the 1950s to a more active, militant, outspoken, liberation movement. Sparked by the Stonewall riots, the movement quickly grew beyond its initial base in New York City and went global. By the end of 1969, the coordinated efforts of the GLF could be seen in cities and universities across the United States. Similar organizations were soon created in other countries around the world, including Australia, Belgium, Britain, Canada, France, Germany, the Netherlands, and New Zealand (Tatchell, 2010).

The following year, 1970, in commemoration of the Stonewall riots, the GLF organized a march from Greenwich Village to Central Park that thousands of men and women attended (Evans, 1970).[1]

Unrest in the United Kingdom

The British policing system also came under pressure and scrutiny in the context of social civil unrest, though it is much compared to the American experience. While the 1993 murder of Stephen Lawrence—which prompted the Macpherson Report and its associated reforms—is the most commonly cited event in explaining the "reinvention" of UK policing, several focusing events preceded the Lawrence murder (discussed in greater detail later in this chapter). The most notable of these focusing events was the Brixton riots of 1981 in South London. According to the London Metropolitan Police, Constable Margottia was assisting a young black man, Michael Bailey, who had been severely stabbed. The young man, thinking he was being arrested, broke away from the constable and fled with the assistance of three other youths. Margottia, assisted by two additional officers, caught up with the youths, detained all three, administered first aid to Bailey, and summoned an ambulance by radio. As the officers waited for the ambulance, a crowd gathered and became aggravated by the seeming lack of medical attention being provided to Bailey. Eventually a group of people hustled Bailey out of police custody and took him to the hospital by car.

Under normal circumstances, this incident might have passed without notice. However, in this case, it became the catalyst for an explosion of social unrest. This incident occurred in the context of the Met's Operation Swamp 81, an initiative to reduce robberies by "overpolicing" the South London community of Brixton, a predominantly black neighborhood. Thus the operation resulted in a predominantly white police force routinely stopping, questioning, and searching a disproportionately large number of young black men (Metropolitan Police, 2011). The stop-and-search efforts were viewed as little more than an excuse to harass and intimidate the youths, which the community was quick to notice.

In the context of Operation Swamp 81, the officers who had tried to help Michael Bailey were viewed with suspicion. Young men threw bricks and bottles at them, and also attacked four police cars that came to their aid. The disturbance lasted an hour and a half, during which time six people were arrested and six police officers were injured. In the meantime, rumors spread that the police officers had refused to help Bailey, that they had tried to prevent him from being taken to the hospital, and even that they had caused his injuries. These rumors further fueled outrage and unrest among the community.

Although the disturbance was relatively brief, the police decided to increase their presence in Brixton overnight. This oppressive response, compounded by a history of mistrust, abuse, and brutality, ignited a night of rioting within the community. The police countered by deploying even more officers to the area, but without initiating a strategy to address the crisis. Over a thousand officers responded to the call, without proper direction and with little communication from police command. Officers did not know whether they were supposed to deter all antisocial behaviors, protect property and life, or suppress only riot-related actions. As then–police sergeant Brian Paddick noted, "we'd never had to deal with a spontaneous riot before. All police officers were told to turn out and I was in charge of ten officers I'd never previously worked alongside" (Wainewright, 2011, p. 4). During the night of rioting, according to the Metropolitan Police (2011), 299 police officers and at least 65 civilians were injured, 61 private vehicles and 56 police vehicles were damaged or destroyed, 28 premises were burned and another 117 were damaged and looted, and 82 people were arrested.

In reaction to the riots, Lord Leslie George Scarman was appointed by the Home Secretary to hold a public inquiry. Lord Scarman reported that the unemployment rate among young black men in Brixton was close to 50 percent, that policing in the community was often "immature and racially prejudiced," and that, given such conditions, the riots were an inevitable response to perceived harassment by white officers ("Obituary: Lord Scarman," 2004). The report's recommendations included increasing the number of minority police officers, creating new community liaison groups, instituting policies to reduce black unemployment, and making racial discrimination by police officers a disciplinary offense.

The unrest continued, and spread, throughout the summer of 1981, fueled by policing practices and economic and social dissatisfaction.

Incidents, uprisings, and riots were recorded at Handsworth in Birmingham, Southall in London, Toxteth in Liverpool, and Moss Side in Manchester. There were also smaller pockets of unrest in Bedford, Bristol, Coventry, Edinburgh, Leeds, Leicester, Gloucester, Halifax, Southampton, and Wolverhampton (Metropolitan Police, 2011).

* * *

Both the Stonewall and the Brixton riots highlight how the wrong approach to policing and law enforcement can have disastrous effects on police agencies and communities. In these cases, the police agencies had not fostered relationships with community leaders, members, and institutions, and the police officers were not culturally competent in the communities they served, lacked diversity and were perceived as outsiders, and were not properly trained to handle unpredictable situations like riots.

These periods of civil unrest in the United States and the United Kingdom were important because they precipitated focusing events—mistakes in policing—and created opportunities for change. The resulting policy innovations and new strategies laid the groundwork for community policing and problem solving, which are critical to inclusion and diversity in law enforcement.

Community Policing

According to Marcia Chaiken (2001), community policing is "a philosophy that promotes organizational strategies, which support the systematic use of partnerships and problem-solving techniques, to proactively address the immediate conditions that give rise to public safety issues such as crime, social disorder, and fear of crime." Community policing is a joint effort between law enforcement and a community it serves to best determine the policing needs of the community. Groups and individuals—including government agencies, nonprofit organizations, businesses, local media, and community members—all have partnerships with the police, which encourage responsiveness and make communities safer.

Police agencies in the United States began experimenting with this new philosophy of policing in the 1980s. These agencies tried to engage community members to jointly address recurring crime and disorder issues through proactive or problem-solving efforts (Diamond and Weiss, 2009). These diffused efforts to change the nature of policing were codified at the federal level in 1994 through the Violent Crime

Control and Law Enforcement Act. As a result of federal support, over 80 percent of the US population is served by a law enforcement agency practicing community policing (US Department of Justice, 2011). In the United Kingdom, efforts to involve communities in local policing began in the 1990s. Given the more unified administrative and command structure of the UK policing system, efforts there have been more uniform than in the United States (Clements, 2008).

Since its inception, policing has been resistant to change, primarily due to its paramilitary origins and hierarchical structure. By exploring the evolution of community policing and the critical incidents that gave rise to it, we can better understand the nature of this resistance and how to overcome it.

Community Policing in the United States: Evolution and Brief History

In modern times, we might think of policing in the United States as having evolved in three strands, each of which has influenced how police agencies understand crime and engage in law enforcement. The first strand is built on the "broken windows" theory, developed by James Wilson and George Kelling (1982), who posited that neighborhoods could quickly deteriorate if proper attention was not given to reducing crime and antisocial behavior. Accompanying research also suggested that citizens' perceptions of crime were more closely related to "signs" of community disorder—such as abandoned buildings and graffiti—than to actual crime statistics. Many communities (such as New York City) began to embrace the idea of more aggressive law enforcement directed against minor infractions such as panhandling, juvenile delinquency, and traffic violations. This type of policing required officers to actively engage community members.

However, this increased and more engaged law enforcement had a disparate impact on many minority groups, particularly black and Latino communities (Roberg, Crank, and Kuykendall, 2000). From the Rodney King incident and Los Angeles riots in 1992, to the police attack on Abner Louima in New York City in 1997, to the shooting of Sean Bell in Queens, New York, in 2006, aggressive, legalistic policing has proven to be an ineffective and unworkable model, harming community-police relations.

In general, police agencies have moved away from models of law enforcement based on the "broken windows" theory, turning instead to community-based theories of crime, which suggest that social order is more the result of informal community processes than of anything police might do (Roberg, Crank, and Kuykendall, 2000). This second strand differs from the first in that it highlights the need for citizens to be a part of policing and problem solving—an idea commonly known as "the co-production of public safety" (Eck and Rosenbaum, 1994).

In recent years, this co-production of public safety has evolved into two general philosophies of policing: problem-oriented and community-oriented. In problem-oriented policing, discrete aspects of policing are analyzed in order to develop new and more effective strategies for dealing with problems. This philosophy places a high value on new responses that are preventive in nature, that are not dependent on the use of the criminal justice system, and that engage other public agencies, the community, and the private sector when their involvement has the potential to significantly contribute to reducing a problem. Problem-oriented policing carries a commitment to implementing the new strategy, rigorously evaluating its effectiveness, and subsequently reporting the results in ways that will benefit other police agencies and that will ultimately contribute to building a body of knowledge that supports the further professionalization of the police (Goldstein, 2001).

Community-oriented policing is the most recent strand in US law enforcement (Roberg, Crank, and Kuykendall, 2000). According to this philosophy, when the police and the community become more closely acquainted, the tension between them can be reduced and local problems can be solved together. Today, community-oriented policing in the United States includes elements of the problem-oriented approach as well.

Given the decentralized nature of police agencies in the United States and the many differences between them, the penetration of community policing across the country remains varied and unclear. One survey of seventy-five police agencies found that levels of implementation of the community-oriented approach varied greatly. For example, at the high end of the implementation spectrum, 78 percent of the agencies surveyed had given officers "discretion and authority," 75 percent had established "community partnerships," and 71 percent had trained all personnel in community policing. However, only 54 percent had established "agency-wide" community policing strategies, only 49 percent had integrated the strategies throughout the entire agency, and only 31 percent had established evaluative processes (US Conference of Mayors, 2000).

Despite such variations in implementation, however, proponents of this approach continue to develop best practices, benchmarks, and procedures. Chaiken (2001) highlights five progressive stages of contemporary community policing. The first stage is to create initiatives that improve responsiveness to citizen requests, including the establishment of special units and centers to handle non-patrol-related requests. The second stage is to involve the community via outreach and targeting to help reduce particular crimes. The third stage is to develop collaboration and cooperation on issues of local concern, including short-term problems driven by citizen concern. The fourth stage is to develop, with input from the community, approaches to the issues of local concern. The fifth and final stage is to codify and institutionalize the policing philosophy and practices into the strategic plans of local communities.

As community policing continues to evolve in the United States—with the support of the federal government—it will no doubt become even more community-specific and community-driven.

Community Policing in the United Kingdom: Evolution and Brief History

As is widely known throughout the United Kingdom, the race-based murder of Stephen Lawrence, an eighteen-year-old black student, changed policing practices throughout the country. Lawrence was attacked and killed in South London in 1993. The police investigation—or lack thereof—was perceived as incomplete, biased, and racist. Despite the emergence of witnesses, the London Met investigation initially yielded no suspects, and thus no arrests were made in relation to the murder. Lawrence's family, friends, and community believed that the police were not interested in solving the murder and pushed them to do more. Though Lawrence's supporters were dissatisfied with the outcome of the investigation, the Met defended its procedures. In fact, a senior Scotland Yard officer, Superintendent Roderick Barker, after conducting an internal inquiry into the investigation, reported that the probe had "progressed satisfactorily and all lines of inquiry had been correctly pursued" (Judd, 2005). As the police attempted to justify their approach, the emergence of new evidence and information (specifically about the Met's treatment of Lawrence's parents) sparked public outcries.

By 1997 the police had determined that Lawrence had been "unlawfully killed in a completely unprovoked racist attack by five white youths" ("Q&A: Stephen Lawrence Murder," 2004). The police arrested five young men, but the suspects refused to answer any questions. The Lawrence family then requested a second internal inquiry via the Police Complaints Authority. Persistent pressure by Lawrence's family, the black community, and the media led to the establishment of a public inquiry into the investigation, four years after Lawrence's death. The findings and recommendations of the inquiry, led by Sir William

Macpherson, were direct and straightforward. In what became known as the Macpherson Report, the Met's investigation into the Lawrence murder was characterized as "marred by a combination of professional incompetence, institutional racism, and a failure of leadership" (Macpherson, 1999). Among the many criticisms noted in the report, particular attention was paid to the inadequacy of the Met's initial response and assistance, to police racism, to the incompetent support offered to the victim's family, and to community concerns. The final two criticisms, regarding victim support and community concerns, are closely related to the reforms that led to the adoption of community policing models and to efforts on the part of the British police to reach out to minority communities.

Prior police practices and approaches had focused on identifying and apprehending criminals, not on the needs or preferences of victims and community members. But because of the refocused attention prompted and guided by the Macpherson Report, the nature of policing in Britain changed. Almost two decades later, most modern police reforms in the United Kingdom can be traced back to the murder of Stephen Lawrence.

Legacies of the Stephen Lawrence Inquiry

To say that Stephen Lawrence's murder and the subsequent events had a profound effect on policing in the United Kingdom would be an understatement. As Phillip Clements (2008) notes, the public inquiry into the Lawrence case led directly to changes in practices of police and public agencies in the United Kingdom—including the passage of the Race Relations Act in 2000 and the Independent Police Complaints Commission, which came into existence in April 2004, replacing the Police Complaints Authority. In addition to these explicit policy changes, scholars often note numerous other legacies that resulted from the Lawrence inquiry, including cultural, governance, political, legal, intelligence, and international effects (Grieve, Hall, and Savage, 2009). Of the six types of legacies identified, three (cultural, political, and legal) had direct implications for community policing and the inclusion of lesbian and gay people in policing in contemporary Britain.

Cultural Legacy

The cultural legacy of the Lawrence inquiry is its impact on the values and mind-set of police agencies. As a result of the inquiry, the Home

Office was required to review its approach to policing and the conse-quences of that approach. Among the many changes that emerged, one of the most important was a redefinition of race-based incidents. Prior to the inquiry, police agencies followed the guidelines of the Association of Chief Police Officers, which placed the determination of a race-based crime solely within the purview of the investigating officer. But given the failure of the police to recognize Stephen Lawrence's murder as race-based, the determination was subsequently shifted away from police and toward the victim and observers. The official definition of a race-based incident was revised as "any incident which is perceived to be racist by *the victim or any other person*" (Home Office, 1999, emphasis added). This revised definition had at least three important cultural implications for police agencies.

First, the new definition represented a straightforward shift to victim-centered policing, also referred to as victim-led, victim-based, or victim-supported policing. With the exception of slight variations, this philosophy is essentially concerned with ensuring that the voices of vic-tims are accounted for in the administration of justice. Traditionally, UK policing was based on the provision that policing should be of the same level and approach regarding all members of the community (Rowe, 2007). Victim-centered policing acknowledged that different members of the community have different needs and make different demands on police agencies. In other words, the diversity of the community requires a more diverse and nuanced approach to policing to ensure that the needs of the whole community are met.

The second implication of the shift toward victim-centered provi-sion of service was an acknowledgment that there are numerous types of victims and that race-based incidents represent just one angle on the issue. In 2000 the Association of Chief Police Officers developed a guide for police agencies that expanded the category of victim-based incidents beyond race to include other attributes, including sexuality, religion, disability, and gender. This shift represented a move beyond race-based incidents to hate-based incidents. As one might imagine, the broader definition allowed for crime reporting from the victim's per-spective and encompassed more types of incidents, including hate-based crimes involving the victim's sexual orientation.

The third implication relates to family liaisons. The shift toward victim-based incidents required a different skill set than most constables possessed. Family liaison officers (FLOs) were trained to help victims and families navigate the criminal justice system and to aid in outreach to various communities to enlist their help in solving other crimes. After formalization of this position following the Lawrence inquiry, 700 people in police service were trained as FLOs in England and Wales (Grieve, Hall, and Savage, 2009). The role of the FLO was important because it was a precursor to other liaison roles in policing depending on the perceived needs of the community, including the role of lesbian and gay liaison officers (GLOs).

Political Legacy

The political legacy of the Stephen Lawrence inquiry is twofold. First, the inquiry demonstrated that a coalition of advocates demanding justice could successfully press for a full and complete investigation via the political process. Advocates for justice—led by Lawrence's parents and family—kept the issue alive for several years after Lawrence's death, despite the fact that they were initially confronted with denial, dismissal, refusal, and suspicion of their motives (Cathcart, 1999). Advocates demanded a thorough investigation, prosecution of the people responsible for Lawrence's murder, acceptance of responsibility by authorities who failed to act, and finally, an inquiry into a system that had failed to fully investigate the case. Their ultimate success was all the more notable given their novice relationship to the political process.

Second, the Stephen Lawrence inquiry provided an opening for minority police associations within the institutional framework of law enforcement (Grieve, Hall, and Savage, 2009). Although minority police associations will be discussed at length in the next chapter, it is important to note here their political legacy contribution in the context of the Lawrence inquiry. As police agencies tried to better understand institutional racism and other maladies in law enforcement, their first inclination was to look within. The shared perceptions of the Black Police Association (BPA) in London yielded valuable insights about police culture, policies, and practices from a minority perspective (Grieve, Hall, and Savage, 2009). Efforts by police agencies to incorporate the views of the BPA gave the group credibility and the ability to expand into a national association throughout Britain (Holdaway and O'Neill, 2007). Working with the BPA also established a pattern of working with associations of minority police officers. In short, the empowerment of the BPA helped normalize the concept of minority associations in policing. Thus, associations like the Gay Police Association and the British Association of Women in Policing were eventually accepted into the institutional framework of law enforcement, in part due to the efforts of the BPA and its assistance in helping address some of the racial issues in policing.

Legal Legacy

The legal legacy of the Lawrence inquiry consists of the laws and policies that were developed, advanced, and implemented as a result. The first law to be influenced by the inquiry was the 1998 Crime Disorder Act. Although this law had been enacted before Lawrence's death, Michael Rowe (2007) suggests that it was the race-based attack on Lawrence and subsequent inquiry that resulted in its actual implementation. Because of its timing and content, the act also served as the first police initiative to address race-based crimes. Police agencies wanted to show that they were taking such crimes seriously, responding to them appropriately, and holding themselves accountable for their actions.

A second legal legacy is the Criminal Justice Act of 2003. This act allowed for a perpetrator's homophobia or bias against physically or mentally disabled persons to be considered during sentencing, and permitted increased penalties accordingly. The Criminal Justice Act also allowed prosecutors to retry people who had previously been acquitted if "new and compelling" evidence were presented to the court. As John Grieve, Nathan Hall, and Stephen Savage (2009) note, this provision effectively abolished the double-jeopardy rule, which had prohibited a person from being tried twice for the same crime. In theory, double-jeopardy provisions discourage frivolous attempts to convict a person of a crime. On the other hand, double-jeopardy provisions have hampered the administration of justice when new evidence is obtained. This has been the case with hate-based crimes, civil rights crimes (such as during the 1960s in the United States), and some international war crimes. In each of these areas, suspension of double-jeopardy provisions has proved to be a powerful tool in administering justice in light of new and compelling evidence.

A third legal legacy of the Lawrence inquiry is the liability provision in the Race Relation Act of 2000, which clarified that the full force of this law applies to police officers and that managerial-level officers are vicariously liable for the acts and omissions of officers serving under them. This provision was intended to ensure that police agencies did not accord inferior treatment to people based on race or ethnic origin in terms of either their provision of services or their use of coercive powers (Bowling and Phillips, 2007).

* * *

The cultural, political, and legal legacies of the Stephen Lawrence inquiry are evident in British criminal justice and law enforcement today. Efforts to improve race relations and police accountability since the inquiry have had a direct and influential effect on policing in all types of communities. For example, efforts to address racism in policing have been broadened to address sexism, homophobia, and religious bias. Victim-based inquiries and investigations, originally applied to race-based crimes, have now been extended to crimes involving other categories of victims, and the understanding of appropriate service provisions has improved. In this connection, lesbian and gay liaison officers are historically linked to family liaison officers, who were the original victim-based service providers. As one lesbian officer noted during a focus-group session in Hampshire:

> That murder [of Stephen Lawrence] led greatly to a lot of the changes around hate crimes, not just in relation to race, but to other hate crimes . . . but primarily to race, and the Crime and Disorder Act that kick-started the [community policing and diversity] schemes that we have in Hampshire, and the liaison scheme that we have in Hampshire. It all came off the back of that at that time. So it's quite, I think, very relevant to the UK to draw back to the Stephen Lawrence murder as being a kick-start. (personal communication, 2009)

Police Community Support Officers

In the United Kingdom, police community support officers (PCSOs) are the embodiment of the community policing model. PCSOs were introduced after the Stephen Lawrence inquiry, in the Police Reform Act of 2002. Classified as support staff, PCSOs are employed, directed, and managed by their local police agencies. Their work complements and supports that of regular police officers by providing a visible and accessible uniformed presence aimed at improving the quality of life at the community level. PCSOs address some of the tasks that do not require a police officer's experience or the power held by police officers—tasks that often take officers away from more appropriate duties (Home Office, 2005). Specifically, PCSOs tackle local antisocial behavior and low-priority issues that nonetheless affect a community's quality of life. Since PCSOs are empowered by their local police agencies, their exact authority varies by locality. According to the Home Office (2005), at a minimum all PCSOs have the following basic community-based powers:

• The power to issue fixed penalty notices for cycling on a footpath, littering, or disobeying dog-control orders.

- The power to record names and addresses related to antisocial behavior and activities and traffic violations.
- The power to enforce tobacco-, alcohol-, and drug-related laws, including seizure of substances in cases of underage or illegal consumption.
- The power to enter and search any premises for the purpose of saving life and limb or preventing serious damage to property.
- The power to enforce traffic regulations, including stopping vehicles, rerouting traffic, carrying out road checks, and seizing vehicles used to cause harm.
- The power to stop and search in authorized areas.

While there has been disagreement over these powers, there appears to be a general consensus that PCSOs can play a critical role in community policing and act as a bridge between community members and police. Because PCSOs have a visible presence in the community and understand the local culture and customs, they often act as victim advocates, conducting follow-ups after a police investigation is complete. Although PCSOs do not have full policing powers, they work closely with police to provide critical information about the community and its members that can be useful when investigating more serious incidents. As PCSOs often describe themselves, they are the "eyes and ears of law enforcement" (personal communication, 2009).

Community Policing: Not a Perfect Model

Despite its many successes, the shift toward community policing has not been problem-free in either the United States or the United Kingdom. Several scholars and practitioners have questioned its use as a model for effective and efficient law enforcement.

One important issue is the extent to which police officers and community members agree on priorities, strategies, and goals. Ivan Sun and Ruth Triplett (2008) found that some community problems are rated as more serious by police officers than by local residents, and that this variation is significantly affected by a community's structural characteristics and its perceptions of the legitimacy of local authorities. Police officers are first and foremost responsible for law enforcement via crime prevention and detection, and it is possible that communities may sometimes lose sight of these policing priorities. For example, in a public disturbance or public order situation, police officers might be required to engage in conventional crowd-control techniques against community members who would otherwise be viewed as partners in community policing.

Voices from the Field

Name: Mark McGregor
Police agency: Wiltshire Constabulary
Rank: Police officer
Length of service: Five years

On training lesbian and gay liaison officers:
"We've very much been seen as the leader, as far as other forces are concerned, in implementing . . . and training [GLOs] . . . and Wiltshire has been used in very many training scenarios around the country as a shining light, where the engagement with the gay community and the acceptance of the role within the police force has been extremely positive."

On the lesbian and gay community's perceptions of community policing:
"From the gay and lesbian community, I would say it's been extremely positive. There's obviously been times when it's not, but on the whole, it's been extremely positive that the police have identified that there's a need, that there's a problem. . . . I have to say, the way we went about promoting junction with the partnering agencies to the gay community, again, was extremely good."

*On the broader community's perceptions
of policing in the lesbian and gay community:*
"I would say it's not been so good, and that's on the basis of: 'Why do gay and lesbian people, why are they being set precedent, why are they having a preferential service over and above? Why are they being identified as having a greater need than people living within general society?'"

Scholars and practitioners have also questioned whether community policing actually works. The assumption has been that community policing is inherently good for both police and communities, yet too few long-term studies of this approach have been conducted. Furthermore, some argue that the metrics used to evaluate community policing (often victimization or incident rates) are not precise enough to determine the model's effectiveness.

Implementation is one of the greatest challenges facing community policing. Even if agreement can be reached about the priorities, strategies, and goals for policing, implementation can be hampered by officers, community members, advocates, or any other stakeholders who have an interest in resisting community policing. Though disagreements about effectiveness and implementation are common in most public programs, community policing presents unique challenges. We can look to at least three factors that make this model of law enforcement less than ideal: change, mistrust, and intergovernmental relations.

Change

In any innovating organization, change comes slowly, and front-line employees—in this case police officers—may be difficult to influence and may resist change. Starting in the 1970s, police agencies began to develop alternatives to the traditional policing model, which emphasized motorized patrol, rapid response to calls for service, and retrospective investigation of crimes (Moore, Trojanowicz, and Kelling, 2000). Various innovations were introduced, including problem-oriented policing, "hot-spot" policing, and community policing. In response to all this change, front-line officers might well believe that community policing is just a fad that will soon be replaced by yet another innovation—and that it therefore does not require serious commitment.

And, of course, managers and supervisors are just as susceptible to resistance as are front-line employees. Management's resistance to change can manifest in ways that specifically affect the implementation of the community policing model. For example, management controls the allocation of human and financial resources; since community policing is a long-term investment and managers are often under pressure to deliver results in the short term, they may resist allocating appropriate resources to the endeavor (Clements, 2008).

Mistrust

The second challenge or barrier is mistrust from communities. In both the United States and the United Kingdom, police have historically had poor relationships with certain communities, such as people of color, the poor, and immigrants, as well as lesbian and gay people. The bad reputation of police agencies in such minority communities is not unfounded, of course, given the history of bias and disproportionate policing. Even in cases where newfound trust has been established, it can be tenuous and can collapse with one critical incident. Moreover, even when community policing is implemented effectively, some elements of the community—especially those engaged in illicit activities—may refuse to buy into the effort. Police may never be able to build trust with gang members or drug dealers, since these elements often try to remain invisible to the broader community as well as to police agencies. The difficulty of community policing is also highlighted by the exclusion of community members who are easily overlooked, including the mentally ill, the hearing-impaired, and the homeless. Though these minority classes often do seek recognition, their concerns are regularly ignored.

Intergovernmental Relations

The final challenge or barrier is intergovernmental relations between police and other agencies. There are numerous imperatives for police to work in partnership with other public agencies and institutions, as well as with nonprofits, and such partnerships are regarded as a key feature of community policing (Clements, 2008). But Jeffrey Pressman and Aaron Wildavsky's (1978) decades-old observation still applies: joint action by mutual stakeholders adds complexity to any endeavor. This complexity of joint action reduces the likelihood of effective implementation. That likelihood is reduced even further if institutions have a history of conflict with police agencies or have conflicting missions, cultures, or values.

* * *

While the number of jurisdictions adopting elements of community policing continues to rise, it is important to remember that this model will not be suitable or even possible in all communities. Policing and law enforcement are continually evolving, and this evolution should be encouraged. Those agencies considering community policing should understand its strengths as well as its weaknesses prior to implementation.

Community Policing in Lesbian and Gay Communities

While lesbian and gay communities have been both over- and underpoliced, relationships between these communities and local police agencies continue to be reformed under the community policing model and its variants.

In terms of overpolicing, relations between lesbian and gay communities and the police have historically been fraught with contention (Williams and Robinson, 2004) due to the uneven and inequitable policing extended to these communities. Across both the United States and the United Kingdom, police officers have often been seen as the active "enforcers" of laws primarily affecting lesbian and gay people, given their harassment of patrons at local gay bars and their arrests of people (mostly men) allegedly engaged in "lewd behavior" (Leinen, 1993; Burke, 1993). Such harassment and arrests have been driven mostly by officers' homophobia. Early research in the 1960s showed that lesbians and gay men were ranked as the second most disliked group by a sample of New York police officers (Niederhoffer, 1967), and this outcome was replicated and validated almost a decade later (Fretz, 1975). The occupational culture of police officers can instill negative attitudes about minority individuals, especially those identifying as lesbian or gay (Leinen, 1993). These negative attitudes have contributed to discrimination, harassment, and in some cases brutalization of lesbian and gay people (Miller, Forest, and Jurik, 2003).

In contrast, underpolicing is the failure to provide a satisfactory level of policing for communities and victims of crime (Storry and Childs, 2002). Underpolicing has also negatively affected community relations. Gregory Herek (1998, 2004) argued that the low reporting of antigay hate crimes—and the high number of such crimes that go unsolved—result not just from lack of interest on the part of the police, but also from the fact that such crimes are sometimes committed by police officers themselves. Community members thus often perceive the police as being antigay, and fear both primary and secondary victimization by officers (Comstock, 1989; personal communication, 2009). Joseph Davis (1992) and David Mitchell (1992) found that lesbian and gay people who approached the police for help tended to receive a negative reception, including a lack of interest in their reports of victimization.

This tumultuous relationship made good policing in the lesbian and gay community virtually impossible. It seriously limited police efforts to monitor and investigate hate crimes, same-sex domestic violence, and drug-related activities. For the most part, lesbian and gay people refused to report crime or to aid police in any substantive way. The unbalanced policing of lesbian and gay populations, the perceived disinterest in complaints from lesbian and gay people, and the high level of police-perpetrated antigay hate crimes combined to create an atmosphere of harassment and intimidation.

In contrast to these historical models of policing, community policing focuses on building relationships between community members and officers, once police accept that all communities—including lesbian and gay communities—have "a legitimate, active role to play in the policing process" (White and Perrone, 2005, p. 29). This "legitimate" role is vastly different from the policing model of the past. Whereas traditional models endow police officers and agencies with the power to enforce the law, the community policing model requires a collaborative process to decide how compliance with laws will be achieved. In this scenario, arrest and prosecution may not be the most effective, efficient, or equitable approach. Furthermore, this new role suggests that police agencies will be better able to serve a community when the composition of the police force reflects the composition of that community. Thus, lesbian and gay people have a right to be an active part of the agencies that police their community. Police agencies in the past allowed themselves to homogenize, and this lack of diversity had a direct effect on the ability of police to meet their mission.

Measurable Outcomes of Community Policing

Understanding the outcomes of community policing can be a challenging task. Despite the increased use of community policing, expected outcomes, common objectives, and valid measures remain elusive when assessing the impact of this model. This is especially the case when attempting to assess the impact on minority officers, especially lesbian and gay officers. Many agencies continue to use performance measures based on other models of policing, including levels of crime and fear, numbers of arrests and citations, and staffing levels (Alpert, Flynn, and Piquero, 2001).

Much of what we do know about community policing comes from case studies of various cities in both the United States and the United Kingdom (Scott, Duffee, and Renauer, 2003; Heaton, 2000; Trojanowicz et al., 1998). These case studies are diverse in their objectives and in their perspectives on community policing. Collectively, however, they provide much-needed information about community policing—particularly about the places where it has been implemented, its stated purposes, its strategic and structural components, the obstacles encountered in its implementation, and occasionally its outcomes (Kerley and Benson, 2000; Kurki, 2000). For example, Robert Lombardo, David Olson, and Monte Staton (2010) explore the largest community policing effort in the United States, the Chicago Alternative Policing Strategy (CAPS), with an emphasis on understanding the change in community satisfaction as a result of the strategy. They found that communities that had implemented CAPS had more favorable perceptions of the police compared to non-CAPS communities.

Unfortunately, the diversity of and variation among the case studies make it difficult to identify more universal patterns of success or failure in community policing. Furthermore, the nature of case studies makes developing consistent performance measures all but impossible. One difficulty is not knowing precisely what is to be measured (Fielding and Innes, 2006). When community policing is operationalized, it can range from neighborhood-watch programs to problem-oriented policing to zero-tolerance approaches. This makes meaningful comparison among the programs problematic.

Despite these challenges, some appropriate measures for community policing have emerged. Of course, traditional measures, including reduction in crime and fear, are appropriate for most law enforcement efforts. These performance measures have historical and political roots, and thus police agencies tend to be most comfortable with them. But other measures—for example, community processes (community organization, cohesion, and cooperative security), community satisfaction, and community trust—also seem intuitively appropriate to evaluating community policing's successes and failures (Kerley and Benson, 2000). These community-oriented measures, unlike traditional measures, are much more ambiguous, and lack the historical and political influence that police agencies have grown accustomed to.

Our best source of information on the community policing of lesbian and gay communities comes from lesbian and gay officers. US and UK officers contacted during research for this book talked about the effects of having lesbian and gay officers engaged in community policing. In the United Kingdom, one officer from the Wiltshire Constabulary summarized it best when he said: "Police officers [who work in the community as lesbian and gay liaison officers] tend to stay much longer and build up their relationship with the communities. . . . [O]nce they've built up with the liaison, they haven't got to build up again with the next person that comes in—they've got *continuity*" (personal communication, 2009, emphasis added).

While traditional measures of police performance remain important for understanding the essential work of law enforcement, new measures that reflect the unique role of police officers in community policing are needed. Scholars are beginning to survey different aspects of this type of police work in the field, but we can already see the important effects that community policing can have on minority or marginalized communities. Community policing efforts can lead to greater connectedness and increased trust on both sides and ultimately improve both the life of the community and the effectiveness of policing.

Conclusion

The history and evolution of policing in the United States and the United Kingdom provide valuable insights into modern inclusion and diversity efforts, both internal and external to police agencies. In some respects, Peel got it right, in 1829, with the idea of putting officers on "beats." Putting officers in local communities, having them engage community members, having them keep watch for unusual situations, and having them depend upon the community for help with law enforcement are all aspects of both beat policing and community policing. In other ways, Peel certainly got it wrong. The top-down command-and-control philosophy has made it more difficult over the years for police agencies to change and modernize. In essence, real change in policing is and was only possible when the leadership found it necessary. Organizational innovation is not likely to occur when individuals are not empowered to bring good ideas forward and test them for empirical value. The paramilitary structure of the police agency has moved it toward use of force in law enforcement.

However, policing is indeed changing. Political, social, and economic pressures have forced police agencies to rethink their approach to law enforcement. We saw this with the Stonewall riots in the United States, and with the Brixton riots and Stephen Lawrence murder in the United Kingdom. These and other similar events have helped to move policing away from an "us versus them" approach and toward a "mutual collaboration" model to meet the needs of all communities.

Note

1. Today, many gay pride celebrations are held during the month of June (such as gay pride marches in Chicago, Houston, Minneapolis, New York City, and San Francisco on the last Sunday of the month), in honor of Stonewall and the launch of the gay rights movement (D'Emilio, 1991).

4

Officer Experiences and Perceptions

Shared perceptions among employees in the workplace can have a profound effect on an organization. These shared perceptions are often the result of individual experiences of employees. An employee who feels that they have been unfairly treated in the organization might share their dissatisfaction with a sympathetic coworker. The coworker may repeat the story to another employee, who might in turn repeat it to a third. Before long, many employees know the story—understand it as fact—and react accordingly. Their reactions can include uncertainty, loss of work satisfaction, on-the-job distraction, and reduced motivation. In the worst-case scenarios, employees can drag down the organization's performance or subvert its mission. Thus organizations that fail to monitor and respond to the shared perceptions and experiences of employees risk failure.

This chapter gathers data about and the shared perceptions and experiences of lesbian and gay police officers. The aggregated data give us a good picture of their work environment, including barriers and opportunities that officers face in terms of equal opportunity and treatment. No doubt, challenges still remain for lesbian and gay officers, but if they share the perception that policing also provides benefits, then organizational failures are less likely. The data were collected from officers in both the United States and the United Kingdom, with 66 officers responding in the former case and 243 responding in the latter. In both cases, these datasets are among the largest ever collected for lesbian and gay officers.

Police Officers in the United States

According to the US Department of Justice, there are over 700,000 uniformed police officers and nearly 15,000 police agencies in the United States (US Department of Justice, 2010). Variations from one agency to the next are many. At one end are a few professional agencies with diverse police forces that match the demographics of the communities they serve. A prime example of this type of agency is the New York City Police Department (NYPD). In 2010, 53 percent of NYPD officers on patrol (22,000) were racial minorities (black, Asian, or Latino), a close match to the 55 percent racial-minority composition of New York City (El-Ghobashy, 2011; US Census Bureau, 2010). In most cases, police agencies have minority officers, but the agencies are not demographically representative of the communities they serve. While the demographics of a police agency rarely match those of its community, efforts (sometimes legally mandated) are under way to remediate this situation; meanwhile, officers in these environments are often trained how to professionally respond to and interact with various constituencies within the larger community. The efforts of these agencies are often undertaken in consultation with the various communities served. At the other end of the spectrum are the "traditional" police agencies, those whose personnel engage in classic law enforcement functions (rapid response to calls for service, arrest, and follow-up investigation) and rarely focus on community involvement, representative police service, or strategic planning to prevent crime.

Although New York City is highlighted as an example of representative police service, the size of a police agency is not necessarily an indicator of its diversity, professionalism, or training. There are large police agencies with generous resources that have low public support, low police morale, and minimal professional training. Conversely, many smaller police agencies have led the country in efforts to diversify and professionalize policing and to garner public support. Most police agencies in the United States, however, lie between these two extremes. Although models for planned change are being implemented at many agencies across the country, the process is long and requires incremental shifts from one policing generation to the next.

Survey of US Lesbian and Gay Officers

The survey on whose results this chapter is based represents an effort to better understand the work environment in which lesbian and gay people in US police agencies operate. The design of the survey instrument was based on surveys conducted for previous studies focusing on the shared perceptions of other minority groups in law enforcement—blacks and women (Bolton, 2003). The instrument was pretested with the help of the New York City Gay Officers Action League (GOAL NY), a professional support organization, and Law Enforcement Gays and Lesbians International (LEGAL International), an umbrella organization for all local lesbian and gay law enforcement professional associations. Pretesting of the survey took place over three monthly meetings during the winter of 2006.

The final instrument was completed in March 2007 and administered at the eleventh annual International Conference of Gay and Lesbian Criminal Justice Professionals, held in Providence, Rhode Island, from June 12 to June 17 of that year. According to the hosting committee, the conference drew 140 participants from sixteen states and two countries, representing over twenty police agencies (personal communication, 2007). The majority of the officers were from the Northeast region, with Boston and New York City representing over a third of attendees.

The four-page survey included three major components:

1. Questions capturing sociodemographic data about the officers and their status in law enforcement.
2. Questions eliciting the officers' perceptions, as lesbian and gay officers, about their workplace environment. (Officers were asked about barriers or obstacles, as well as access points or openings, to equal employment opportunities—for example, whether or not they received their first-choice assignments.)
3. Questions focusing on elements of work specific to the law enforcement environment, including questions about workplace relationships with external and internal entities.

The survey was administered over a two-day period at the conference hotel, where a separate room was set up specifically to administer the survey. Survey data were also collected at each major gathering of officers at the conference, including plenary sessions, guest lectures, and meals.

The results presented in this chapter are drawn from surveyed officers' responses to the following four questions:

1. Why did you choose a career in law enforcement?
2. Have you experienced any barriers related to equal employment opportunities?

3. Have you experienced any unique access related to equal employment opportunities?
4. In what ways, if any, have you been treated differently in law enforcement?

These questions created the opportunity for participants to discuss their rationale for entering into an environment traditionally hostile to homosexuals (Belkin and McNichol, 2002), and how unique barriers or access had affected their careers.

Demographics of Survey Respondents

Table 4.1 shows demographic information for the 66 officers who completed the survey. This high response rate of 47 percent (66 officers out of the 140 attending the conference) suggests that a robust cross-section of the conference population was surveyed. While it is impossible to assess whether the respondents are representative of the conference attendees, of law enforcement personnel, or of the general population, a prima facie review of the race and educational attainment data indicates a close match to the general population (US Department of Commerce, 2010; US Census Bureau, 2010).[1]

Table 4.1   Demographics of US Survey Respondents

	Number	Percentage
Gender		
Female	20	30
Male	46	70
Race		
Black/African American	6	9
Hispanic	10	15
White/non-Hispanic	48	72
Mixed	2	3
Education (level completed)		
High school	10	16
Community college	21	33
Undergraduate	20	32
Graduate	12	19
Rank		
Patrol	36	55
Supervisor/command	30	45

Note: N = 66. Numbers may not sum to 66 due to nonresponse. Percentages may not sum to 100 due to rounding.

Table 4.2 highlights the sexual orientation–related demographic information gathered by the survey. Not surprisingly, the majority of officers identified as gay or lesbian, and 84 percent considered themselves openly gay or lesbian with everyone in their lives—friends, family, and coworkers. Given the nature of the conference, the number of officers here who report being open about their sexual orientation is likely higher than among the broader police population. Respondents' relationship status was almost equally divided: 42 percent reported being single and 46 percent reported being in a relationship (including state-recognized domestic partnerships, marriages, and civil unions, as well as relationships not recognized by the state). The remaining officers reported being in some other type of relationship status.

Reasons for Choosing Law Enforcement

Table 4.3 shows the reasons respondents chose law enforcement as a career. There was a high level of agreement among respondents: job security, career opportunities, and civic duty were the top three reasons given, with 41 percent of respondents choosing each of these reasons.[2] Salary and

Table 4.2 US Survey Respondents' Sexual Orientation and Relationship Status

	Number	Percentage
Sexual orientation		
Gay	62	94
Straight	0	0
Other	4	6
Relationship status		
Single	26	42
Recognized partnership (marriage, civil union, domestic partnership)	18	29
In a relationship	6	17
Other	7	11
Level of "outness"		
Out to everyone (friends, family, and coworkers)	55	84
Out to friends and family	8	12
Out only to select people	3	5
Not out	0	0

Note: $N = 66$. Numbers may not sum to 66 due to nonresponse. Percentages may not sum to 100 due to rounding.

**Table 4.3   US Survey Respondents' Reasons for
Choosing Law Enforcement Careers**

	Number	Percentage
Job security	26	41
Career opportunity	27	41
Family tradition in law enforcement	11	17
Salary, wages, benefits	25	38
Adventure	22	33
Civic duty	27	41

Note: N = 66. Multiple choices allowed.

benefits followed closely, with 38 percent of respondents choosing this reason. Previous research had suggested that family and friends are influential when selecting a career in law enforcement (Ermer, 1978; Lester, 1983). Among these respondents, however, having family members in law enforcement was not especially important: only 17 percent said they entered policing because of having a family member on the force.

Barriers and Access Related to Equal Employment Opportunities

Police agencies have had varying degrees of success in their efforts to diversify and professionalize the law enforcement environment, but notable changes have taken place in police agencies across the United States. For many agencies, change has come because of legal mandates forcing them to include racial minorities and women. These efforts have their origins in the Equal Opportunity Act of 1972, which extended the Civil Rights Act of 1964 to cover public employment and prohibit discrimination on the basis of race, color, religion, sex, or national origin (Equal Employment Opportunity Commission, 2007). After these laws were enacted, potential and existing employees demanded their enforcement, challenging nearly every aspect of personnel practices in policing (Walker, 1985). While these mandates have had some success in diversifying the policing workplace through hiring practices, many other personnel-related issues have never been adequately addressed, and despite over thirty-five years of judicial, legislative, and executive mandates, barriers still exist in the law enforcement work environment.

Samuel Walker spoke to these issues in the context of promotion for minority officers:

[E]ven though civil service systems impose nominally objective procedures for promotion, informal subjectivity plays an important role. . . .
[P]erformance ratings, no matter how they are quantified, involve a
high degree of subjective evaluation by a supervisor. Certain assignments, moreover, offer greater opportunities for an officer to distin-
guish him- or herself, whereas others are regarded as "dead end"
assignments. Selection for these assignments is a discretionary matter
in most agencies. (1985, p. 567)

Beyond obeying mandates that provide the foundation for equal
access in the law enforcement environment, many agencies have gone
further by embracing efforts to change the culture of their organizations.
These efforts include diversity initiatives, community policing models,
and representative bureaucracy. Such efforts, in conjunction with societal and cultural changes, have made it more acceptable and beneficial to
be an openly lesbian or gay officer in some agencies. As David Sklansky
(2006) suggested, lesbian and gay officers are transforming the profession. In this sense, unique access or opportunities might exist for lesbian
and gay people in law enforcement. These access points seek to enhance
options for lesbian and gay people in much the same way that affirmative action and equal employment opportunity mandates enhanced
options for minorities and women in the past.

Figure 4.1 presents data on the equal employment barriers that the
lesbian and gay survey respondents reported facing in the law enforcement workplace. These officers experienced the lowest levels of discrimination in those areas where agencies have minimal discretion: firing (2 percent) and hiring (8 percent). The low levels of discrimination
in hiring, firing, and training suggests that Walker's observations about
discrimination and supervisory discretion, made in 1985, apply to lesbian and gay people as well. The low level of discrimination in mentoring may be attributable to officers finding informal mentorship via other
outlets—professional associations, for example. Respondents reported
discrimination in promotion as the most commonly faced barrier to
equal employment opportunity (21 percent), followed by assignments
(17 percent) and evaluation (15 percent).

Figure 4.2 identifies unique access that the lesbian and gay survey
respondents experienced in the workplace. As with barriers, individual
experiences varied greatly. As a group, the officers were most advan-
taged by being lesbian or gay in terms of assignments (28 percent).
This advantage comes from lesbian and gay officers' requests for
assignments within their communities and administrative support for
those requests, which could include community policing within lesbian

Figure 4.1   Equal Employment Barriers Faced by US Survey Respondents

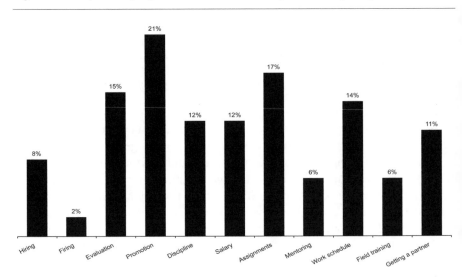

and gay–dominated neighborhoods and assignments in training or liaison units. In cases where assignments are seen as barriers, officers noted being denied postings that they perceived would enhance their careers, but that would not commonly be thought of as inclusive or diverse, such as homicide units. The officers reported lower (but still significant) levels of unique benefits in mentoring (11 percent) and work schedule (9 percent). Beyond these benefits, few officers reported other advantages to being openly lesbian or gay in the workplace. Given that workplace barriers were reported much more frequently compared to workplace access points, the differential treatment experienced by lesbian and gay officers becomes especially important in characterizing their shared attitudes.

Differential Treatment in the Workplace

The survey revealed how acutely lesbian and gay people in law enforcement can feel that they are treated differently in their day-to-day experience in the workplace. Discrimination in promotion, assignments, and evaluations poses formidable barriers to equal employment opportunities, but attitudinal barriers—mistreatment by others in law enforcement—can be institution-wide, and negative attitudes can have a detrimental impact on lesbian and gay officers. And, of course, these attitudes can have a deleterious effect on their employment opportunities as well.

Figure 4.2   Access Points Reported by US Survey Respondents

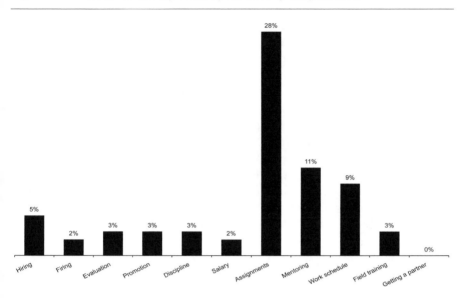

Table 4.4 shows the frequencies with which the lesbian and gay survey respondents experienced attitudinal barriers to equality in the workplace. They reported homophobic comments as the most frequent attitudinal barrier (67 percent). As a population that may not be visible to others, these officers may very well have been exposed to the honest attitudes of other officers, who use such comments to reinforce the established or entrenched cultural norms of police agencies. Being treated like an outsider (51 percent) and feeling social isolation (48 percent) were also common complaints—perhaps less common than homophobic comments because in order to establish an insider-outsider dynamic, the gay and lesbian officers would first have to be visible to all their colleagues.

Table 4.4   Differential Treatment Reported by US Survey Respondents

	Number	Percentage
Outsider	33	51
Tokenism	28	43
Social isolation	31	48
Homophobic talk	44	67
Repeated harassment	22	34
Retaliation	16	25

Note: N = 66. Multiple choices allowed.

Interpreting the Survey

The demographic information collected in this survey suggests that the experiences of lesbian and gay officers in the United States are in many ways very similar to the experiences of some of their heterosexual counterparts in law enforcement. For example, racial minorities experience similar incidents in terms of racist talk and social isolation (Bolton, 2003). The challenges that agencies face regarding racial and gender diversity also apply to lesbian and gay representation on police forces. In most police agencies, women, racial minorities, and lesbian and gay people remain underrepresented (Sklansky, 2006). For example, nationally, women represent only about 16 percent of uniformed police officers (US Department of Justice, 2010). Such underrepresentation has many contributing factors, including poor recruiting strategies, persistent institutional and other barriers, and lack of leadership.

Lesbian and gay police officers in the United States are also drawn to law enforcement for many of the same reasons that heterosexual officers are (Ermer, 1978; Lester, 1983). Law enforcement is a stable, respectable profession that can offer a route to the middle class. The availability of career opportunities, job security, and the chance to serve one's community offer as much appeal to gay and lesbian people as to others. These responses are telling in the context of the officers' overall workplace experience. Despite the many challenges that lesbian and gay officers encounter—including homophobic talk and biased performance evaluations—they believe that these challenges can be overcome or that the benefits of police service outweigh the costs.

Lesbian and gay officers report experiencing more barriers than opportunities in law enforcement. These barriers are strengthened by the different treatment that lesbian and gay officers receive. The homophobic talk they hear, the outsider status they suffer, and the feelings of isolation they endure all have a direct effect on their employment opportunities. James Croteau, Mary Anderson, and Bonnie VanderWal (2008) have noted that lesbian and gay people are often forced to create a faux heterosexual persona, avoid sexual-identity labeling, or keep their sexual orientation hidden as coping mechanisms in the workplace. In many cases, lesbian and gay officers use these identity-management coping mechanisms to optimize employment opportunities and minimize barriers.

In many ways, this distinguishes the experiences of lesbian and gay officers from those of other minority groups who enter law enforcement. Racial minorities and women enter into the field with minority status, as they are visible minorities. When harassment, discrimination, or other malfeasances occurs, we can attribute it to one or more minority statuses (as a woman, or as a person of color, or both). As an invisible minority group, lesbian and gay people have different coping strategies and manage their minority status based on the workplace climate. Of course, people are often assumed to be lesbian or gay, and are treated accordingly depending on the context and climate. In these situations (when a person is not able to manage her or his minority status), the experiences of racial minorities, women, and sexual minorities are more similar than different.

Police Officers in the United Kingdom

In the United Kingdom, policing is governed at the local level, by a police authority, usually consisting of three local judges, nine local councilors, and five independent or community members (House of Commons, 2010). The police authority also has a legal duty to ensure that the police agency is financially sound. In addition to the forty-three police agencies overseen by individual police authorities, there are also several independent agencies, including the British Transport Authority, the Central Motorway Policing Group, the Civil Nuclear Constabulary, the Ministry of Defense Police, the Port of Dover Police, the Port of Liverpool Police, the Serious Organized Crime Department, and the Scottish Drug Enforcement Department. Northern Ireland and Scotland have somewhat different ways of governing their police agencies: in the former, the Police Service of Northern Ireland is supervised by the Northern Ireland Policing Board; in Scotland, each police agency is overseen either by the local authority or by a joint board of the relevant authority from all other agencies.

As of March 2009, there were 243,126 full-time police and staff working in the forty-three police agencies in the United Kingdom. Police officers accounted for 59.1 percent of this total, police community support officers 6.8 percent, traffic wardens 0.2 percent, designated officers 1.3 percent, and other police staff 32.6 percent (House of Commons, 2010). In addition to these police and staff, there were 14,251 special constables providing a voluntary police resource to police agencies and local communities in England and Wales (House of Commons, 2010).

Survey of UK Lesbian and Gay Officers

The questions asked in my UK survey of lesbian and gay officers were identical to those in the US survey, although the language was sometimes altered to be relevant to the UK experience. Unlike the US survey, the UK survey was conducted online, over an eight-week period in August and September of 2009. After the survey was sent, reminder e-mail messages were sent at two-week intervals over those eight weeks. The survey pool was drawn from the e-mail listserv of the Gay Police Association (GPA). According to the association, this list reaches more than 5,000 lesbian and gay police officers, community support officers, and staff (personal communication, 2009). It is estimated that the survey instrument reached 2,500 members of the list.[3]

Demographics of Survey Respondents

Table 4.5 shows demographic information for the 243 officers who completed the survey, out of an estimated 2,500 contacted (a response rate of 9.7 percent).[4] As with the US data, it is impossible to assess with certainty whether the respondents are representative of UK lesbian and gay officers in general, or of the GPA's membership, though a prima facie review of the race data indicates a close match to the general population of the United Kingdom.[5] However, the demographic information does differ in several important ways. First, the proportion of survey respondents who are women (38.7 percent) is higher than the proportion of nationally serving officers who are women (22 percent) (Office of National Statistics, 2010). Next, the educational level of survey respondents is higher than the general educational level among police officers nationally. For survey respondents, about 25 percent of officers have university degrees or higher, compared to about 20 percent for the general police population (Office for National Statistics, 2010). Finally, we see a cross-section of police ranks represented in the survey, with the majority of respondents (32.9 percent) serving as front-line police constables.

Table 4.6 highlights the sexual orientation–related demographic information gathered by the survey. Not surprisingly, the majority of officers identified as lesbian or gay, and 81.5 percent considered themselves openly lesbian or gay with everyone in their lives—friends, family, and coworkers. Of the officers responding to the survey, 70.8 percent reported being open about their sexuality with everyone at work—superiors, subordinates, and coworkers. Over 66 percent of respondents reported being in a relationship (either a formal, state-recognized relationship, or an informal one).

Table 4.5 Demographics of UK Survey Respondents

	Number	Percentage
Gender		
Male	140	57.2
Female	94	38.7
Race		
Black or black British/African	1	0.4
Mixed: white and black Caribbean	1	0.4
Mixed: white and Asian	2	0.8
Other mixed background	2	0.8
White British	205	84.4
White Irish	9	3.7
Other white background	12	4.9
Prefer not to say	1	0.4
Education (level completed)		
Diploma, A level	92	37.9
Diploma, O level	13	5.3
Degree (other)	40	16.5
Foundation degree	6	2.5
First degree (bachelor's)	38	15.6
Master's degree	22	9.1
Doctoral degree	1	0.4
Other	12	4.9
Rank		
Police constable	80	32.9
Detective constable	10	4.1
Sergeant	29	11.9
Detective sergeant	5	2.1
Inspector	15	6.2
Chief inspector	4	1.6
Police support	28	11.5
Administration	21	8.6
Other	27	11.1

Note: $N = 243$. Numbers may not sum to 243 due to nonresponse. Percentages may not sum to 100 due to rounding.

Reasons for Choosing Law Enforcement

Table 4.7 shows the reasons that respondents chose law enforcement as a career.[6] Career opportunity was ranked highest among the options, with 32 percent of respondents identifying this as their main reason for entering law enforcement, followed by civic duty (15 percent) and job security (14 percent). The three reasons least often identified for entering law enforcement were family tradition, compensation, and adventure.

Table 4.6 UK Survey Respondents' Sexual Orientation and Relationship Status

	Number	Percentage
Sexual orientation		
Homosexual (lesbian or gay)	226	93.0
Bisexual	11	4.5
Other	3	1.2
Relationship status		
Single	67	27.6
Divorced	4	1.6
Legal partnership	59	24.2
In a relationship	101	41.6
Other	2	0.8
Level of "outness" in community		
Out to everyone	198	81.5
Out only to friends	15	6.2
Out only to select people	12	4.9
Not out	8	3.3
Level of "outness" at work		
Out to everyone	172	70.8
Out to select people	19	7.8
Out to at least one person	1	0.4
Not out	6	2.5

Note: $N = 243$. Numbers may not sum to 243 due to nonresponse. Percentages may not sum to 100 due to rounding.

Table 4.7 UK Survey Respondents' Reasons for Choosing Law Enforcement Careers

	Number	Percentage
Job security	33	14
Career opportunity	77	32
Family tradition in law enforcement	10	4
Salary, wages, benefits	8	3
Adventure	27	11
Civic duty	36	15
Other	28	12

Note: $N = 243$. Numbers may not sum to 243 due to nonresponse. Percentages may not sum to 100 due to rounding.

Barriers and Access Related to
Equal Employment Opportunities

Like their counterparts in the United States, British police agencies have experienced varying degrees of success in their efforts to create equal employment opportunities and to diversify their forces. However, the United Kingdom has undertaken comparatively greater efforts to professionalize its police agencies and make them more responsive. The most prominent and best known of these efforts emerged in response to the public inquiry into the murder of Stephen Lawrence (Home Office, 1999). As is widely known throughout the United Kingdom, the race-based murder of Lawrence in South London in 1993 changed policing practices throughout the country. Although the police investigation did lead to a prosecution, it was perceived as incomplete, biased, and racist. Persistence and pressure by Lawrence's family and the black community led to the establishment of a public inquiry to investigate his murder and the policing procedures used in the case, led by Sir William Macpherson. (For more details on the Lawrence inquiry and Macpherson Report, see Chapter 3.) Although those efforts were primarily race-related, they provided the foundation for other diversity efforts. One recent effort is the National Police Learning Requirement for Race and Diversity Training. This training initiative, established by the Home Office (the UK's national policing and law enforcement agency) but delivered by local agencies, has three main aims: to raise awareness about individual officers' responsibility for inclusive behavior; to make participants aware of the diversity of twenty-first-century Britain with respect to race (the initiative's primary focus), gender, disability, age, sexual orientation, religion, and beliefs; and to provide necessary skills and information to officers to adopt inclusive practices within the workplace and when working with the community (Clements, 2008).

With regard to employment and sexual orientation, the guiding effort has been legislation. The Employment Equality Regulations, which came into force in the United Kingdom in 2003, cover discrimination, harassment, and victimization in the workplace and in vocational training settings, and mandate equal access to employment opportunities such as promotion and training.

Figure 4.3 presents data on the equal employment barriers that the lesbian and gay survey respondents reported facing in the law enforcement workplace. The most commonly cited barrier, reported by 13 percent of respondents, involved discrimination experienced when joining or transferring into a police agency. UK lesbian and gay officers also reported discrimination or barriers in work schedules, promotion, and postings (10 percent each). The barriers least often reported involved getting a partner (3 percent), benefits/salary (1 percent), and firing. Little comparative data exist, but in the general UK population, similar levels of discrimination are reported in terms of race and promotion (Equality and Human Rights Commission, 2010).[7]

Figure 4.4 identifies unique access that the lesbian and gay survey respondents experienced in the workplace. As with barriers, individual experiences with access varied greatly. Of the officers responding to the survey, 25 percent reported unique access or benefits related to being a lesbian or gay officer—far fewer than those reporting barriers. The access or benefit most commonly reported was training (9 percent), followed by mentoring (6 percent). Equal percentages of officers reported beneficial postings and ease of getting a patrol partner (3 percent each). Few equal opportunity benefits were reported in the areas of promotion, benefits/salary, or work schedule (1 percent for each of these areas). Given that workplace barriers and access were reported at varying levels by respondents, the differential treatment experienced by lesbian and gay officers becomes especially important in characterizing their shared attitudes and perceptions about law enforcement.

Figure 4.3 Equal Employment Barriers Faced by UK Survey Respondents

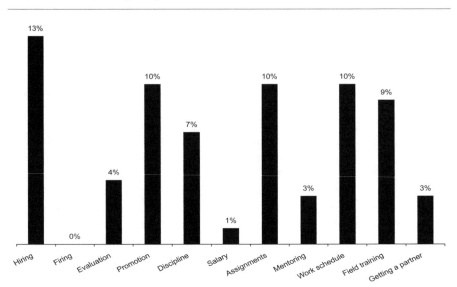

Differential Treatment in the Workplace

Like the US survey, the UK survey also reveals a less than ideal work-place. On any given day, a lesbian or gay person might encounter words, behaviors, or actions that negatively affect the work environment. Of course, these negative factors have an impact on the lesbian or gay offi-cers, but they also affect other officers as well as agency staff and man-agement. Employment barriers for one group can negatively affect the entire organization. For example, straight female officers may assume an unfriendly environment based on the treatment of lesbian and gay officers. Additionally, lesbian and gay staff and management might interpret the environment as hostile when these officers are negatively discriminated against. In total, negative factors are not just detrimental to the individual officers; they are detrimental for the entire agency.

Table 4.8 shows the frequencies with which the lesbian and gay sur-vey respondents experienced attitudinal barriers to equality in the work-place. Half of the officers (50 percent) reported homophobic talk as the most frequently faced attitudinal barrier. Being outed in the workplace followed closely, with 34 percent of officers reporting that their sexual orientation had been revealed against their wishes. Being treated like an outsider (24 percent) and tokenism (being selected as the single minori-ty to stave off claims of discrimination) (25 percent) were also common complaints.

Figure 4.4 Access Points Reported by UK Survey Respondents

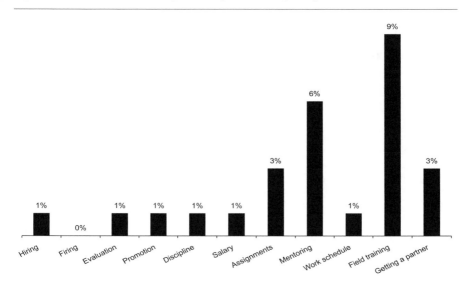

Interpreting the Survey

The UK survey data suggest that the work lives of British lesbian and gay officers remain less than ideal. As noted earlier, many officers join their agency because of the perceived career opportunities. For the most part, these career opportunities are thwarted by the realities on the ground. When lesbian and gay officers enter the agency, they experience discrimination along a number of fronts, and this discrimination in equal opportunity is often paired with day-to-day harassment in the form of homophobic talk and differential treatment. But the data suggest that the Employment Equality Regulations are being implemented effectively; civil service protections appear to have reduced the likelihood that lesbian and gay officers will be discriminated against in salary and benefits. Furthermore, levels of discrimination—while not completely eliminated—match closely the discrimination levels for other groups, namely racial minorities.

Comparing the US and UK Surveys

The results of the US and UK surveys of lesbian and gay officers suggest that working in law enforcement is more challenging for lesbian and gay officers in the United States than in the United Kingdom. Both groups identify important barriers that may affect equal opportunity in the workplace. In the United States, the most important barriers are unequal opportunities in evaluation, training, and promotion. In the United Kingdom, the chief barriers involve challenges faced when join-

Table 4.8   Differential Treatment Reported by UK Survey Respondents

	Number	Percentage
Outsider	59	24
Tokenism	61	25
Social isolation	45	19
Homophobic talk	121	50
Repeated harassment	37	15
Retaliation	14	6
Property damage	24	10
Being outed at work	83	34
Other	14	6

Note: $N = 243$. Multiple choices allowed.

ing an agency or transferring to a new post, work schedules, promotions, and assignments. These UK barriers, however, were reported much less frequently in the United Kingdom compared to the United States, and were reported in the United Kingdom at frequencies similar to those experienced by other minority officer groups, not just lesbian and gay officers.

That said, both US and UK officers did report some unique opportunities granted to them. Although these opportunities were reported much less frequently than were barriers, the responses point to a trend toward a more inclusive and diverse law enforcement environment (Gillespie, 2008). Previous research suggests that benefits or opportunities for lesbian and gay officers would have been inconceivable just two decades ago (Buhrke, 1996; Burke, 1994; Leinen, 1993).

This trend appears to be confirmed by the final set of questions asked in each survey, which focused on the general police work environment and the respondents' perceptions about their professional relationships. Survey participants were asked about interactions with others in law enforcement as well as with community members. Officers in both the United States and the United Kingdom reported similar levels of agreement on five of the six questions.

First, when asked whether their job advancement opportunities were the same as those of nonlesbian and nongay officers, 48 percent of US officers and 58 percent of UK officers said yes. So, while officers in both surveys pointed to individual instances of discrimination (perhaps a one-time event), at least half believed that the overall environment afforded them the same opportunities that it did to others in law enforcement.

Second, when asked whether they had good relationships with non-lesbian and nongay coworkers, supervisors, and subordinates (if applicable), 71 percent of US officers and 72 percent of British officers said yes. This suggests an overall climate that is basically friendly and inclusive. Given the large proportion of lesbian and gay officers who reported being openly gay in each survey, their response to this relationship question suggests support for Eden King, Clare Reilly, and Michelle Hebl's (2008) assertion that more supportive work climates can be achieved through timing and method of disclosure of sexual orientation. These supportive work climates can even be achieved in traditionally hostile environments when close interpersonal relationships are developed.

Third, in addition to having good relationships inside the police agencies, officers had good relationships in the nongay communities in which they served, with 69 percent of US officers and 60 percent of UK officers reporting this experience. While it is not clear how often sexual orientation–related issues arise when officers are in the field or what level of "outness" lesbian and gay officers exhibit when they are on patrol, this response suggests that most officers do not feel constrained by sexual orientation when carrying out their day-to-day work. We might also infer that lesbian and gay officers believe that they are respected by people and institutions in their communities when carrying out their jobs.

The fourth question generated the largest difference between the United States and the United Kingdom in shared perceptions of lesbian and gay officers. When asked about their work relationships within the gay communities they served, 60 percent of US officers reported good relations, while only 43 percent of UK officers reported the same. It is not clear why this variation was the largest, but it may be a function of location and local demographics. Most of the officers who participated in the US survey were from metropolitan cities—including New York City, Boston, and Los Angeles—which tend to have geographically concentrated lesbian and gay communities. The UK survey population differed significantly in this respect. As noted earlier, lesbian and gay officers serving in the country's most populous city, London, were generally unable to participate in the survey. Thus, most of the respondents were from smaller communities that lacked "geographic" gay subcommunities in their jurisdictions. A comment from an officer who participated in one of the UK focus-group sessions strengthens this assertion: "We mustn't forget that there is hardly a gay community, as in a gay scene, within Wiltshire or Swindon. And we need to be mindful that even if people are open about their sexual orientation, they may not necessarily be on the scene. So, though we're going in and we're engaging more with the scene base, what about all the others? What about all the other community that's out there that we're not engaging with?" (personal communication, 2009).

Fifth, when asked whether they were more effective than nongay officers when working with lesbian and gay suspects and prisoners, officers from both countries generally said no. Only 39 percent of US officers and 40 percent of UK officers thought that they were more effective than their nongay counterparts in this regard. Although measuring "good police work" is difficult and inherently subjective, many officers would argue that they "know it when they see it." This is part of police socialization, which is commonly described as a "blue-walled mosaic" (Wilkins and Williams, 2005). The profession reflects and projects a sense of fraternal support and fidelity, which reinforces police culture. And police culture includes the belief that being a good officer—usually

Voices from the Field

Name: Jason Cortes
Police agency: Metropolitan Police Department (Washington, D.C.)
Rank: Police officer
Length of service: Ten years

On outreach and partnerships in the community:
"There are youth groups, transgendered groups that we form these alliances with. So you could call the HIPS: Helping Individual Prostitutes Survive, because they were transgendered sex workers, and the best people to go to are the ones who work the streets, who work with those people, like HIPS. When we have a lot of youth [who] get kicked out of their homes, so there's this youth organization, this youth advocacy group, and they don't necessarily have to be gay or GLBT groups, they can be friendly. There are some that are allied."

On when an incident is not a hate crime:
"People start calling on Mondays and start, 'I was walking down the street and somebody called me a faggot. I know they hang out at 14th and U Street all the time. I can pick them out. I want to report this as a crime.' And, of course, I explain that it's not a crime, it's an incident. We do report on that, we do document that. It's something that we do track, we do keep track of all that. And we'd like to know and get as much information as we can, but it's not a crime. I mean, to call a person a faggot is not a crime."

*On the lesbian and gay community's perceptions
of community policing:*
"Well, from the outside perspective, like from the outreach perspective, I think the response from the community has been tremendous. I haven't seen too much negative, except for people who really just don't like the police to begin with, and they're always suspicious. There have been a few."

meaning conducting good police work or policing in a professional manner—is the standard by which all should be judged. Thus it makes sense to assume that lesbian and gay officers have been socialized to believe that any "good officer" should be able to work effectively with any suspect or prisoner, regardless of specific personal characteristics. One UK police officer said it this way:

> So, I like the fact that I'm a GLO [gay liaison officer], because it helps me relate to that person, and they can see I'm a GLO and I'm not there because I'm gay. And also, I think it helps them, sort of, have that boundary for me, but as for being more effective, I don't think so at all. It doesn't make me more effective. I just might know a bit more about the community and things like that. But as for effective skills, it's just up to the officer. (personal communication, 2009)

Finally, the officers were asked about their support network on the job. This broad question was an attempt to identify levels of friendship and intimacy for lesbian and gay officers in the workplace. Implicitly, the question was asking whether there were people at work with whom the officers could talk, in whom they could confide, and with whom they felt comfortable sharing time. As Nick Rumens (2008) noted, the formation of good relationships has many implications for both the worker and the workplace, including implications for psychological and emotional support, motivation and feelings of self-worth among employees, and evaluation and promotion consideration. Certainly, friendship and intimacy can help police officers deal with difficult working conditions (Korczynski, 2003). Such relationships can also help officers make better sense of their work environment and increase the likelihood for career advancement (Willis, 1977; Kanter, 1977). In short, support networks create shared perception, workplace culture, and opportunities. Of the lesbian and gay cops who responded to the surveys, 51 percent of UK officers and 48 percent of US officers reported having a good support network in their agency.

Conclusion

Though it is impossible to draw universal truths or even generalizations about the lives of lesbian and gay officers based on a survey sample of just over 300 nonrandom respondents, we can improve our understanding of the varied and complex policing environment from this sample. The data from the two surveys suggest that lesbian and gay officers in both the United States and the United Kingdom face many of the same opportunities and barriers. The aggregate picture for the UK policing system appears somewhat more favorable than that for the US system, but this is most likely a function of the particular populations who responded to the survey. What is clear from both datasets is that the work environment for lesbian and gay officers is complex and complicated, which reinforces the reality that both positive and negative experiences can exist in the workplace and that even negative shared perceptions won't necessarily deter committed and dedicated officers. Since most officers join the police for career opportunities and job security, it makes sense that many will tolerate the less-than-ideal conditions often associated with law enforcement.

Notes

1. According to the US Census Bureau (2010), educational attainment for the general population in 2010 was as follows: high school, 86.7 percent; some college, 57.0 percent; associate's or bachelor's degree, 39.0 percent; master's degree, 7.6 percent; doctorate or professional degree, 2.9 percent. Racial demographics for the general population were as follows: white, 63.7; Hispanic and Latino, 16.3 percent; black or African American, 12.6; mixed race (mestizo, mulatto), 6.2 percent; Asian, 4.8 percent; two or more races, 6.2 percent; American Indian or Alaska Native, 0.9 percent; and Native Hawaiian or other Pacific Islander, 0.2 percent.

2. Respondents were able to select more than one reason for entering law enforcement.

3. Members of the London Metropolitan Police and a few other agencies were unable to participate in the survey. According to the GPA, some police agencies in the United Kingdom do not allow receipt of e-mail messages that contain links to websites, and some still filter out e-mails based on keywords such as *gay* and *lesbian* (personal communication, 2009). Thus I was not able to survey these police agencies online.

4. Response rates for online surveys (as for postal surveys) vary greatly—from 5 to 40 percent—based on numerous potential influences, including survey length, respondent contacts, design issues, research affiliation, and compensation (Sheehan, 2001).

5. According to the United Kingdom's Office for National Statistics (2010), the ethnic breakdown of the general population in 2009 was as follows: white (British, Irish, other), 92.0 percent; Asian (Indian, Pakistani, Bangladeshi, other South Asian, Chinese), 4.4 percent; black (Caribbean, African, other), 2.0 percent; mixed, 1.2 percent; other, 0.4 percent.

6. Respondents were allowed to select only one reason for entering law enforcement.

7. In terms of promotion in the United Kingdom, ethnic minorities report experiencing discrimination. Specifically, blacks (African, 9 percent; Caribbean, 8 percent) and Asians (Indian, 5 percent; Chinese and other, 4 percent; Pakistani, 3 percent) are more likely to feel they have experienced discrimination based on race compared to whites (1 percent) (Equality and Human Rights Commission, 2010).

5

Unique Roles,
Unique Contributions

Lesbian and gay officers report a number of contemporary opportunities and barriers in police agencies. In devoting their lives to public service, these officers have helped to change the nature of the police work and the law enforcement environment. We know, for example, that lesbian and gay officers have been involved in training other officers, acting as liaisons with community groups, and supporting fellow lesbian and gay officers for professional development. Given the historical invisibility of lesbian and gay people, including lesbian and gay police officers, it is impossible to know their full contribution to policing. We can, however, get a better sense of the lives of lesbian and gay officers by understanding the broader historical, social, political, and legal contexts of their known contributions to policing.

In both the United States and the United Kingdom, the decision to serve as an openly lesbian or gay officer is highly variable and remains a very personal decision with numerous implications. Openly lesbian and gay officers experience varying levels of support in the workplace, and a hostile environment does not necessarily mean that officers will keep their sexual orientation hidden.

In the early 1980s, lesbian and gay police officers began meeting outside their agencies, forming professional associations and networking within the law enforcement ranks. Today, countless lesbian and gay officers in Western countries serve openly in their agencies, some serving at the highest ranks of law enforcement. For example, until his retirement in 2007, Brian Paddick was the United Kingdom's most senior gay police officer, having served as deputy assistant commissioner for the London Metropolitan Police (White, 2008). In 2009, the city of Tampa, Florida—

with an urban population of nearly 3 million—selected an openly lesbian woman, Jane Castor, to serve as its chief of police (Melloy, 2009).

Factors Influencing Broader Acceptance

In recent years, the presence of openly lesbian and gay police officers—some in the early stages of their careers—has become much more common. A number of factors help to explain the emergence of openly gay women and men in policing, including media portrayals, nondiscrimination laws, and changing social norms.

Media Portrayals

The role of the media in influencing public opinion is well documented (Birkland, 1997; Kingdon, 1995). Organizational action on certain issues may be dictated—either promoted or constrained—by public opinion. That being the case, the media's ability to influence public opinion must translate, at some level and to some degree, into an ability to influence organizational action. *Framing* is a way of packaging and positioning an issue so that it conveys a certain meaning (Menashe and Siegel, 1998). Communication sources, such as news organizations, use framing to define and construct political issues or public controversies (Nelson, Clawson, and Oxley, 1997). Robert Entman explains this best:

> The distinction between "what to think" and "what to think about" is misleading. Nobody, no force, can ever successfully "tell people what to think." . . . The way to control attitudes is to provide a partial selection of information for a person to think about, or process. The only way to influence what people think is precisely to shape what they think about. . . . Influence can be exerted through selection of information, but the conclusions cannot be dictated. If the media (or anyone) can affect what people think about—the information they process—the media can affect their attitudes. (1989, p. 349)

The effects of framing have been demonstrated in studies of public opinion and gay rights policies (Lewis and Rogers, 2000; Nelson, Clawson, and Oxley, 1997; Yang, 1999), alcohol policies (Wagenaar and Streff, 1990), affirmative action (Fine, 1992), and environmental policies (Vaughan and Seifert, 1992). While media framing may not have direct influence on which issues come to public attention, it can influence how the public comes to understand an issue and can affect public opinion about the issue. And if organizational leaders are influenced by public opinion, then they are also influenced by how issues are framed in the media.

Over the past two decades, television—perhaps the most important player in media framing—has introduced a number of gay police roles. No doubt influenced by the larger social environment, these portrayals of gay officers have become more favorable over time. The first gay police officer role debuted in the United States in 1987 in the show *Hooperman* (Jensen, 2009). In this show, Officer Rick Silardi (played by Joseph Gian) was a San Francisco cop who was openly gay with his coworkers but who often had to thwart the sexual advances of his female policing partner. The inclusion of a gay officer as a central character represented a major milestone for US television. By 2003, gay police officers were accepted as commonplace, and these characters' sexuality was fully integrated into their portrayals. For example, the NBC sitcom *Will and Grace* featured Officer Vince D'Angelo (played by Bobby Cannavale) as namesake character Will's police officer boyfriend. Also in 2003, the HBO drama *Six Feet Under* introduced Officer Keith Charles (played by Mathew St. Patrick) as the partner of one of the show's main characters. In both cases, the police officers lived openly gay lives. More recently, the TNT drama *Southland* has featured Officer John Cooper (played by Michael Cudlitz) as perhaps the most modern version of a gay police officer so far represented on television. Cooper is perfectly at ease with his sexuality. The show portrays him as a "cop first"—he identifies far more closely with his fellow police officers than he does with the gay community. Without being a central theme of the show, Cooper's homosexuality is handled casually and without stigma (Jensen, 2009).

The portrayal of lesbian police officers on television has also trended in a positive direction. In 1997, ABC's police drama *NYPD Blue* introduced a minor lesbian character, Officer Abby Sullivan (played by Paige Turco). Sullivan's storyline focused on her and her partner's desire to secure a sperm donor. Unfortunately, this storyline ended with Officer Sullivan's intimate partner being killed and Sullivan being attacked and wounded by a disillusioned ex-girlfriend (Warn, 2004). In addition to the Officer Sullivan character, *NYPD Blue* also introduced two ambiguously lesbian police officers. The first was introduced in 1995, with Detective Adrianne Lesniak (played by Justine Miceli) transferring to the Fifteenth Precinct and finding herself the object of sexual advances from a fellow male police officer, James Martinez (played by Nicholas Turturro). To escape his advances, she told him she was gay, which temporarily made her wonder if she actually was—until she eventually concluded that she was just bitter and disillusioned with men, and not attracted to women (Warn, 2004). In 2004, Detective Kelly Ronson (played by Jessalyn Gilsig) was introduced. Her character could be described more accurately as bisexual, but several episodes highlighted her relationships with other women.

The most recent, and arguably the most realistic and complex, lesbian police officer character on television was Detective Shakima "Kima" Greggs (played by Sonja Sohn) in the HBO series *The Wire.* As one of the show's main characters, Detective Greggs was introduced in the first season, 2002, and her story was integrated into all of the show's major episodes. The character had problems with fidelity, alcohol, and relationships, but she was generally portrayed as complex and balanced. In fact, Sarah Warn (2004) noted that in *The Wire*'s second season, Greggs was the only stable character on the show.

One of the longest-running and most well-known television shows about the US criminal justice system was the drama *Law and Order.* The main series ran for twenty seasons (from 1990 to 2010), with several successful spin-offs and adaptations, include *Special Victims Unit, Trial by Jury,* and *Criminal Intent.* The show was set and filmed in New York City, and it often dramatized real-life events. The dramatizing approach allowed the show to raise contemporary and sometimes controversial topics. It is not clear whether this "ripped from the headlines" approach followed or led cultural trends; however, given its long history and television prominence, its portrayal of gay characters in law enforcement is important.

Over the course of the main show, there were numerous episodes that featured gay characters or gay-themed plots (Lo, 2005). These characters and themes where were often episodic and tangential to the ongoing narrative of the show. It was not until 2009 that a confirmed-gay major character entered in the series, Special Agent George Huang, M.D. (played by B. D. Wong), as part of the *Law and Order* spin-off show *Special Victims Unit.*

Over the twenty-year evolution of *Law and Order,* at least four gay-themed topics emerged: HIV/AIDS, hate crimes, being "outed" as a homosexual, and marriage equality. When the series first aired in 1990, the HIV/AIDS crisis was at a critical stage, and was also thought of as an exclusively "gay" disease. One of the first episodes of the first season was about a gay man who admitted to mercy-killing men who were dying of AIDS in San Francisco and Los Angeles. Over time, as the HIV/AIDS crisis became less prominent culturally, and became decoupled from gay men, the topic also receded in the television show (Lo, 2005).

The second gay-themed topic was the issue of hate crimes, featured in one of the few episodes that included a lesbian or gay police officer.

In the third season (1993), a gay police officer was wounded in a shootout and died because his backup did not arrive in time. It was later revealed that the backup officers responded slowly because the injured officer was gay. In this dramatization, the backup officers were acquitted, based on a psychiatrist's court testimony that homophobia was pathological and uncontrollable.

By 2001, *Law and Order* was approaching hate crimes in a very different way. In this season, a gay foster father was beaten by the biological father of his adopted child, whom the biological father then kidnapped. During the attack and kidnapping, the biological father used antigay slurs, which became the basis for a hate crime charge.

Several *Law and Order* episodes also highlighted crimes committed in the context of people who were exposed as lesbian or gay. These episodes usually focused on politicians. In a 1992 episode, a gay city councilman was blackmailed and murdered by his lover. In a 1995 episode, another gay city councilman was murdered by a heterosexual city councilman. The events in the latter episode appeared to be loosely based on the Harvey Milk murder (Lo, 2005). In the fifteenth season (2005), an episode focused on a secretly gay governor in Connecticut who was managing his outing amid a number of political scandals. Despite the fact that by 2005 the cultural stigma of "coming out of the closet" had diminished greatly, the dramatization still revolved around a murder (the governor's wife).

Finally, the issue of marriage equality for homosexuals also made its way into the scripts of *Law and Order*. In the final season (2010), a lesbian was forced to "adopt" her partner as a way to form a family union. When the two women became suspects in a murder investigation, the adoption was exposed as a sham, though a necessary one in the absence of marriage equality. The question of spousal privilege was raised but rejected, since the couple were not legally married.

Thus the *Law and Order* series highlighted a number of gay characters and gay issues for the television viewer. Although the series gave very little representation to lesbian and gay officers (only one episode), its representation of lesbian and gay people in general can be characterized as considerate and fair (Lo, 2005). In exposing its American audience to considerate portrayals of lesbian and gay people, *Law and Order* also exposed viewers to the idea that lesbians and gays could serve within law enforcement.

While British television has an equally diverse and complicated history of depicting lesbian and gay characters, its history is less extensive compared to American television. The most famous portrayal was gay sergeant Craig Gilmore (played by Hywel Simons) in *The Bill*. This police procedural television series focused on the lives and work of one shift of police officers—at Sun Hill—rather than on any particular aspect of police work. The show, aired from 1984 to 2010, was the longest-running police television drama in British history (*"The Bill* Is Slashed," 2009). Like *Law and Order* in the United States, *The Bill* enjoyed ongoing popularity and several spin-offs. At its high point, the show was aired in over fifty-five countries (*"The Bill* Will Be Cut Back," 2009).

Sergeant Craig Gilmore was introduced in the show in 2001 as the modern face of policing—Gilmore was confident and ambitious, yet disinterested in office politics ("Sergeant Craig Gilmore," 2010). With his introduction, he became the first regular gay police character on British television ("UK: When Soaps Go Gay," 2010). The Gilmore character was openly gay, and sexuality issues appeared to take a backseat to policing issues—Gilmore was not portrayed as a gay police officer, but rather as a police officer who happened to be gay. He came from a close-knit family in Wales who knew he was gay, and faced the same relationship challenges as his heterosexual counterparts, including ending a long-term relationship, embarking on a new relationship with a troublemaker, and attempting to establish a personal relationship with another police officer, Constable Luke Ashton (played by Scott Neal). Before exiting the show, the Gilmore and Ashton characters made television history in portraying the first gay kiss between uniformed officers on British television ("UK: When Soaps Go Gay," 2010). The kiss also marked the first time *The Bill* courted controversy, as over 300 people complained about the gay embrace ("Sergeant Craig Gilmore," 2010).

These television shows and their plot lines can be viewed as having framed gay-related issues and affected attitudes about sexual orientation and policing. It can be argued that the media have helped to normalize the idea of lesbian and gay police officers. While not telling viewers *what* to think, the media have influenced *how* we think about lesbian and gay cops—an influence that includes communicating the basic ideas that lesbian and gay officers exist, that they have personal and professional lives, and that the concepts of homosexuality and policing are not mutually exclusive.

Nondiscrimination Laws

Although legal protections for lesbian and gay people continue to expand, discrimination on the basis of sexual orientation continues to be a social and policy problem (Colvin and Riccucci, 2002; Riccucci and Gossett, 1996). In 2001, the New York State Pride Agenda conducted a survey of 1,891 gay and lesbian individuals across the state. The survey's findings confirmed previous research about discrimination based on sexual orientation, finding that more than one-third of respondents (36 percent) had experienced some form of job-related discrimination based on sexual orientation within the previous five years (Pride Agenda, 2001). Specifically, the authors of the Pride Agenda reported that 8 percent of respondents had been fired, 27 percent had been verbally harassed at the workplace, 7 percent had been physically harassed, and 10 percent had been given negative performance evaluations because of their sexual orientation (Pride Agenda, 2001).

A UK lesbian and gay advocacy organization, Stonewall, found that nearly one in five lesbian and gay people, almost 350,000 workers in Britain, have experienced bullying from their colleagues because of their sexual orientation (Stonewall, 2010). Almost 4 million people (13 percent of the British work force) have witnessed verbal homophobic bullying in the workplace, and over 1 million people (4 percent of the national work force) have witnessed physical homophobic bullying at work (Stonewall, 2010). These US and UK findings closely match the results of other studies that have attempted to measure sexual orientation–based employment discrimination (Levine, 1989; Simon and Daly, 1992; Badgett, 1995; Croteau and Lark, 1995; Riccucci and Gossett, 1996; Colvin, 2004).

Currently, twenty-seven US states have laws prohibiting employment discrimination based on sexual orientation (Human Rights Campaign, 2010). These state statutes and executive orders range from basic protection for public employees in hiring, firing, and promotion, to comprehensive laws that ban discrimination based on sexual orientation in housing, credit, public accommodations, education, and employment. Provisions that address public employment discrimination in hiring, firing, and promotion are universal among states with nondiscrimination policies, and thus protect local and state police officers. To date, there is no federal-level law prohibiting employment discrimination against lesbian and gay people.

In December 2003 the Employment Equality Regulations, which ban discrimination on the grounds of sexual orientation in employment, went into effect in the United Kingdom. The legislation, which specifically bans direct and indirect discrimination, harassment, and victimization, is the result of the United Kingdom's implementation of the European Union's 2000 Employment Framework Directive, which required member states to ban employment discrimination based on sexual orientation by the end of 2003 (Stonewall, 2010). The UK legislation covers both public and private organizations.

The passage of nondiscrimination legislation has helped diversify police agencies in both the United States and the United Kingdom. In the United States, given the added job security provided by state and local laws focusing on public employees, lesbian and gay officers are now more likely to reveal their sexual orientation and serve openly. This logic applies to police officers in the United Kingdom too. Although the national UK nondiscrimination law went into effect in 2003, older UK laws and regulations have also been interpreted to include sexual orientation nondiscrimination within their protections (Clements, 2008).

Changing Social Norms

The proliferation of characters representing lesbian and gay police officers on television and the passage of nondiscrimination laws are both connected to a larger progressive shift regarding homosexuality in Western societies. Since the 1970s and the birth of the modern gay rights movement, public opinion about homosexuals has mostly moved toward integration and away from isolation. Public opinion data reveal the contentious nature and complexity of the debate surrounding gay rights. While prima facie evidence indicates that public opinion of gay men and lesbians has improved dramatically, a closer look shows a more complicated picture, with public support for policies related to sexual orientation depending on the specific policy area (Lewis and Rogers, 2000; Yang, 1999). According to Alan Yang (1999), the areas in which public support in the United States is strongest are housing and employment. Between 1977 and 1996, support for equal employment rights among Americans rose from 56 to 84 percent. More recently, in 2008, *Newsweek* reported that 87 percent of the American public supported equal employment opportunities for lesbian and gay people and 82 percent supported equality in housing (Princeton Survey Research Associates International, 2008).

While public opinion generally supports extension of tangible social benefits to lesbian and gay people, support for lesbian and gay rights drops drastically when it comes to the issue of marriage equality versus civil unions. Between 1998 and 2010, support for partnership recognition in the United States increased, with support for civil unions rising from 39 to 66 percent. In the same period, support for same-sex marriage also rose, but much less dramatically, from 34 to 47 percent (Gallup, 2010a).

Recent public opinion research about lesbian and gay rights in the United States has focused largely on military service and the "don't ask, don't tell" policy. Between 1998 and 2010, support for lifting the ban on service by openly lesbian and gay people in the US armed forces rose from 57 to 69 percent (Gallup, 2010b). This support was also found among active service members. When the "don't ask, don't tell" law was repealed in December 2010 by President Barack Obama, 70 percent of service members believed that the impact of the repeal would be positive, mixed, or of no consequence at all to military readiness (Stolberg, 2010).

Women in Policing as Trailblazers

It is hard to imagine contemporary advances in policing by lesbian and gay people without acknowledging the sacrifices of previous generations of women and racial minorities in law enforcement. While women and racial minorities often faced insurmountable levels of discrimination, harassment, and in some cases violence in police agencies, the recruitment and retention of women has had a profound effect on policing procedures in both the United States and the United Kingdom. As one US police chief noted, "the presence of women has done more to change the culture of police agencies than any other effort. Women actually helped to professionalize the police by making men act like grown-ups at work" (public discussion, 2010). Building on his sentiment, I believe that the inclusion of women, more than any other effort, has paved the way for lesbian and gay police officers to serve openly in many police agencies.

Although women have a long history in policing, their entrance in the 1970s and 1980s has had a direct effect on policing today. This entrance was coupled with equal employment legislation and evolving ideas about women in the workplace. While these factors have helped to make the work lives of women more equitable, they have not succeeded in eliminating all bias against women in policing. In fact, women still face many of the same challenges today. For example, one-third of women police officers still report being made to feel unwelcome by male counterparts (Seklecki and Paynich, 2007). While structural forms of discrimination have been aggressively targeted and eliminated, the informal structures remain. This includes the "outsider" status that continues to haunt women (and other minorities). As noted earlier, acceptance into what has traditionally been a white, male, and presumed-heterosexual occupation has affected women, people of color, and lesbian and gay people (Hassel and Brandl, 2009; Martin and Jurik, 2007; Miller, Forest, and Jurik, 2003).

Voices from the Field

Name: Sarah Pond-Robbins
Police agency: Hampshire Constabulary
Rank: Police officer
Length of service: Fifteen years

On recruitment of lesbian and gay liaison officers:
"The general perception about it at that point would have been that the police were homophobic. They wouldn't have felt comfortable coming forward, and a lot of staff that were in the organization were sort of underground and didn't feel comfortable being out in the organization . . . when the issues [of the GLOs] first came out. Although it wasn't designed just for gay officers, some people didn't want to put themselves forward for it because the perception was, they'd be gay because of that stigma that was attached."

On how Hampshire began collecting information about homophobic crimes:
"About 1997, the Crime and Disorder Act was introduced and it introduced the aggravating factors for race and religious aggravated crime. What it didn't do, at that time, was bring into light other hate crimes. So homophobic, transphobic hate crime wasn't given the same kind of parity in legislation. So Hampshire Constabulary looked at the situation and said, 'What can we introduce for the victims of homophobic/transphobic hate crime to ensure that their incident—which is an aggravated offense, which is a hate crime—is given the same parity that the legislation has offered the race and religiously motivated hate crime?' So they introduced . . . lesbian and gay liaison officers."

On being among the first cohort of lesbian and gay liaison officers:
"[It was like] double jeopardy because you have all women around here, at the moment, and you kind of got—you're fighting the female thing and the gay thing. . . . I think that you're known, because you have to stick your head above the crowd because you are invisible and when you are known then that will go with you always, and also because I guess you're allowed to be who you are and who you want to be, which gives you that confidence and that ability to know that you're recognized and hopefully found to be credible for the whole encompassing bits because you don't have to worry about the baggage of not being out."

continues

Voices from the Field continued

On schools and homosexuality:
"They're still very, very wary of promoting anything having to do with homosexuality and same-sex relationships. And there are very, very, very few schools that will actively open their arms and say, 'Yeah, come on in and let's have these sessions, and let's teach the kids all of this.' Anything that they do, I mean we have safe partnerships. We have, I think you still get on around the county. We have a few officers who are now paid for by the schools who are going in to the schools as school liaison officers."

In both the United States and the United Kingdom, the road for women in contemporary policing has not been easy. In 2009, women accounted for only 16 percent of uniformed officers in the United States, up from 13 percent in 2001 (Lonsway et al., 2002; US Bureau of Labor Statistics, 2009). The data for the United Kingdom are not much better, where women accounted for only 23 percent of police officers in 2007. These numbers are especially low given four decades of activism and legislation to open opportunities for women in policing.

Assumptions About Gender, Sex, and Policing

Although women have been involved in policing since the 1910s, for most of this history this involvement had been relegated nearly entirely to "social work." The dominant (and male) belief was that women were less physically and emotionally able to handle the demands of law enforcement (Bell, 1982). As Judith Bardwick and Elizabeth Douvan (1972) suggested, the presence of women in law enforcement indicated that the profession was not as demanding and physically challenging as perceived.

The perception of policing as masculine created a gendered form of cognitive dissonance. In order to alleviate this dissonance, police officers often pushed the idea that if a woman were a good officer, she must be a lesbian (and more masculine than a heterosexual women). To some degree, women who entered policing may not have engaged in what was considered to be stereotypically feminine behavior of the day (Rabe-Hemp, 2008). Thus, in some cases, female officers exhibited stereotypically masculine behavior in an effort to better fit within the male-dominated policing world.

This perspective conforms to sex role theory, which argues that sex roles are imparted and reinforced, beginning in childhood and continuing throughout adulthood, through interactions with family, friends, social institutions, and the media (Adler, 1999; Connell, 1985). According to the theory, men are raised to be goal-oriented and aggressive, whereas women are raised to be passive and dependent. Those who do not adhere to these behaviors are marked as deviant, serving to remind others of the importance of conforming to gender expectations (Garcia, 2003; Adler, 1999).

Assumptions about sex, gender, and policing are so ingrained in society that the stereotype of female officers as lesbians still endures today. As Richard Seklecki and Rebecca Paynich (2007) noted, female officers still report being insulted and called homosexual, despite our contemporary understanding of law enforcement.

Cultural Norms in Policing

There is a belief in policing that a good officer has certain knowledge, skills, and abilities regardless of demographic characteristics. As Paul Willis (1977) noted, the skills required of a good police officer include a well-developed capacity to communicate, extensive knowledge of the beat and the law, and a willingness to go "beyond the call." As the belief goes, the officers who exhibit such skills will succeed in law enforcement— regardless of demographic background—and will be judged solely on their skills. This is not to say that officers will be given the training or opportunity to exhibit good policing skills; nor does it mean that performance evaluations or promotions will acknowledge these skills. It means only that an officer's peers will accept that officer as one of them.

Thus, some women who entered policing adopted some of the traditional masculine or authoritarian traits of policing, established themselves as good officers, and were praised and promoted within the ranks.[1] Many of these women were in fact (or were perceived to be) lesbian. Regardless of sexual orientation, their presence and promotion began to affect police culture. This was aided by legislation that enforced equal opportunity efforts and, more importantly, anti–sexual harassment efforts. In the United Kingdom, this took the form of the Sex Discrimination Act of 1975 and the subsequent tribunals that investigated violations of the law, including the Launay (1984) and Halford (1990) cases. In the United States, it was the Civil Rights Act of 1964 and the related court cases, including *Meritor Savings Bank v. Vinson* (1986). Inquiries, summary judgments, consent decrees, and lawsuits against police officers and agencies were all instrumental in moving male police officers away from the "old boy" system and some of its traditional ideas about the nature of policing. In the 1980s and 1990s, police agencies had to improve their training for officers beyond the skills of the job; officers had to be professionalized and taught how to work with women and minorities within law enforcement.[2]

The Importance of Women for Lesbian and Gay Policing

As noted in Chapter 4, women were overrepresented in my surveys of both US and UK lesbian and gay police officers. In the US survey, women represented 30.0 percent of respondents; in the UK survey, they represented 38.7 percent. This was in contrast to the national percentages of women in policing the United States and United Kingdom—15.5 percent and 23 percent, respectively (US Bureau of Labor Statistics, 2009; Office for National Statistics, 2007). In terms of openly lesbian and gay officers who have been promoted to leadership posts in the United States, women outnumber men by about three to one (see Table 5.1). This disparity in representation did not happen by chance. In fact, assumptions about gender, and cultural norms and assumptions regarding policing, have helped to make serving as an openly lesbian officer more common than serving as an openly gay officer.

Table 5.1   Openly Lesbian and Gay Police Chiefs

	Location	Post	Year Elected or Appointed
Margo Frasier	Travis County (Tex.)	Sheriff	1996
Mindy Pengel	San Francisco (Calif.)	Deputy police chief	1997
Brian Paddick	London (UK)	Deputy assistant commissioner	2000
Serge Muyters	Antwerp (Belgium)	Deputy police commissioner	2000
Susan Jones[a]	Healdsburg (Calif.)	Police chief	2001
Ron Forsythe	Suisun City (Calif.)	Chief of police	2002
Lupe Valdez	Dallas County (Tex.)	Sheriff	2004
Sharon Lubinski[b]	Minneapolis (Minn.)	Assistant chief of police	2006
Jane Castor	Tampa (Fla.)	Chief of police	2009
Raymond Gregory	Riverside County (Calif.)	Sheriff captain	2009
Kelley Fraser	West Hollywood (Calif.)	Sheriff captain	2010
William Pace	Randolph (Mass.)	Chief of police	2010
Denise Schmitt	San Francisco (Calif.)	Assistant chief of police	2010

Source: Compiled from jurisdictions with current and active websites.
Notes: a. In 2010, Jones retired from Healdsburg, but continued in police service as the interim chief in Cotati.
   b. Lubinski left the agency in 2010 to become a US marshal.

With the aid of voluntary and involuntary efforts to diversify police agencies, women who had entered policing and had proven themselves to be "good" officers were promoted within law enforcement. The history here is anecdotal, but as more women entered into policing, lesbians may have joined the ranks in numbers disproportionate to their presence in the general population. Regardless of the numbers, real or perceived, the women who entered policing were competent, hardworking, and dedicated to law enforcement. The traits of "tough," "good," and "lesbian" merged, giving the latter a more positive connotation within police culture. Perhaps the most successful women officers at the time expressed these traits. The positive social construction of lesbians in policing has had an interesting impact, with lesbian officers being perceived as better officers than heterosexual women (who are perceived as more feminine) and as better officers than gay men (who are perceived as effeminate). As one gay male officer from my US survey noted:

> Cops believe that gay [male] officers are lowest on the totem pole. If a straight officer is getting a new patrol partner, he prays for a straight partner, then a lesbian—because they are considered tough and will have your back. If he can't have either of those, he'll take a straight woman. Gay men are considered too queenie to be good police officers. (personal communication, 2009)

Though much organizational change is still needed, women have been instrumental in helping to reform and professionalize police agencies. As agencies move toward community policing, ideas about what makes for a "good" officer continue to evolve, and the belief that policing is a masculine and authoritarian occupation continues to dissipate. As police agencies continue to diversify, they will increase their exposure to an even greater range of officers who, regardless of demographic background, display the traits needed to succeed in law enforcement.

Lesbian and Gay Officers: Types of Service

The individual lesbian and gay police officers who serve openly with regard to their sexual orientation are the foundation of the movement to diversify police agencies. The decision to serve as an openly lesbian or gay officer has many implications. As Judith Clair, Joy Beatty, and Tammy MacLean (2005) note, stigma in the workplace leads to negative outcomes for employees. As shown in Chapter 3, serving openly can affect an officer's job evaluation and his or her promotion opportunities.

It can also subject the officer to a hostile work environment in which he or she may experience social isolation and be exposed to homophobic talk. For this reason, many officers choose to reveal their sexual orientation only after they feel secure on the force. Historically, this has meant that few officers have entered police service as openly lesbian or gay. Instead, they have avoided the issue or tried to appear heterosexual. A number of officers who participated in my focus-group research confirmed this observation. In the United Kingdom, one officer from Wiltshire, with nearly twenty years of service, noted: "It's easier for [gay officers] to say they're not gay and carry on with their lives than to actually identify themselves as being gay and bring on the problems that they perceive, or not necessarily that they perceive but that it brings with it" (personal communication, 2009).

Concealing one's sexual orientation has psychological and political costs. Psychologically, it may create denial, self-directed homophobia, negative identity development, and anxiety associated with feeling like a fraud (Clair, Beatty, and MacLean, 2005; Herek, 2004; Shallenberg, 1994; Wickberg, 2000). Police officers, who form strong bonds with other officers and policing partners, are even more susceptible to this psychological damage. Psychologically, concealing one's sexual orientation inhibits organizational change. Individuals and groups within organizations are less likely to express homophobic tendencies if they know a person who is lesbian or gay. By not disclosing their sexual orientation, lesbian and gay officers might be complicit in promoting a homophobic environment.

Despite these continuing challenges, many social, political, economic, and organizational factors have converged to create opportunities for lesbian and gay people to serve openly in law enforcement, and the presence of such officers on police forces has affected both police agencies and the wider lesbian and gay community. With regard to the latter, openly lesbian and gay officers serve as role models for other community members who may be interested in pursuing careers in law enforcement. These officers can also engender the community's acceptance of the police, because their presence suggests that the police agency is diverse, representative of the community, and worthy of its support. As with other minority groups, the presence of lesbian and gay people in a police agency enhances the organization's legitimacy.

Openly lesbian and gay officers impact police agencies in a number of ways. First, since one of the strongest predictors of an individual's support for gay rights is knowing a lesbian or gay person personally, the mere presence of openly lesbian and gay officers in the agency—

interacting with the policing community—has a beneficial effect (King, Reilly, and Hebl, 2008). For fellow officers, homosexuality ceases to be an abstract concept, and lesbians and gay men become real people. Second, individual lesbian and gay officers can also informally communicate with management about external and internal matters, including the development of sensitivity-training modules and identification of potential human resource problems.

As mentioned earlier, I consider the presence of openly lesbian and gay officers as essential to the process of making police agencies more diverse and inclusive. These officers can advocate for a community that is sometimes invisible and usually underserved. They can act as informal bridges between the police and the community. And they can help sensitize police agencies to lesbian and gay issues. The development of the gay and lesbian liaison unit in Washington, D.C., would not have been possible without the initial input and support of openly lesbian officers, and a similar story applies to the Wiltshire and Hampshire constabularies in the United Kingdom, where openly lesbian and gay officers used their free time to develop voluntary training sessions for police officers and community groups, and worked with police management to raise the profile of community issues.

Without the pioneering efforts of openly lesbian and gay officers— some of whom began serving openly before this was common—none of the subsequent developments would have been possible, including the emergence of liaison officers, resource groups, and specialized units in police agencies.

Liaison Officers

Liaison officers act as conduits or intermediaries between police agencies and specific communities or constituency groups. Their primary responsibility is to help their constituency groups understand and navigate the criminal justice system. Family liaison officers help crime victims and their families. Latino liaison officers work with Hispanic communities, often engaging in activities designed to reduce community mistrust of the police. They are also called upon to translate important information for community members who may not sufficiently understand English. As has happened for other communities, liaison officers for lesbian and gay communities have emerged as conduits between the police and the people.

The concept of liaison officers originated with the community policing movement (Clements, 2008). In the United Kingdom, the systematic training and deployment of liaison officers was a direct result of the public inquiry into the murder of Stephen Lawrence (Grieve, Hall, and Savage, 2009; see Chapter 3 for more details on the Lawrence murder and Macpherson Report).[3]

Although many police agencies now use liaison officers, their deployment varies greatly. This is especially true for lesbian and gay liaison officers (GLOs). These liaison officers can be found in all types of police agencies. From the largest metropolitan agencies in the United States and United Kingdom, such as those of London and Los Angeles, to small rural police agencies, such as those of Hampshire, England, and Fargo, North Dakota, GLOs interact with and engage community members and police agencies. In their most typical roles, liaison officers serve as public relations officers, acting as the "face" of policing organizations in their interactions with the lesbian and gay community as a whole or individually. GLOs may also act as spokespersons for the police in matters related to hate crimes or same-sex domestic violence (Stiffler, 2010).

But GLOs also have more integrated roles, sometimes working full-time to foster mutual understanding between the police and the lesbian and gay community. On the police side, GLOs work to formally train officers regarding the lesbian and gay community and its unique needs. On the community side, GLOs are visible and accessible representatives, interacting with community members and helping them navigate the criminal justice system. While the basic interaction is mostly one-way (the police agency communicating with the community), the more integrated approach attempts to establish two-way communication. In addition, not all GLOs are uniformed police officers; some may be support or administrative staff. In fact, in the United Kingdom, community support officers are often designated as the liaison officers for local police agencies (personal communication, 2009).

The most highly integrated use of GLOs involves officers who can participate in the investigative process. In this scenario, officers not only advocate for the lesbian and gay community, and train members of the police agency; they also serve on investigation teams.[4] In such a capacity, liaison officers contribute both to the core policing function (law enforcement) and to active community engagement. For example, GLOs might be called in to participate in a hate crime investigation, possibly by interviewing the victim or other community members. In this role, liaison officers can employ their unique knowledge of the community and their relationship with residents to improve the effectiveness of law enforcement.

The level of engagement of lesbian and gay liaison officers and the amount of support they receive depend on the police agency. Neither the size of the local community nor the size of the police agency are reliable indicators of the extent of a liaison officer's role. For example, the New York City Police Department—which serves more than 8 million residents, including one of the largest lesbian and gay populations in the United States, and maintains a force of over 35,000 uniformed officers— uses liaison officers only in the basic capacity of public relations. Many smaller agencies that serve much smaller communities, however, employ their GLOs beyond such basic capacity. For example, in the United Kingdom, the Wiltshire Constabulary, which serves about 450,000 residents and maintains a force of about 1,400 officers, deploys GLOs to engage and support community members who have been victims of gay-related crimes (Wiltshire Constabulary, 2010). And some police agencies, large and small (including those of Hampshire, England; Washington, D.C.; and Los Angeles, California), integrate GLOs into their work in a more systematic manner. Table 5.2 highlights variations in the scope and mission of GLOs in various US, UK, Canadian, and Australian communities.[5]

Resource Groups

Lesbian and gay resource groups provide additional opportunities for police agencies to collaborate with the lesbian, gay, bisexual, and transgender (LGBT) community. Though such resource groups are not common in the United States, in the United Kingdom they usually include liaisons as well as other members of the police community who have an interest in the LGBT community, and they represent a higher level of commitment and involvement on the part of police agencies than do liaison officers alone. Often, other individuals, groups, and organizations in the lesbian and gay community are invited to join the resource group. In general, the aim of these resource groups is to coordinate efforts to reduce homophobia (both internal and external to the police agency) and to advise the police agency on any matter affecting the LGBT community. To achieve these general aims, resource groups engage in specific activities such as acting as advising supervisors who are experiencing issues regarding sexual orientation with their staff (Hampshire Constabulary, 2010); appraising police actions and operations at a strategic level, including advising on proposed police actions and operations that may impact or raise concerns within the LGBT community (Nottinghamshire Police, 2010); communicating with the LGBT community about local situations

Table 5.2 Communities with Lesbian and Gay Liaison Officers, and Their Missions

	Liaison Mission
Arlington County (Va.)	Improve the relationship between the police agency and the LGBT community.
Atlanta (Ga.)	Empower the LGBT community and provide a forum for citizens and business owners to express their concerns.
Dallas (Tex.)	Foster a stronger relationship between the police agency and the LGBT community in order to reduce complaints, solve more crimes, and increase acceptance of openly gay officers.
Doset (UK)	Increase the LGBT community's confidence in the police agency in order to encourage reporting of hate crimes and incidents.
Fargo (N.D.)	Collaborate with LGBT community leaders and residents to design and implement public safety and outreach programs that establish a closer, more effective dialogue with the police agency.
Gloucestershire (UK)	Assist officers with the investigation of homophobic and transphobic incidents.
Hampshire (UK)	Increase the LGBT community's confidence in the police agency in order to encourage reporting of hate crimes and incidents, and improve the agency's service delivery to the community.
Ottawa (Canada)	Increase the LGBT community's confidence in the police agency and improve the agency's service delivery to the community.
Queensland (Australia)	Ensure policing services are accessible to all members of the LGBT community.
Tasmania (Australia)	Increase the LGBT community's confidence in the police agency and improve the agency's service delivery to the community.
Victoria (Australia)	Increase the LGBT community's confidence in the police agency and improve the agency's service delivery to the community.
Washington, D.C.	Provide twenty-four-hour police response to the LGBT community.
Wiltshire (UK)	Liaise with and support the LGBT community when its members become victims of crime.

Source: Compiled from jurisdictions with current and active websites.

that might put its members at risk (Nottinghamshire Police, 2010); and examining external and statutory matters impacting the LGBT community, as well as reviewing and improving the investigation and prevention of homophobic hate crimes (Metropolitan Police, 2010).

The work of resource groups epitomizes the community policing approach. The relationship between community and law enforcement is bidirectional: when communication occurs, trust is built on both sides. Such groups and similar efforts also have a community capacity-building effect. Community members and resource groups can work with law enforcement agencies and with other community groups to become actively engaged in policing. This model is also beneficial to the police agencies, both internally and externally. Internally, the resource groups help to create a more diverse and gay-friendly workplace. Association with a resource group can also lead to feelings of acceptance and respect among officers, which can improve productivity (Button, 2004). Externally, resource groups enable police agencies to deploy themselves more efficiently and effectively. By working with the lesbian and gay community, the police agency can differentiate issues that can be handled without law enforcement from those that require police action. For example, a resource group might develop a coordinated plan to reduce or eliminate public sex incidents that does not require police engagement. Joint action in this area might produce the same desired outcome (reduced incidents) without bringing more people into the criminal justice system. Such cooperation empowers both police agencies as well as the lesbian and gay community.

Lesbian and Gay Policing Units

Like resource groups, units (or teams) represent an integrated approach to lesbian and gay community policing. The idea of designating specialized units is not new to police agencies, as their use regarding gangs, drugs, and organized crime has long been a staple of modern policing. However, only recently have specialized units been created to serve constituencies such as the lesbian and gay community.

Of the various roles in which lesbian and gay officers serve, the specialized unit role is the rarest. The major difference between resource groups and specialized units concerns their primary focus. For resource groups, engagement is the prominent focus, while specialized units, although they also engage the community as constituents and as partners in policing, tend to focus on measurable outcomes (such as reducing crime or improving response times).[6]

This focus on measurable outcomes appears to have grown out of critical incidents in local communities (Stiffler, 2010), including bias or hate crimes, bar raids, media exposés, and sex scandals. For example, the reporting—or lack thereof—of hate crimes in Washington, D.C., was a catalyst for the creation of the Metropolitan Police Department's lesbian and gay unit (personal communication, 2010; see Chapter 6). A rising number of bias crimes also led to the creation of such specialized teams in several communities in the United Kingdom, including Hampshire and Wiltshire (personal communication, 2010). And the creation of the lesbian and gay unit in Fort Worth, Texas, was instigated by a bar raid and the community outrage and media scrutiny that followed. As Scott Stiffler (2010) notes: "Police agencies tend to be reactive rather than proactive. When a crisis arises, the bureaucracy thinks about what it can do to avoid this in the future."

While the impetus behind the establishment of these specialized units varies, their internal and external activities have been instrumental in creating more diverse and gay-friendly policing environments, building trust between police and communities, and managing public safety by reducing crime and enhancing law enforcement.

Measurable Outcomes in Policing

One of primary hallmarks of lesbian and gay specialized units is their active involvement in policing and investigative work. The investigation of crimes committed by and against members of the community is what differentiates these units from resource groups and GLOs. While there is much variation in the level of involvement in investigations that such units are accorded, there are some roughly discernible patterns. In some police agencies, members of the local lesbian and gay unit will take a leadership role, investigating same-sex intimate-partner violence or hate crimes. In cases involving murder or sexual abuse, however, members of the lesbian and gay unit might work with members of other specialized units (homicide units, sexual abuse units) to ensure that all units have the resources needed to complete an investigation.

In some instances, an outside agency will request assistance from the police force's lesbian and gay unit because the agency lacks investigators who are knowledgeable about the kinds of crimes committed against lesbian and gay people. Because of the unit's ongoing presence in the community, unit members are often able to obtain information from people who might not ordinarily share with outsiders. For example, members of the community might be reluctant to discuss cases involving illicit drugs or public sex with unknown law enforcement personnel. Finally, because members of these units are comfortable in environments not usually frequented by other law enforcement officers—including bars, restaurants, community associations, and adult-oriented businesses—they may be asked to participate in investigations via outreach and communication within these environments.

Because specialized lesbian and gay units participate in investigations in measurable capacities, outcomes are easier to observe than for resource groups or GLOs. To measure the effectiveness of a unit, gay-related and non-gay-related crimes and incidents are compared. For example, the increased reporting of gay-related hate crimes in communities like Washington, D.C., and Wiltshire, England, has been attributed to the community trust-building and investigative work of specialized units. The ability to solve homicides with suspected involvement of lesbian or gay people provides another measure of unit effectiveness. In this case, the number of solved homicide cases might vary based on known sexual orientations. For instance, according to officers interviewed for my study, the lesbian and gay unit in Washington, D.C., solves homicide cases at a higher rate than does the regular homicide unit.

Conclusion

Whether a lesbian or gay officer serves as the "only gay cop" in their agency, as a public relations liaison, as a member of a resource group, or as a member of an investigative unit, their contribution to a more diverse and gay-friendly law enforcement environment is important. Without officers who were willing to serve openly, police agencies would never have begun offering community-related training to non-gay officers or conducting positive outreach initiatives to the community. Furthermore, these officers have helped create models that meet the primary goals of community policing, including better outcomes and greater trust among members of the community. They have also contributed to the most prominent aspect of policing—law enforcement and crime prevention. By engaging the lesbian and gay community, police agencies ensure support from the community and aid in meeting their missions.

Notes

1. The advancing women employed numerous coping strategies to succeed in this policing culture. Most of them advanced despite the cultural, institutional, and other barriers that would have hindered their success.

2. For a fuller discussion on gender and policing, see Brown and Heidensohn, 2000; Garcia, 2003; and Miller, 1999.

3. One complaint levied against the police in their investigation of the Lawrence murder was the lack of support extended to the Lawrence family through liaison officers. Police use of family liaison officers was revamped in conjunction with broader reforms that emerged from the Lawrence inquiry. This resulted in hundreds of family liaison officers being trained and deployed throughout Britain. Such officers are now part of the standard complement of services available to victims and their families.

4. Forces with a number of GLOs often have both uniformed officers and support staff who act as liaisons. Of course, only uniformed officers are included in police investigative work.

5. No comprehensive list of gay and lesbian liaisons, or communities with such liaisons, exists.

6. The differences in the responsibilities of units, resource groups, and liaison officers are fairly fluid. Many liaisons help with investigative policing, and many units are instrumental to community outreach. In this sense, local police forces are laboratories of innovation, with each community determining what is needed for success.

6

Urban and
Rural Contexts

Police agencies are as diverse as the communities they serve.
Although variations in size, population, socioeconomic status, demographics, politics, and cultural values make generalizations about all
agencies and communities impossible, we can gain unique perspectives
into policing by exploring specific communities. This chapter explores
the efforts of two agencies to improve policing in lesbian and gay communities. The first case is a large, urban US city with its own lesbian
and gay–oriented investigative team. The second case is a small, rural
UK community with lesbian and gay liaison officers. Each case represents law enforcement's efforts to balance its policing obligations with
the demands placed upon it by the community it serves.

The stories of these two police agencies and their communities are
based on several focus-group interviews I conducted with police officers, as well as archival data. Central to this discussion is the role that
critical incidents play as catalysts for change.

Washington, D.C.,
and the Metropolitan Police Department

This case explores and explains the evolution of Washington, D.C.'s
Metropolitan Police Department (MPD) from gay-community foe to
gay-community ally. In many ways, Washington is emblematic of the
typical modern US city—home to extreme wealth as well as extreme
poverty. As the nation's capital city, much of its autonomy is constrained
by the federal government, except where local law enforcement is con-

cerned. Its local government tends to be politically liberal, whereas surrounding suburban areas (and the federal government) are more conservative. With nearly 600,000 residents, Washington is considered a major US city, yet is not among the twenty most populous cities in the country (US Census Bureau, 2010). Washington is also demographically and socioeconomically complex. According to the US Census Bureau (2010), its population is 55 percent black/African American (compared to 12 percent of the US population) and 8 percent Hispanic/Latino (compared to 14 percent of the US population), making Washington a "majority minority" city (and the leader of this trend nationally). In terms of socioeconomic status, 17 percent of the city's population lives below the poverty line (compared to 14.3 percent of the US population), while its median income is $58,906 (compared to $50,221 for the US population). It is within this complex context that the MPD operates.

The Metropolitan Police Department includes more than 4,400 members—approximately 3,800 uniformed police officers and more than 600 civilian employees. The agency has over thirty specialized units: from traditional units and harbor patrol, to community outreach, including its Gay and Lesbian Liaison Unit (GLLU). The MPD's mission is "to safeguard the District of Columbia and protect its residents and visitors by providing the highest quality of police service with integrity, compassion, and a commitment to innovation that integrates people, technology and progressive business systems" (Metropolitan Police Department, 2011a).

Nearly 25 percent of all MPD uniformed officers are women, one of whom, Cathy L. Lanier, made history when she was named the first female MPD chief in 2007. Approximately 70 percent of uniformed officers are black, Hispanic, or Asian, which closely mirrors the makeup of the resident population it serves. At present, no data exist on the extent of sexual diversity in the MPD.

Like many other police agencies in the United States, the Metropolitan Police Department historically had a tumultuous relationship with its constituents in the lesbian, gay, bisexual, and transgender (LGBT) community. High levels of mistrust on the part of the community and ambiguous policing directives from the MPD impaired effective community policing. Historically, the LGBT community had been largely closed to law enforcement and much other public service delivery. This insular situation helped to breed and foster criminal activity within the community.

Due to a number of critical incidents and visionary leadership, the MPD developed a more practical policing model that built trust, improved policing efforts, and sensitized the broader police agency to the unique public service needs of the LGBT community. The primary component of the agency's LGBT policing-strategy reform was the creation of its Gay and Lesbian Liaison Unit.

Challenges of Policing "Invisible" Communities

Prior to the reforms instituted by the Metropolitan Police Department, the LGBT community in Washington was in many ways invisible to the police and other public service agencies. Whether they provide social, health, or police services, service agencies must know something about the communities they serve, and they must be able to identify and communicate with individuals and groups inside those communities. In the case of Washington, prior to reforms, focus was on various racial communities because they were more easily identifiable. Such efforts missed out on the nuanced composition of each community, and the less visible community members. No doubt, service delivery to some communities is much easier than to others, and the most difficult communities to serve are those that are invisible to providers. Table 6.1 identifies the ways in which a community might be rendered invisible to service providers.

Several factors can contribute to a community's visibility or lack thereof. These factors fall into three general categories—social taboos, community norms, and institutional barriers—and can contribute to community invisibility both individually and collectively. In some cases, communities engage in active efforts to remain invisible. For example, individuals and communities who engage in activities that are socially taboo or illegal—homosexuals, undocumented immigrants, drug addicts, sex workers, gang members—might attempt to remain invisible in order to isolate themselves from the larger society. Since their behaviors are considered taboo or illegal, they have an incentive to avoid police and other public service providers.

Second, individuals and communities whose lifestyles or activities lie outside the larger community's norms—homeless people, alcohol abusers, unwed teenage mothers—can also be rendered invisible, even though these activities are not necessarily illegal. As Anne Schneider and Helen Ingram (1993) suggested, the social construction of a population can affect the level of service delivery it receives.

Finally, institutional barriers might render individuals and communities invisible. Institutional barriers embedded in policies or procedures restrict the information available to us about some populations. For example, as far as I am aware, there are no representative public surveys that ask about respondents' sexual orientation, and thus we have very little generalizable data about the lives of lesbian and gay people.

In addition to the invisibility created by social taboos, community norms, and institutional barriers, there are other factors that may affect delivery of public goods and services. One is a community's level of *permeability*. Some communities are more "open" and others more "closed." While open communities are more or less easily accessible to outsiders, closed communities are not. Barriers to entry such as different languages, different cultural beliefs, and geographic isolation can hinder service delivery, as is the case with some separatist communities, some immigrant communities, and some religious sects. The LGBT community, while largely invisible to outsiders, is not tightly closed in this sense, because it is fairly easy for outsiders and service providers to enter the community's common institutions, such as community centers, restaurants, bars, businesses, and churches.

Table 6.1   Factors Affecting Public Service Delivery

	Definition	Example
Visibility		
Invisible	Not immediately visible to the larger community or to public service providers	Sex workers
Visible	Generally visible to the larger community and to public service providers	Asian American communities
Permeability		
Closed	Community organizations are not accessible to noncommunity members or to service providers	Non-English-speaking immigrant communities
Open	Community organizations are accessible to noncommunity members and to service providers	Lesbian, gay, bisexual, and transgender communities
Vulnerability		
Vulnerable	Lacking proper resources or political power to influence public policy	Mentally and physically disabled people
Invulnerable	Having proper resources or political power to influence public policy	Wealthy people

Another factor that can add to the difficulty of effective service provision is a community's level of *vulnerability*. Many communities lack the political influence, financial resources, or numerical size needed to attract public services. These communities may have a history of being denied public support, which contributes to their vulnerability. For example, people with mental or physical disabilities were long neglected in the United States, and it was only with intervention of the courts and passage of the Americans with Disabilities Act (1990) that tangible and measurable service provisions began to flow to these communities.

From a public policy perspective, delivering services to an invisible, closed, *and* vulnerable community can be very challenging indeed. Foreign-language-speaking immigrants without proper documentation exemplify such a community. The language barrier makes the community closed; its members' immigration status makes it invisible (because of both social taboos and institutional barriers); and since it also lacks political influence, resources, and an easily measurable population (even if large), it is also vulnerable.

This vulnerability can manifest itself in the form of exploitation, most commonly exploitation in employment, where wages, benefits, and health and safety standards are subverted. Public officials, including police officers, may also engage in exploitation of a vulnerable population, since it has limited resources and power to retaliate.

Policing the largely invisible lesbian and gay community presents some additional challenges. Unlike members of some racial or ethnic communities, lesbian and gay people are not necessarily identifiable by sight. And unlike religious enclaves or some immigrant communities, the LGBT community is not necessarily restricted to a certain geographic area. Lesbian, gay, bisexual, and transgender people are integrated into every part of broader society: they can be found among the affluent and the poor, among the young and the old, and among all racial, ethnic, and religious groups. Some LGBT people are open, known, and visible; others are hidden, unknown, and invisible within the larger community and sometimes within the LGBT community itself. Overall, we can classify the LGBT community as largely invisible, mostly open, and somewhat vulnerable.

Traditional policing has proven to be ineffective in the LGBT community. Police officers cannot conduct thorough investigative work if they do not know whom to talk to or where community members are located. Thus, because most lesbian and gay people do not live in "gay" neighborhoods, geographic policing is not optimal for the LGBT community. According to the US Census Bureau, households that identify as same-sex are present in all seven of Washington, D.C.'s police districts. In 2010 the 5,146 same-sex couples counted in Washington represented 1.8 percent of the city's population, but of course the 2010 Census counted only openly gay and lesbian couples who self-identified as same-sex partners. Because so many other LGBT people, including single LGBT people, were overlooked, many scholars believe that census data undercounts the national LGBT population by as much as 62 percent (Human Rights Campaign, 2011b).

The Role of Critical Incidents and Leadership

As mentioned earlier, police agencies and LGBT communities in the United States have had a long and uneasy relationship. From beat cops harassing owners and patrons of gay bars, to sting operations in public sex environments, to inappropriate interventions in intimate-relationship disturbances (with both accuser and accused often being arrested), there are well-founded reasons for the lesbian and gay community's distrust of the police. Washington, D.C., is no different from other cities in this respect.

Critical incidents and leadership are two important factors that contributed to changes in policing by the Metropolitan Police Department. There were three critical incidents and two acts of leadership, in particular, that led to the creation of the city's Gay and Lesbian Liaison Unit.

Critical incidents. The first critical incident—one exemplifying the poor relations between Washington's public service providers and its LGBT community—occurred in 1995. In August of that year, Tyra Hunter, a preoperative male-to-female transsexual, was severely injured in an auto accident. First responders arrived on the scene and proceeded to treat Hunter's wounds. In the process, one paramedic cut away her pants, revealing her as a biological male. The first responders then refused to continue treating her, and she was also initially denied treatment in the emergency room. Several hours after the accident, Hunter died. None of the first responders was held responsible for her death, despite the fact that medical experts estimated an 86 percent likelihood of survival had her wounds been treated (Southern Poverty Law Center, 2003). Although this incident centered on firefighters and emergency medical technicians, the police were viewed as complicit in Hunter's death given that none of the first responders were arrested or found criminally negligent.

While Hunter's death did not immediately trigger changes in policing procedures, it did prompt activism among the LGBT community.

When no first responders were held responsible for her death, the LGBT community actively protested and kept the issue at the top of the public agenda. Community organizations such as the Gay and Lesbian Activists Alliance (GLAA) and Gay Men and Lesbians Opposing Violence (GLOV) testified before city investigative committees and targeted Washington's fire chief as culpable (Southern Poverty Law Center, 2003). Other LGBT and LGBT-allied organizations were also active in seeking justice for Hunter and her family, including the D.C. Coalition of Black Lesbians, Gay Men, and Bisexuals; the Gay and Lesbian Alliance Against Defamation (GLAAD); Transgender Nation; the American Civil Liberties Union; and the National Gay and Lesbian Task Force. Community vigils were held and media attention (gay and nongay) was continuous and persistent. In this sense, Hunter's death was a critical incident within the LGBT community. As one community activist noted, "these days, most people understand that hate crimes are message crimes. Most people know that when a transgendered [*sic*] person is victimized, it does not just affect her friends and family—it terrifies a whole community of people who can't help feeling they might be next" (Southern Poverty Law Center, 2003, p. 3).

The second critical incident occurred in 1997. That year, Lieutenant Jeffrey Stowe of the MPD was charged in US District Court with extortion and embezzlement. Stowe was accused of blackmailing married men whom he believed to be living secretly gay lives. To carry out his scheme, Stowe identified vehicles that appeared to belong to men with families—vehicles with child safety seats in them—parked outside gay clubs. Starting with license plate numbers, he traced the owners using law enforcement computer databases and the Internet. Lieutenant Stowe then contacted the men and demanded money to remain silent. All of Washington (both the LGBT community and the broader community) was shocked when the news of Stowe's extortion broke. The investigation against Stowe reached the highest levels of the police agency, and ultimately resulted in the resignation of then–police chief Larry D. Soulsby, who was a close friend and former roommate of Stowe's. It was believed that Soulsby had used his influence to protect Stowe. Despite the chief's efforts, in 1998 Stowe was sentenced to forty-eight months in prison for extortion and embezzlement.

To an even greater degree than the Hunter incident, the Stowe incident intensified the tension between the MPD and Washington's LGBT community. To many LGBT community members, Stowe's actions were no different than the bar raids and intimidation tactics carried out by police during the pre-Stonewall era (see Chapter 3). Sharen Shaw

Johnson, of the Washington-based group Gay Men and Lesbians Opposing Violence, captured the sentiment of the LGBT community at the time: "This hardly is surprising. . . . [M]embers of our community are being victimized or re-victimized by the very people entrusted with ensuring their safety: the police" (Gay and Lesbian Activists Alliance, 1998).

The third and perhaps best-documented critical incident occurred in 1998, putting the issue of hate crimes on the public agenda in Washington, D.C. A hate crime is defined by the MPD as "a criminal offense committed against persons, property or society that is motivated, in whole or in part, by an offender's bias against an individual's or a group's race, religion, ethnic/national origin, gender, age, disability or sexual orientation. Hate crimes include not only violence against individuals or groups but also crimes against property, such as arson or vandalism, particularly those directed against community centers or houses of worship" (Gay and Lesbian Liaison Unit, 2008).

In 1998, the two jurisdictions surrounding the city—Virginia and Maryland—reported 169 and 282 hate crimes, respectively, for the previous year (Fillichio, 2006). By contrast, Washington, D.C., with a population of over half a million people at the time, officially recorded just two hate and bias–related crimes for the entire year (see Table 6.2). (Meanwhile, the community-based organization GLOV documented eighty-six victims of antigay violence in Washington in the previous year [Gay and Lesbian Activists Alliance, 1998].) The comparative data highlighted a disparity that could not be easily explained away by politicians or police administration, and sparked an outcry among the LGBT community—who knew, as did the police, that the reported numbers were too low to be true, most likely due to a large percentage of unreported crimes against lesbian, gay, bisexual, and transgender people. Given the close proximity of the three jurisdictions, the disparity suggested poor performance by the MPD and poor oversight by the political entities, embarrassing both groups.

These three critical incidents acted as focusing events for both the LGBT community and decisionmakers in the MPD. For the LGBT community, these incidents helped to mobilize its members and increase their visibility. With increased visibility, the community was able to garner more public support and police agency attention. For the MPD, these incidents put LGBT issues on the public agenda, and thus on the agenda of elected officials and decisionmakers. Each incident, by increasing the visibility of the LGBT community, increased the pressure for action by the MPD.

Leadership. The critical incidents of 1995, 1997, and 1998 created an opportunity for the MPD to change its relationship with Washington's LGBT community. Two acts of leadership helped facilitate that change. First, in 1999, two lesbian police officers (Kelly McMurray and Berdette Williams) put a forward a proposal to the MPD to improve relations with the LGBT community. The proposal was designed to address two main problems: the lack of training for police officers about hate and bias crimes, and the lack of trust within the LGBT community toward the police, which discouraged the reporting of such crimes (Fillichio, 2006).

The MPD's chief of police at the time, Charles Ramsey, was sensitive both to the outrage among the LGBT community (the city finally settled with the Hunter family in 1999) and to the disparity in the reporting of hate and bias crimes. In 2000, Ramsey appointed Officers McMurray and Williams as liaisons to the LGBT community. These new liaisons coordinated internal training for police officers about hate and bias crimes and conducted outreach to the lesbian and gay community about the importance of reporting such crimes. The benefits were immediate and measurably evident. During the unit's first year of operation, as a result of its training and outreach, reporting of hate and bias crimes doubled.

Table 6.2   Hate Crimes Reported in Washington, D.C., 1998–2009, by Basis of Bias

	Ethnicity	Race	Religion	Sexual Orientation	Disability	Total
1998	0	1	1	0	0	2
1999	0	0	1	3	0	4
2000	1	2	0	2	0	5
2001	0	3	2	5	0	10
2002	3	2	0	9	0	14
2003	1	9	2	17	0	29
2004	4	14	2	29	0	49
2005	1	6	7	28	0	42
2006	3	8	5	36	1	53
2007	2	3	6	26	0	37
2008	2	5	0	30	0	37
2009	1	3	0	24	0	28

Source: US Federal Government, US Department of Justice, Federal Bureau of Investigations, "Uniform Crime Reporting: Hate Crime Statistics." Retrieved November 7, 2011, from http://www.fbi.gov/about-us/cjis/ucr/ucr#cius_hatecrime.

Note: Figures for 2009 are preliminary and have not yet been reported to the FBI.

Despite this early success, the unit and its staff faced a number of challenges, including structural, institutional, and cultural challenges within the MPD. The liaison officers felt that the unit was not realizing its full potential, in part because of the relatively low rank of Officers McMurray and Williams and in part because they were female. After a year of operation, the founding officers made additional recommendations regarding the unit to the MPD and Chief Ramsey, including devotion of more resources, assignment of some male officers, and provision of higher-ranking leadership. According to Sergeant Brett Parson, the founding officers had told the MPD that in order to make the unit successful, "you need a gay boy, you need a gay boy that has some rank, and you need a gay boy that has rank and doesn't give a damn what people think about him" (personal communication, 2009). By fall 2001, with the assignment of Parson to command, the unit had its first openly gay, full-time, male police sergeant. It was also received an official title: the Gay and Lesbian Liaison Unit.

To contextualize the leadership in this case, we can consider the leader-member exchange theory. Unlike other theories of leadership, leader-member exchange does not focus on internal traits or behaviors, or qualities of leaders. Instead, it focuses on the relationships between those who lead and those who follow (Truckenbrodt, 2000). Leader-member exchange theory suggests that people in authority are likely to form different working relationships with different subordinates. High-quality relationships are characterized by trust, open communication, and information sharing. Low-quality relationships tend to be limited to contractual-type obligation. In this context, the relationship between Chief Ramsey and Officers McMurray and Williams can be understood as high-quality. The officers were given some latitude in working with the lesbian community, as well as with other members of the MPD. Their assessment of what was needed to make the community partnership work was brought to Ramsey honestly and openly, with the belief that he would act appropriately on the information. We see the results of another high-quality relationship with the appointment of Sergeant Parson as first official head of the Gay and Lesbian Liaison Unit.

The MPD's Gay and Lesbian Liaison Unit

The Metropolitan Police Department's Gay and Lesbian Liaison Unit is staffed by openly gay, lesbian, and transgender members of the agency and their allies. The GLLU has three main mission objectives: to provide educational outreach to the LGBT community, to educate fellow police officers about the LGBT community, and to actively participate in day-to-day crime-fighting responsibilities (Harvard University Kennedy School of Government, 2006).

To meet these objectives, the GLLU engages in several community and policing activities, including advising the chief of police on issues involving the LGBT community; representing the MPD at community gatherings, civic meetings, government functions, and other events; participating in Washington, D.C.'s Hate Crimes Task Force; visiting gay–owned and operated businesses, corporations, associations, and other groups that seek the support or assistance of the GLLU; providing support and assistance to law enforcement investigations that involve members of the LGBT community; providing support to other city agencies with regard to law enforcement within the LGBT community; engaging in recruitment efforts for both uniformed and reserve police officers by operating an MPD booth at local gay pride festivals; training and educating members of both the MPD and the LGBT community (including safety training for the latter); and serving as a resource for other police agencies nationwide (Gay and Lesbian Liaison Unit, 2008). Unlike other liaison units, the GLLU is specifically designed to be community-focused and highly visible, emphasizing collaboration between community and law enforcement to improve policing and public safety.

Because of the efforts of Sergeant Parson as unit commander, the GLLU currently has six full-time officers plus numerous part-time officers and volunteers from the community. Although the unit is located in the gay-identified neighborhood of Dupont Circle, its outreach and police work are not geographically restricted. It responds to calls from all over the city and all seven policing districts. The GLLU's support hotline is staffed twenty-four hours a day, seven days a week. At present, no other police agency in the United States has an LGBT unit designed to operate like Washington, D.C.'s GLLU.[1]

Measuring Success in Washington

One of the challenges of providing public services to an invisible community is the difficulty of collecting and maintaining information about the community and of establishing measures of efficiency and effectiveness. That is to say, it is often hard or impossible to know how well a particular public service is meeting the needs of the target population. In the case of the Washington, D.C., LGBT community, accurate measures remain elusive, but the Metropolitan Police Department has tried to adapt to and compensate for this reality.

Data are elusive because of the relative invisibility of the LGBT community. No data exist that can provide us with a sense of its exact size, nor do we have information about the likelihood that lesbian, gay, bisexual, and transgender people will report crime or want to interact with the MPD. We do, however, have a few indirect measures of success that can shed some light on the efforts of the police agency and its Gay and Lesbian Liaison Unit.

First, the creation of the GLLU raised the profile of internal, community-related crimes such as same-sex intimate-partner violence (domestic violence). As recently as 2000, no same-sex domestic violence cases had been reported to the MPD, but since then, over 460 cases of same-sex domestic violence have been investigated by the GLLU (personal communication, 2009). This change can be attributed to three efforts by the GLLU: training officers to recognize the signs of such violence, increasing levels of trust toward the unit among individuals and community organizations, and guiding victims of domestic violence through the criminal justice system.

In addition to increasing attention to same-sex violence issues, the GLLU has been instrumental in increasing the reporting of hate and bias crimes. As noted earlier, in 1998 only two hate and bias–related crimes were recorded by the MPD (and neither was related to sexual orientation). Here again, officers have since been taught how to recognize the signs of such crimes and how to complete the related paperwork to ensure proper investigation. Since 1998, the reporting of gay-related hate and bias crimes has increased from none to around 30 annually. Since 2005, bias crimes related to sexual orientation have been the most frequently reported type of hate crime in Washington, accounting for 73 percent of all hate crimes in 2009 (US Department of Justice, 2010). From a measurement standpoint, the increase in such reports is a positive outcome, for it suggests growing and sustained trust of the MPD and the GLLU. As former chief Ramsey has noted, "For the law enforcement community, that [increased reporting] is real progress—not because of the occurrence, but because they were reported, a clear indication that gays and lesbians who've been victimized once know they will not be victimized again when they report the crime to us" (Fillichio, 2006). In 1998, according to Gay Men and Lesbians Opposing Violence, thirteen of twenty-three reports of sexual orientation–related crimes made by lesbian, gay, bisexual, and transgender people were met with indifference or verbal abuse from MPD police officers. In sharp contrast, today the GLOV refers *all* victims directly to the GLLU. As Ramsey has suggested, LGBT community members now believe that the GLLU will take their reports seriously.

We can also measure the success of the GLLU by reviewing its closure rate for homicide cases. Nationally, murders are solved at a rate of about 70 percent. In Washington, D.C., the success rate is significantly lower, hovering at about 50 to 60 percent (Southern Poverty Law Center, 2003). Since the murder of Eric Plunkett at Gallaudet University in 2000 (see Chapter 1), the GLLU has been involved in a number of murder investigations involving lesbian, gay, bisexual, or transgender victims, suspects, or witnesses. To date, the closure rate for homicide cases with GLLU assistance is 95 percent (personal communication, 2009). While it is not possible to detangle the GLLU's 95 percent average closure rate from Washington's overall closure rate of 50 to 60 percent, it is also not possible to separate the city's closure rate from the national closure rate. However, we can generally assume that the GLLU's higher homicide closure rate contributes positively to both the city's and the nation's closure rates.

While no solid measures exist regarding the GLLU's full impact on policing, training, and trust-building efforts in the LGBT community, we can use several indirect measures to evaluate the unit's effectiveness in these areas. For example, the MPD's increased awareness of same-sex domestic violence, the increased reporting of hate and bias crimes, and the high closure rate for LGBT-related murders all point to a positive impact for the GLLU on both the community and the police agency.

Learning from the Washington Experience

The Metropolitan Police Department's Gay and Lesbian Liaison Unit offers an exciting and interesting case study of how public services (especially police services) can be provided to an invisible community. Although all communities are different, we can draw some generalizations from this case to enhance policing in the lesbian and gay community.

Reach out to community groups and service providers. Most communities, whether visible or invisible, have some institutions and service providers of their own—for example, churches that provide meals to the homeless community, support organizations for people with addictions, and advocacy organizations that promote a particular community's agenda. These groups may not always appear to be a police agency's natural allies, but they are critical for identifying invisible communities and helping to assess those communities' needs, and their work within the community will be invaluable as a police organization attempts to establish trust. The MPD's GLLU worked closely with community groups, especially during its inception, and the unit now has a long-standing working relationship with both the Gay and Lesbian Activists Alliance and Gay Men and Lesbians Opposing Violence.

Conduct internal training. Invisible communities are often invisible for a reason. Members might be engaging in "antisocial" or illegal activities, and service providers might have to overcome stereotypes or negative assumptions about the community in need of services. The ability to work effectively with an invisible community might require training to equip service providers with special knowledge or skills, as well as outreach to build community trust.

Keep track of critical incidents. Critical incidents can occur anytime and anywhere. An incident's effect on individuals, institutions, or an entire community cannot be known until after the incident has occurred. By establishing a method for tracking emerging problems and their effects, a service provider can learn to respond more quickly. And, of course, patterns in critical incidents are valuable predictors of potential problems. Knowledge of these patterns can enable preventative action.

Consider the leadership. As we saw with the MPD, leadership can emerge from any part of an organization. Fostering a climate that encourages collaboration and inventiveness among service providers can help cultivate leadership, initiative, and expertise, all of which are important in responding to critical incidents, taking preventative action, and implementing planned changed. Establishing such a climate requires high-quality working relationships between leaders and subordinates.

Develop measures of success and failure. After determining the problems in the community that need to be addressed and finding collaborative partners, a service provider should develop measures of success and failure. These measures can be benchmarks, targets, or goals to be met by the community and the police agency. At a minimum, survey data should be collected both before a solution to a problem is applied and then again after, which will allow both the police agency and the community to evaluate the solution's success.

* * *

This case study highlights how critical incidents and leadership created an opportunity for Washington, D.C.'s Metropolitan Police Department to better serve one of its invisible communities. To improve its policing, the MPD had to reduce the level of mistrust within the LGBT community. The MPD accomplished this by establishing a visible and helpful presence in the community, by increasing the number of properly trained police officers, and by meeting with community leaders and organizations. As the GLLU's commander, Sergeant Brett Parson, noted, the biggest challenge for the unit's liaison officers has been "walking the tightrope between [being] advocates for the community and [being] enforcers" (personal communication, 2009). Meeting this challenge has been one of the GLLU's major successes.

By taking advantage of opportunities created by critical incidents and responding positively, the MPD has been able to provide better policing for Washington, D.C.'s lesbian and gay community and the city as a whole. The efforts of the MPD and the successes of its Gay and Lesbian Liaison Unit show that some invisible communities can be made more visible, and that increased visibility makes it possible to improve service delivery.

Wiltshire, United Kingdom, and the Wiltshire Constabulary

Regarding service delivery to the LGBT community and other invisible minority groups, police agencies in the United Kingdom face many of the same challenges as do police agencies in the United States. The current social and political status of LGBT people in both countries still presents challenges to those providing services to a community that, though permeable, is vulnerable and only partly visible. As the Wiltshire Constabulary's policy statement on homophobic and transphobic incidents notes, "Gay, bisexual, and transgender people are particularly vulnerable to threatening behavior, abuse, and attack because of their actual or perceived sexual orientation, gender identity or lifestyle" (Wiltshire Constabulary, 2005).

Based on archival data and a focus-group session with several Wiltshire lesbian and gay liaison officers (GLOs) and staff members, this case study focuses on the recruitment, selection, and training of GLOs and the use of partnerships in community policing.

According to the United Kingdom's Government Office for the South West (2010), Wiltshire covers an area of 3,255 square kilometers (1,257 square miles) and has a population of more than 635,000. Wiltshire, however, has one of the lowest population densities in south-western England (Wiltshire Constabulary, 2010) and, as a primarily rural community (with the exception of the city of Swindon), has few minority residents, composing only 5 percent of Wiltshire's population, half of whom belong to visible ethnic minorities. One-quarter of the county's population identifies itself as religious, with backgrounds including Buddhist, Hindu, Jewish, Sikh, Muslim, pagan, Roman Catholic, Protestant, and Evangelical, among others (Wiltshire Constabulary, 2010). Regarding sexual orientation and gender identity, the government of Wiltshire operates under the assumption that between 5 and 7 percent of the county's population are lesbian, gay, bisexual, or transgender.

The Wiltshire Constabulary has 1,200 police officers and 1,000 police staff (including community support officers). The police management team consists of one chief constable and five chief officers. Day-to-day policing services are delivered through two territorial divisions: Wiltshire and Swindon, each of which is led by a chief superintendent (Wiltshire Constabulary, 2010). The constabulary is one of forty-three districts that report to the Home Office. As noted earlier, the United Kingdom has a unified police administration that brings all policing under one command structure. But although the command structure is unified, chief constables have wide discretion in implementing policing directives.

Wiltshire's Lesbian and Gay Liaison Officers

The first GLOs in Wiltshire were recruited in 1999 on a voluntary basis. In the beginning, officers had to attend specialized training to become GLOs—training that included learning about the LGBT community and its unique problems, and about the implications of service delivery to invisible communities.

GLOs have four major objectives: (1) to provide an environment in which community members can freely discuss LGBT-related incidents or issues, (2) to ensure confidentiality and sensitivity toward the concerns of community members, (3) to connect community members with external sources of support, and (4) to raise awareness about the LGBT community among the police and improve officers' understanding of and interaction with LGBT victims, witnesses, and offenders. At the core, GLOs are tasked with increasing support for lesbian and gay people, building community capacity, and improving relations between the police and public.

Currently, 150 people in the Wiltshire Constabulary are trained as GLOs. They can be contacted directly via local police stations throughout the county, but most often they are referred to members of the community by investigating officers. GLOs can also be contacted through local community organizations that coordinate with the Wiltshire police.[2]

The Role of Critical Incidents

Given Wiltshire's demographics and rural character, its need for GLOs did not become apparent until a number of critical incidents converged concerning the LGBT community. The first was the public inquiry into the murder of Stephen Lawrence and the resulting policy changes recommended in the Macpherson Report (see Chapter 3). Although the inquiry was primarily concerned with race, the issues it raised regarding the equitable delivery of police services and the need for improved police-community relationships extended beyond communities of color. Concurrent with the development of GLOs in Wiltshire (and other constabularies) was the development of numerous other liaison roles, including roles devoted to community and race relations, victim support, services for the disabled, and support for senior citizens (Wiltshire Constabulary, 2010).

Second, while policy changes connected to the Stephen Lawrence inquiry were being implemented, community organizations were simultaneously pushing for more support from the Wiltshire police. One such organization, the Men's Sexual Health Service (MSHS), played a critical role in this push for reform. Prior to 1999 and the creation of GLOs, the MSHS was the primary organization collecting information on hate and bias crimes involving lesbian, gay, bisexual, and transgender people. The MSHS operated a data-collection system and encouraged community members to report incidents both to itself and to the police. However, the MSHS was more successful than the police at gathering this information, because the police were not viewed as trustworthy by the LGBT community, nor as responsive to its needs (Wiltshire Constabulary, 2010; personal communication, 2010). Even as late as 2005, according to a study conducted by the MSHS, some victims of gay-related hate crimes reported a distrust of the police and a belief that nothing would be done about their cases; respondents in that study cited unwillingness to disclose their sexuality as a reason for not reporting hate crimes to the police (Weatherburn et al., 2005). In addressing this lack of trust, the MSHS used its survey data to increase the visibility of the LGBT community and to highlight gaps in service delivery.

A third incident that drove the development of GLOs resulted from the experiences of lesbian and gay officers in the field. Despite lacking quantitative police data about bias and hate incidents involving LGBT people, GLO observations in the field suggested a gap in services to the community. Lesbian and gay officers observed that such crimes were not always recognizable by fellow officers and that community members were reluctant to report them. In an act of leadership, several officers approached police management and community organizations and formed the Lesbian, Gay, Bisexual, and Trans Action Group. This group—a partnership designed to address homophobia and improve services to the community—consisted of community members, police officers and staff, and members of other relevant agencies and organizations, including the Crown Prosecution Services and the Men's Sexual Health Service (Wiltshire Constabulary, 2010).

Members of the action group reported a number of goals for the partnership, including increasing the level of trust between community and police, sharing information and good practices, increasing police and public awareness of the partnership work, identifying solutions to community problems, supporting lesbian and gay police staff and officers, promoting the reporting of hate crimes, and providing advice on critical incidents (Wiltshire Constabulary, 2010; personal communication, 2010).

Overall, Wiltshire's approach was self-reinforcing and affirming. By promoting quality data collection within the LGBT community, encouraging proactive efforts among community members, and increasing the visibility of the community to service providers, Wiltshire's GLOs were able to amplify their call for LGBT support, creating a dynamic exchange among the community, the police, and lesbian and gay officers within the agency.

Together, these three incidents helped to establish GLOs in Wiltshire. The changing policy environment, the changing police environment (especially the move toward community policing), the efforts of community groups, and internal efforts by police officers created an ideal climate for addressing the needs of the LGBT community and improving police-community relations.

Recruitment of GLOs

When establishing gay and lesbian liaison teams, chief constables usually recruit volunteers. If too few people volunteer for the post, the chief constable can assign officers to GLO teams. In Wiltshire, both forms of recruitment presented challenges. In the beginning, officers volunteered to join the GLO team. Given the traditional sociopolitical nature of this rural community and the traditional values held by untrained police officers, the experiences of the first GLOs were less than ideal. These first liaison officers were assumed to be gay and were sometimes subjected to the very homophobic harassment and discrimination that the GLO post had been created to address.

As one focus-group participant noted: "We had issues at the early stage that anybody that wanted to be GLO must be gay, and I think there were some kickbacks [negative consequences] for early people . . . from colleagues, and homophobia that went on within the force that needed to be dealt with. That is to say that fellow officers and staff penalized police who became GLO and it meant that you were gay. The thought was, you could only be interested in supporting gay people if you're gay yourself."[3] Most senior GLOs reported verbal harassment, personal property damage, and discrimination by police management. These initial reports conform to the quantitative data gathered about the shared experiences of lesbian and gay officers in the United Kingdom.

Furthermore, there was initial confusion about the need for GLOs and about the role they would play in investigative work. Some rank-and-file officers questioned the "preferential" treatment given to the lesbian and gay community, arguing that the needs of the general society were just as great. A bigger challenge, however, was presented by the officers who accepted the need for GLOs and acknowledged their role in policing. Too often, these officers viewed GLOs as having been designated to handle *all* issues related to the LGBT community. This assumption, in theory, would have allowed these officers to abdicate their investigative responsibilities if they thought one or more persons involved a crime was lesbian or gay. As one focus-group participant noted, the general view among officers was: "We've got GLOs. We don't have to deal with any homophobic incidents anymore. We can pass it to a GLO."

Of course, this was not the role envisioned for the GLOs, and the first of them had to work hard to avoid falling into it (personal communication, 2010). The GLO training had been designed to provide these liaison officers with specialized knowledge that would enable them to advise and support nonliaison officers, not to assume responsibility for the latter's investigative work.

In response to initial miscommunications and misunderstandings about GLOs, both police management and GLO team members advocated for more visibility, not less—especially in regard to openness and availability in the LGBT community. While some police constables and supervisors were skeptical about the usefulness of GLOs, the liaison officers were generally positively received in the lesbian and gay community.

As one senior liaison officer elaborated in a focus group: "So, all the GLOs, they wanted to be visible. They don't want to hide. Once they got the role, they wanted to be visible. They wanted to be visible in a way that was a communication to people within Wiltshire that may be gay, not out, or anything, to know that actually there are police officers, because we did advertise it. . . . It was a very high percentage that wanted to be visible."

Recruiting enough officers also presented challenges for Wiltshire. The general consensus was that 10 percent of the work force should receive training as GLOs. When only volunteers were used, the distribution of GLOs throughout Wiltshire was haphazard and uneven. Some stations in the county had twenty-four-hour GLO coverage and support, while others had no coverage at all. As one focus-group participant noted:

> One of the targets, initially, with the GLO role is to work on the basis of 10 percent of the overall work force being trained as GLOs. And I think that that target, if you like, was taken too literally, on the basis of, we need to train 10 percent of the work force as quickly as possible, irrelevant of their skills or devotion. And, I think, [there was a] lack of understanding of where those GLOs . . . need to be placed . . . from an operational point of view. So, it is great having 10 percent, but it's not when the majority of that 10 percent is not an operational front line where they're needed the most.

Recruitment challenges have continued to hinder the GLO program in Wiltshire. Because of the social stigma attached to the post and the constabulary's inability to recruit enough officers, a number of alternatives have been tested. The first was to assign uniformed police officers to the GLO posts. As we shall see, this effort had negative consequences. The second option was to assign support or administrative officers—specifically, community support officers. This latter effort met with generally positive consequences. Each alternative has had important implications for GLOs and community policing.

Assignment of Officers to GLO Posts

As mentioned, chief constables have the option of either recruiting or assigning officers to fill GLO posts. After the initial recruitment effort became problematic, the Wiltshire Constabulary, in coordination with the existing GLOs, decided to fill the remaining posts by assignment. This approach, it was thought, would reduce the associated sexual orientation stigma, since any officer might be assigned to a GLO post. By assigning uniformed officers, local police stations around the county could also ensure that enough officers would be trained as GLOs to cover shifts throughout the day.

But a number of problems arose. First, rather than being dedicated to the mission and goals of the GLO program, some officers viewed the assignment as just another responsibility, and many did not take the role seriously. Other officers attended the training only to improve their chances for promotion, without ever engaging in the work associated with the position. As one focus-group GLO noted: "So it's a bit of a tick box for promotion exercises as well, for some, which is quite clear. They came on the course, it was then evidence for their write-up, and you never saw or heard of them since, sort of thing. So, it became a quite acceptable and popular way to improve your chances."

Second, of the officers who completed the GLO training and were dispatched throughout the county, not all were equally committed or qualified to liaise with the lesbian and gay community. While many of the new GLOs had good intentions, members of the LGBT community did not feel that the officers created an environment conducive to reporting sexual orientation–related incidents. One focus-group GLO noted: "It's the rural nature of this county that . . . we know that homophobia is inherent within those organizations. And you've got to remember that a high percentage of police officers and police staff that are recruited to a force will be from the communities, so you will get those sorts of attitudes coming in."

The move from volunteers to assigned personnel weakened the energy of Wiltshire's GLO program. The volunteer officers were viewed as more committed to policing with the LGBT community. According to senior GLOs, these officers were also active in developing and improving the training for other officers. While many of the assigned officers performed their duties professionally and contributed to the GLO program's mission and goals, their commitment was lackluster, which also stifled innovation in the training sessions.

In 2009, GLO training was temporarily suspended in anticipation of a new model of policing with the LGBT community, under which diversity liaison officers (DLOs) would handle outreach to the LGBT community as well as to other minority groups in the county.

Training of GLOs and DLOs

Between 2001 and 2009, Wiltshire officers interested in becoming GLOs participated in five hours of additional training. In theory, the five-hour course would prepare an officer to conduct outreach to the LGBT community as well as to train other officers about sexual orientation–related incidents. As noted, implementation of the GLO training was less than ideal, with problems related to the recruitment and assignment of qualified police officers forcing the training to be temporarily suspended. More recently, the constabulary has begun to incorporate LGBT issues and community policing problems into training for diversity liaison officers, who in theory should be able to liaise with any and all minority groups, not just the LGBT community.

There appears to be disagreement in Wiltshire over the value and use of DLOs as opposed to GLOs. Several focus-group participants argued that lesbian and gay people and other sexual minorities have unique needs and thus require specialized services and support. On the other hand, some members of the focus group believed that all officers should be trained and expected to work with any member of any community. One participant noted in expressing what seems to be the dominant view about GLOs and DLOs:

> The forces, as a whole, are looking at changing the role from the GLO to actually having diversity liaison officers [so that] the diversity liaison officers represent all strands of diversity. This is where the force is pushing . . . at the moment. So few of us are outspoken as to why we shouldn't be moving . . . that way, but the reason being that there [should be] no minority group[s] that aren't represented or [don't] have a liaison officer. The idea being that, if you were a diversity liaison officer, you could liaise for, whether it be a hate crime because of race, disability, gender, sexuality, whatever it may be. . . . But certainly my argument is, perhaps being a gay person myself, and some people are saying that it doesn't matter, [that] as long as you're a police officer, you should be able to liaise with anything . . . [though] [y]ou may not be able to freely discuss a sexual act between same-sex people. . . . I strongly support the role of [the] DLO, but I think the GLO is quite a specific role in the type of incidents and the type of terminology and the types of things they'd have to discuss.

Although DLOs represent a new trend in liaison officers, members of the focus group were optimistic about the possible return of GLO training and about the Wiltshire Constabulary ultimately having both types of officers. One effort of the GLO program has been to strengthen relations with LGBT community groups and to increase the number of local partners providing services to that community. The GLO program has also established close relations with police community support officers (PCSOs) with the aim of helping PCSOs develop GLO skills. Members of the focus group believed that by working with local organizations and expanding the pool of GLOs to include PCSOs, the constabulary could maintain the trust that has been built between the LGBT community and the police. The PCSOs, who are at the front line of police and community relations, would provide lesbian and gay victims with an important link to the constabulary. This model would free officers to pursue investigative components while the PCSOs ensure community participation and victim support. At present, 147 PCSOs are working in Wiltshire.

As one focus-group member noted regarding the PCSOs: "One of the areas that [the constabulary] wants to promote when we do bring the training back in is our PCSOs. They're the heartbeat of our neighborhood policing team. They are the people that are out there within our communities now." Another focus-group member echoed that perspective:

> Because even though [PCSOs] may not be investigating officers—it's not part of their role—they can still form the liaison between the victim and the police officer, and sometimes it's easier to fit with a PCSO because they're not involved fully with the investigation side of it. Or they do investigation so they can liaise much better than perhaps a police officer can, and the police officer can't put the burden of the investigation onto the PCSO. So, if it's used correctly, it could be a real step forward.

Measuring Success in Wiltshire

Despite the challenges faced by the Wiltshire Constabulary in implementing its GLO program, several successes can be identified: improved reporting of hate and bias crimes, improved community relations, and improved community-based policing alternatives.

Improved reporting of hate and bias crimes. As noted, prior to 1999, most sexual orientation–related hate crimes in Wiltshire were not reported to the police. Those that were reported were instead conveyed to a local nonprofit, the Men's Sexual Health Service. Reporting to the MSHS was more common because the police were believed to be hostile toward lesbian and gay people.

The GLOs have been instrumental in changing community perceptions of the police agency. One trend in particular is noteworthy when measuring the success of the GLO program in this respect: the number of hate crimes reported in the county has increased. Most community groups, associations, and police agencies in Wiltshire agree that a large

Voices from the Field

Name: Sharon Abbott
Police agency: Wiltshire Constabulary
Rank: Police officer
Length of service: Nineteen years

On the visibility of lesbian and gay liaison officers in the community, and the decision to wear rainbow pins on their uniforms as a sign of commitment:

"GLOs actually came back to the office and said, 'We want to be more visible. We want to be able to walk through a town or villages.' And, obviously, [since] the rainbow flag is universal, people would recognize it. They don't have to say anything, it's just this knowledge that, 'I am a GLO, I am someone that can help.' . . . They wanted to be visible, . . . [to communicate] to people within Wiltshire that may be gay, not out, . . . that actually there are [GLO] police officers, because we did advertise it. It went to the media. It did actually get well received by our local media. It felt to me—it was a very high percentage that wanted to be visible. And the option is, you don't have to wear these [rainbow pins], but you give them one, should they want to. But it's really strong. I've done this training, and I'm actually quite proud. I've got this knowledge, this understanding, and these skills. I want to be able to go out there and do it. They also understood through their training that sometimes you want to give some quiet, unobtrusive information to people that they exist . . . but, it's something subtle that actually gave the awareness, and they wanted to be open, that they had that skill, and they were available should anybody want some help or support from Wiltshire police. And that actually came from the GLOs themselves; they really wanted that."

On the importance of GLOs in recruitment for Wiltshire police:

"We recognize there's groups within Wiltshire, or the police service in this country as [a] whole, [who] are under-represented . . . and we have used our GLOs on recruitment days. . . . On Wednesdays, GLOs will go along and they'll talk about the support that Wiltshire [provides]—both externally and internally—because one of the things we've said is, 'We can never get it right externally if we don't have an understanding, and [if] we don't improve things internally [regarding] homophobia.' And, I think, with the GLO role (and our colleagues see this), sending GLOs to awareness days, we have actually promoted

continues

Voices from the Field continued

what it is, on the whole—a gay-friendly organization. It will be like anywhere else. You get the odd stupid comment on a poster, but that can be put on a table and be dealt with. But, there is a recognition within the organization that this role does matter."

On whether or not lesbian and gay officers are better at working with gay suspects, victims, and witnesses:
"I think we've got some very competent police officers. And, I think to have such police officers, it doesn't matter what your sexual orientation is. They're very professional, and they want to do a really, really good job. . . . [I]t does actually matter to the organization as a whole if you've got perceived heterosexual staff going out there, dealing with homophobic crimes and incidents, whether it's suspects or victims, witnesses or whatever. You're in a professional job, and getting the right result at the end of it. That's a very powerful message, not just internally to the organization, but to our community. . . . [T]he message across the board is: Wiltshire police want to get it right, irrelevant of whether they're gay, they're heterosexual, or whatever. The message is: you matter."

---

number of these cases go unreported. However, trust in the police has begun to improve, given the increasing number of cases reported directly to the police instead of through the MSHS and other partnering agencies. As one such agency member noted during a focus group: "we saw a decrease in the number of hate crimes reported to us and an increase to the police. So that was significantly different. Also, of the ones that were reported to us, there wasn't that much reluctance to report to the police."

The increased reporting of hate crimes is partly a function of better reporting by investigating police officers. Since more officers have been trained to identify hate and bias crimes, they are better able detect them. GLOs in Wiltshire often conduct training for police and staff about indicators of same-sex domestic violence, bullying, and other bias incidents. As in other jurisdictions, improved understanding means that more cases will be reported (Colvin, 2000).

Improved community relations. Given the relative invisibility and vulnerability of Wiltshire's lesbian and gay population, very little public opinion data for the community exist. There are, however, indications of improved relations between the community and the police. In addition to the increased reporting of crimes to the police by lesbian and gay people, there has been an increase in the number of openly lesbian and gay people participating in the Lesbian, Gay, Bisexual, and Trans Action Group, which suggests greater comfort between the LGBT community and the police. Finally, in a 2005 MSHS survey of lesbian, gay, bisexual, and transgender people in Swindon, 50 percent of respondents indicated a willingness to work with officers to help break down barriers and encourage the community to open up to police (Weatherburn et al., 2005).

Improved community-based policing alternatives. GLOs have been instrumental in bringing to life the notion of community-based efforts to solve common problems. One area in which progress has been made in Wiltshire concerns public sex environments (PSEs). Traditional police methods of dealing with complaints about PSEs have proven unsatisfactory, ineffective, and costly. Too, the historical police practice of targeting PSEs frequented by men who have sex with other men had created friction between the lesbian and gay community and the police. In 2004, Wiltshire's GLO team joined with several other members of the county's community partnership to develop a plan to manage PSEs more fairly and humanely.

The plan's strategic goals for were fourfold: (1) to establish a framework for Wiltshire Constabulary officers to work in partnership with other agencies to find effective solutions to complaints about PSEs, (2) to develop a professional, graduated approach for dealing with PSEs when complaints were received, (3) to adopt a problem-solving approach for addressing complaints about PSEs, and (4) to establish a clear, transparent public document detailing how complaints about PSEs would be dealt with by the constabulary (Weatherburn et al., 2005).

Because the GLOs worked with members of the LGBT community to develop policies on which all stakeholders could agree, the solutions arrived at were more effective, satisfactory, and cost-effective compared to traditional policing methods. In 2005 the Lesbian, Gay, Bisexual, and Trans Action Group developed a PSE policy and procedures manual for the constabulary, which has become a model for PSE management in many communities in the United Kingdom. Lesbian and gay groups have praised the nondiscriminatory nature of the rules it lays out for police action regarding PSEs. One focus-group member shared her thoughts about the new policies:

Probably one of the other areas where we've had success was around our public sex environments. And that was probably where we were having a lot of our conflicts and a lot of our issues and stuff. Obviously, public sex environments have moved on in recent times. It's not just gay men. . . . Historically, it was perceived that the police service would harass gay men because they knew where the public sex environments were within the county. They would be policed a lot more. And at times we actually probably went a little bit—some things happened and maybe shouldn't have been done historically. With the GLO role, what we were able to do with the GLO staff was actually say, "Look at these." Public sex environments will exist; they will always exist. It's about managing them and managing them in a way for people's safety, and that they don't come into conflict with other members of society. . . . There's a public sex environment policy that all police forces need to follow . . . and Wiltshire did play a big part in putting that together with other forces. We did say, and it was down to how we approached these sites, and, again, we did it with partner agencies. We didn't just go flying in there. And there are guidelines about how we police those sites. If an incident happens within those sites, there's a protocol for how police officers should deal with it. And it was twofold. It's about protecting the public whether you use the sites or whether you live in that area. The other side of it is, it prevented police officers from getting complaints of harassment against them. . . . When we educated the police officer, they're obviously aware what that site is.

Learning from the Wiltshire Experience

Despite the challenges faced by the Wiltshire Constabulary, its experience is for the most part a success story. The constabulary has recruited and assigned a number of quality GLOs, improved policing in the county, and increased citizens' faith in police and government. We can learn a number of important lessons based on Wiltshire's challenges and success.

Recruitment matters. When it first began recruiting GLOs, Wiltshire took a passive approach: interested officers had to volunteer for the program. But active recruitment requires goals, strategy, and planning (Dresang, 2009). In fact, Evan Berman and colleagues (2009, p. 55) note several important questions that should be considered when designing a recruitment strategy: Does the process embody the organizational goals and aims? Are enough strategies being used to reach a broad range of those who might be qualified and interested? Is the process aggressive enough to encourage the best candidates to apply? Is the process sufficiently clear and nonbureaucratic that would-be recruits are not discouraged? And perhaps most important, do applicants feel good about the recruitment process?

Wiltshire's haphazard approach to identifying and recruiting officers was inadequate. There were not enough strategies to reach the broadest possible pool of candidates, and the process was not aggressive enough to ensure that the best candidates applied. As one focus-group member noted: "We put out that we're running so many GLO courses this year, please send your nominations in. Now I don't think that worked. Rather than saying, 'Where do we need these officers to be trained?' they just put out, 'Who would like to be a GLO?' and those who put their hand up we sort of nominated."

Selection matters. If an organization has successfully engaged the talent pool via recruitment, it should end up with a large group of first-rate candidates (Riley, 2002). But Wiltshire gave little attention to its selection of GLOs. They either volunteered or, worse, were randomly selected by the local station chief. Berman and colleagues (2009) identify four critical stages for successful selection: (1) making an assessment regarding who is qualified and who is not, (2) screening the most highly qualified people, (3) selecting a single candidate for each opportunity, and (4) confirming the qualifications and ability of the candidate after the offer.

The Wiltshire Constabulary could have made a better effort to develop some selection criteria for the GLO candidates. No meaningful distinctions were made about who was qualified and who was not. People assigned to the post were not always sufficiently educated on matters important to the LGBT community, which affected the level of service provided as well as the public's perception of the GLOs.

Training matters. Besides developing a pool of high-quality candidates and selecting top candidates from that pool, proper training is also critical. The development of internal and external training materials was a collaborative effort that included the perspectives of front-line officers, individual community members, and partnership organizations. The work of the Lesbian, Gay, Bisexual, and Trans Action Group was particularly important, because it also drew resources from outside the jurisdiction. While some staff and officers who were not GLOs did not understand the role of or need for GLOs, those who received the training reported positive results.

Moving forward, Wiltshire might consider adding levels of training for officers and staff. For example, it is possible to design one level of training for diversity liaison officers and another, more specialized level of training for lesbian and gay liaison officers. In this scenario, DLOs would be generalists and GLOs would be specialists. Such a model might also be used with police community support officers, who could be trained to assist with victim support and community relations while allowing GLOs to assist with the investigative portion of an incident involving lesbian and gay people.

* * *

Despite inherent barriers to inclusive and diverse policing, the Wiltshire Constabulary has made important progress through its focus on the LGBT community. Its efforts have sensitized police and constabulary staff to issues important to the community, including same-sex intimate-partner violence and hate crimes. But these successes have not come without costs. The first GLOs were subjected to harassment and discrimination, due in part to the culture of policing and in part to the social demographics of the Wiltshire community. And GLOs were not recruited and trained in a consistent manner, thus making their integration more difficult.

Yet regardless of the barriers and costs, Wiltshire's community approach stands as a model for all of law enforcement. The constabulary's commitment shows us that even the smallest of communities can take on issues of inclusion and diversity in policing.

Conclusion

Despite the tangible differences between the two communities explored here—American versus British, urban versus rural, majority minority versus majority white, dispersed and uncoordinated LGBT versus politically engaged LGBT—many of the essential issues remain the same. For example, police officers have to be trained in proper community policing techniques, and taught how to interact with unique communities. They have to be trained to see community members as partners in their policing efforts. Both studies show the importance of leadership and management support. In Washington, D.C., the leadership of the chief of police contributed greatly to the success of the liaison unit. In Wiltshire, less support resulted in several unintended consequences, like GLOs who were not committed to the liaison unit's gay-friendly approach to policing or were negligent in their role as liaison officers.

What is clear from each case is that community policing can work, even with some invisible communities. In both the United States and the

United Kingdom, police agencies face a number of challenges in providing services to the LGBT community. Beyond invisibility, lack of trust between the police and the community can further complicate the environment. And lack of proper planning, leadership, and training can critically hinder service delivery. As we will see in the next chapter, police support—for all officers—via formal and informal organizations, provides one of best approaches to ensuring successful integration and participation of lesbian and gay officers.

Notes

1. Many other jurisdictions have gay and lesbian liaisons, but none has a unit dedicated to outreach and positive change. Elsewhere, the role of liaison is usually focused on public or agency relations, not community outreach and training.
2. This is often the case when a community member is uncomfortable contacting the police directly about an issue or incident.
3. All quotations in the remainder of this chapter are drawn from personal communications and focus-group sessions with police officers in the Wiltshire and Hampshire constabularies.

7

Professional
Police Associations

The acceptance of openly lesbian and gay officers in police agencies has helped to change institutional behaviors and attitudes. Changes to long-held conceptions of the archetypical policeman exemplify the application of gay rights in the context of a public organization. The mobilizing efforts of lesbian and gay police officers, mirroring those of the larger gay rights movement, have included the formation of professional, political, social, and legal associations, but with a focus specific to law enforcement. In terms of policing, lesbian and gay officers have used the professional association as the basic unit for organizational change.

In the United States, fraternal associations have long existed for police officers (Walker, 1992). These associations have historically been organized along racial or ethnic lines (Roberg, Crank, and Kuykendall, 2000), with local associations often coexisting alongside regional and national associations. For example, there are two national organizations for African Americans in law enforcement—the National Organization of Black Law Enforcement Executives (NOBLE) and the National Association of Black Law Enforcement Officers (NABLE)—in addition to local organizations, such as New York City's 100 Blacks in Law Enforcement Who Care and San Francisco's Officers for Justice. Local associations are often created to meet the unique needs of officers in particular communities. As police agencies have become more diverse, the number of such associations has grown at both the national and local levels.

Rod Githens and Steven Aragon (2009) have identified four categories of lesbian, gay, bisexual, and transgender (LGBT) employee associations: conventional, internally responsive informal, organized unofficial, and queer/radical. Each is defined in part according to its relationship to its broader environment. *Conventional associations* are commonly commissioned or approved by employing organizations and usually emphasize connections to the goals of the employer, such as diversity or employee satisfaction. *Internally responsive informal associations* are usually not officially recognized, are loosely structured, and are responsive to needs of constituents on an organic or "as needed" basis. *Organized unofficial associations* are formed outside the workplace and usually seek change both within the workplace and throughout the broader society. Finally, *queer/radical associations* are focused on broader social changes and have little desire to formalize their relationships with other institutions. As Githens and Aragon note about all of these types of associations, "The groups typically exist to bring about some type of change. Change can be aimed toward improving organizational effectiveness or toward broader social goals, which can include the betterment of society" (2009, p. 26). While organizational goals and societal goals might seem contradictory, in many cases they are actually complementary. Thus, lesbian and gay police associations may have the complementary goals of providing social support for officers and of improving policing within the LGBT community.

Of all the factors aiding the acceptance and integration of openly lesbian and gay police officers, gay professional associations are arguably the most significant, because they operate as both external and internal mechanisms for change within law enforcement. These associations have been important to both individual lesbian and gay officers and the police agencies they work for. For individual officers, the associations provide support and advice and create a sense of community or group identity (Holdaway and O'Neill, 2007). For police agencies, such associations create partners for diversity training and access points for community policing within the lesbian and gay community.

These lesbian and gay professional associations were not immediately embraced by law enforcement. This was especially the case in the United States. Police administration and management as well as rank-and-file members engaged in numerous activities to hamper the efforts of lesbian and gay associations. For example, in 1996 the New York City Police Department (NYPD) refused to let the Gay Officers Action League (GOAL) celebrate the contributions of lesbian and gay officers to the force (Sudetic, 1996). While it was common for other associations to honor the accomplishments of their members, GOAL's request to do the same was rejected.

Other professional police associations also fought the efforts of lesbian and gay officers to organize. When GOAL attempted to join Brotherhood-in-Action, an umbrella organization for fraternal police organizations, the latter chose to disband rather than accept GOAL's membership (Purdum, 1987).[1]

Despite initial resistance, however, many of the major US police agencies now recognize and coordinate with lesbian and gay professional organizations. This represents a shift in policing and in the role of identity-based professional associations, aided at times by legal and political action where resistance is strong and persistent—such as in New York City and Boston.

Emergence of Lesbian and Gay Professional Police Associations in the United States

In the United States, a number of lesbian and gay professional police associations emerged in the late 1970s. The first two formed on the coasts—the Golden State Peace Officers (GSPO) in the west, in California, and the Gay Officers Action League in the east, in New York City. Following the founding of these organizations, similar groups around the country and the world began to form. To help catalog and coordinate the efforts of the many groups, the Law Enforcement Gays and Lesbians International (LEGAL International) was formed. LEGAL was the umbrella organization that supported member groups and provided assistance to nascent lesbian and gay professional associations and organizations.

Golden State Peace Officers

On the West Coast, a group of lesbian and gay officers began gathering on a social basis in Los Angeles in 1979. Six years later, the social group had evolved into a more formally structured, broader-based group called the Golden State Peace Officers. The GSPO was not limited to police officers. Men and women from all criminal justice and police agencies were included. Besides offering lesbian and gay officers the opportunity to socialize, the association provided professional and charitable support for lesbian and gay–related causes.[2] At its height, the GSPO had members or representation from twenty-eight police agencies throughout California (Burke, 1993). Although no longer an active statewide organization, the GSPO spawned a number of progeny across

California, most notably the Gay Peace Officers Association of Southern California (GPOA). The GPOA represents over 400 police officers, deputy sheriffs, federal agents, deputy district attorneys, and firefighters in the greater Los Angeles area, offering its members career training opportunities, legal representation, emotional support, and the ability to network and socialize without fear of discrimination or retribution. The GPOA also provides diversity training to police and sheriff agencies throughout southern California (Gay Peace Officers Association, 2010). Although the GPOA represents a major advancement in the establishment of a lesbian and gay voice in law enforcement, the Gay Officers Action League (GOAL) and Law Enforcement Gays and Lesbians International in New York have truly transformed policing across the United States and in several additional countries around the world.

Gay Officers Action League

The same year that the GSPO was established on the West Coast, police officers in New York City were informally gathering to consider establishing a professional association of their own. The Gay Officers Action League was founded by NYPD sergeant Charles Cochrane and retired detective Sam Ciccone. Their idea was that GOAL would represent lesbians and gay men in police service and would receive the same recognition, rights, benefits, and privileges accorded to the more traditional fraternal groups. These groups had for many years influenced and dominated police policies and practices across the country. Lesbians and gay men in the NYPD had no such advocates. The issue of sexual orientation and policing was thrust onto the public agenda when Sergeant Cochrane, a fourteen-year veteran of the NYPD, spoke in favor of a gay rights bill while testifying at a city council hearing. His testimony followed that of a Patrolmen's Benevolent Association (PBA) vice president who had denounced the bill and denied the presence of any homosexual police officers on the force. Sergeant Cochrane, in his rebuttal testimony, announced: "I am very proud of being a New York City Police Officer, and I am equally proud of being gay" (Quindlen, 1981). In 1982, Cochrane and Ciccone incorporated GOAL, making it the first officially incorporated nonprofit police fraternal society in the world to represent lesbian and gay people (Gay Officers Action League, 2006).

To expand its membership, GOAL opened itself to anyone serving in any police agency, whether uniformed officers or civilian staff. Since then it has evolved from a fraternal association into an activist organization that represents the interests of its members in all agencies of the criminal justice system. But when the NYPD first began to address the question of gay recruitment, in 1984, GOAL met with fierce opposition from other fraternal organizations and from the Patrolmen's Benevolent Association, whose president publicly declared that gay people "could not hold the dignity and image of a police officer" (Gay Officers Action League, 2006). It wasn't until May 1987, at the persistent urging of GOAL, that the NYPD began a concerted effort to actively enlist qualified lesbian and gay candidates. Also for the first time, high-ranking police officials met with GOAL leaders to discuss recruitment strategies for upcoming police exams as well as career opportunities for lesbians and gay men already in the agency. Soon after, GOAL members were invited to Boston to testify at hearings that resulted in Boston's mayor enacting a nondiscrimination policy and the Boston Police Department actively recruiting in the gay community.

GOAL next began to secure the creation of a liaison position within the NYPD for the purpose of fostering communications between the agency and the lesbian and gay community. It created posters to recruit gays and lesbians into police service and sent members into the community to promote the effort, and it developed a team of lesbian and gay police officers who led sensitivity training courses for police recruits at the NYPD academy.

But despite the positive contributions of GOAL and its members, the NYPD and other fraternal associations continued to discriminate against GOAL, and against lesbian and gay officers. GOAL was denied many of the rights and privileges afforded to other police fraternal and ethnic organizations (Jirak, 2001). For example, it was denied permission to hold a cultural festival at One Police Plaza, denied permission to invite the NYPD marching band to participate in New York City's gay pride parade, and even denied authorization to march in uniform in that parade. In response, GOAL filed a civil rights suit against the NYPD, which was settled in GOAL's favor in 1996.

GOAL also engaged in proactive legal action. In 1998 it filed suit against the Puerto Rican Police Department, La Uniformada, which has islandwide policing jurisdiction. As an unincorporated territory of the United States, Puerto Rico is bound by the US Constitution. In this context, GOAL challenged La Uniformada's Regulation 29, which barred its police from associating with lesbians and gay men. On September 30, 1998, a US District Court judge ruled the regulation unconstitutional on the ground that it furthered no state interest and violated the First Amendment.

Since 1998, GOAL's relations with rank-and-file NYPD officers, other police fraternal associations, and police management have been mostly amicable. In 1999, fifteen years after the president of the Patrolmen's Benevolent Association had denounced recruitment of gay people into the NYPD, members of the PBA board appeared at a GOAL meeting seeking votes for their reelection bids. In 2002, GOAL was admitted into the Committee of Police Societies (COPS), an umbrella organization comprising all recognized NYPD religious, ethnic, and fraternal organizations (Gay Officers Action League, 2006).

GOAL chapters and GOAL-affiliated organizations have sprung up across the United States, as well as internationally.[3] Some of these associations are formally constituted, with membership dues and elected officers, while others are informal groups that focus primarily on fostering a sense of community. Each affiliated organization continues the struggle to gain legitimacy and respect for its membership and to raise awareness of issues affecting lesbians and gay men within the criminal justice system.

LEGAL International

The emergence of these various professional organizations representing lesbian and gay police officers, coupled with their members' desire to meet with their counterparts from other agencies and to collaborate to advance the rights of lesbian and gay people in law enforcement generally, led to plans for international expansion. In 1994, GOAL sponsored a conference for lesbians and gay men in law enforcement, which was held in New York City in conjunction with the Gay Games. The success of this conference led to the creation of Law Enforcement Gays and Lesbians International, an umbrella organization that serves member groups around the globe and coordinates conferences and training for lesbian and gay people in law enforcement, including police officers, deputy sheriffs, firefighters, parole and probation officers, prosecutors, jurists, and criminal justice support personnel, as well as all other law enforcement officers, managers, and executives who are interested in creating a positive working environment for an increasingly diverse work force. As with GOAL, LEGAL has formed chapters and affiliates in many parts of the United States. For example, Alabama LEGAL was formed in January 2006 by a small group of gay law enforcement officers who envisioned and developed a way for LGBT law enforcement officers across the state to meet others in the field for support, networking, and fellowship. Today, Alabama LEGAL has members from all areas of one of the most conservative states in the country.

Other Associations

Although GOAL and LEGAL have emerged as the most visible professional associations for lesbian and gay police officers, numerous smaller organizations have been established over the years to support officers and to promote acceptance and diversity in policing in the United States. One example is Pride Behind the Badge (PBB), which was informally founded in Los Angeles in 1988 (Burke, 1993) and formalized in 1991. The group originally met on a monthly basis, acting primarily as a social and support organization for lesbian and gay people in law enforcement and other first-responder roles. Today, PBB is not affiliated with any other lesbian or gay police association. It exists as a social organization and promotes events and gatherings via its website. PBB's forums, message boards, and e-mail listservs help to provide a virtual community for lesbian and gay police officers. Another organization, the Society of Law Officers (SOLO), was formed in San Diego in 1990. The aim of SOLO was to provide a "discreet" professional network for lesbian and gay officers, along with social activities for its members (Burke, 1993). Despite its more circumspect mission, SOLO did promote itself among other groups. A third important organization was the Lesbian and Gay Police Association (LGPA) of Chicago, founded in 1991. Like other lesbian and gay officers around the country, officers in Chicago felt that their fraternal organizations—as well as the city's police department—were not meeting their needs. While few lesbian and gay officers were open about their sexual orientation at the time, the LGPA operated as a safe place for both openly and secretly lesbian and gay officers. Although it was founded much later than GOAL and the GSPO, the LGPA faced many of the same challenges and obstacles that those two associations had faced a decade earlier. For example, the LGPA had to advocate for the right of lesbian and gay officers to wear uniforms during pride parades. As well, the police union and police department resisted recognition of the LGPA, which fought and won the right to post lesbian and gay–related notices in the police bulletin. The LGPA was even instrumental in Cook County's decision to offer same-sex domestic-partner benefits in 2003. In 2005 the LPGA merged with a local GOAL chapter and became LGPA-GOAL Chicago. The merger was designed to increase membership and strengthen the operational capacity of the organization.

In the United States, lesbian and gay police associations emerged as what Githens and Aragon (2009) term "organized unofficial associations." Organized unofficial groups typically form outside an organization to bring about social change or equity within their members' place of employment. While not necessarily focused on organizational effectiveness (meeting the mission of the employing organization), the goals of such associations are not incompatible with that mission. We see this most clearly in the original efforts of GOAL in New York City. Since working through the police union or other fraternal associations was not an option for lesbian and gay officers, GOAL was formed to advocate for equality based on sexual orientation. Even though GOAL's members were police officers, its unofficial (external) status allowed it to engage in an adversarial relationship with the city, the NYPD, and the police union, and to use social pressure, bring lawsuits, influence public opinion, and support legislation to advance equity for lesbian and gay people in law enforcement.

Emergence of Lesbian and Gay Professional Police Associations in the United Kingdom

Traditionally, most British police associations have been based on religion, such as the Christian Police Association (Clements, 2008). Recently, however, new police associations based on diversity and inclusion have emerged, including associations serving people of color and other minority groups. We can trace the origins of these associations back to the public inquiry into the murder of Stephen Lawrence and the resulting Macpherson Report (Grieve, Hall, and Savage, 2009; see Chapter 3). The reforms recommended in the report and enacted in its wake created a window of opportunity for broader and more inclusive changes in policing. In this context, the employee associations that emerged in the United Kingdom functioned differently from those in the United States.

The United Kingdom currently has only one professional police association for gay and lesbian officers—the Gay Police Association (GPA), founded in 1990 as the Lesbian and Gay Police Association (LAGPA).[4] Of the four categories of employee organizations identified by Githens and Aragon (2009), the GPA most closely resembles the "conventional" type—it is a formally structured, officially sanctioned group that supports diversity and organizational effectiveness. However, the road to such recognition and support by the British police was not an obvious one for the GPA.

The Gay Police Association's original mission was threefold: (1) to work toward equal opportunities for lesbian and gay police officers, (2) to offer support and advice for lesbian and gay police officers, and (3) to work toward better relations between the police and the gay community (Burke, 1993). The GPA's creation roughly coincided with the creation of other lesbian and gay police associations around the world. As with those other associations, its impetus was need-based, and the GPA was originally informal in structure (Burke, 1993). The first gatherings of the GPA were social and supportive in nature. As more officers found their way into the group, a committee was formed with the intention of revealing the association's existence to both the London Metropolitan Police (the Met, for which most of the original members worked) and the National Police Federation of England and Wales (the United Kingdom's national police union). Members of the GPA planned to quietly introduce themselves to the policing world and to the LGBT community in order to gain support and establishment.[5]

Despite the GPA's surreptitious efforts to gain support inside policing and the gay community, in January 1991 the editor of *Police Review* leaked word of the existence of a group of gay police officers to the press. This premature launch of the association created a media spectacle—one *Police Review* article went so far as to suggest that acceptance of the gay association would pave the way for a "police bondage association" (Burke, 1993). But it also put a number of legitimate issues on the public agenda. For example, several newspaper articles acknowledged the open hostility that many gay officers encountered in policing (Kirby et al., 1991).

The media controversy also threatened to scuttle any support the association was hoping to garner. Some senior officers who had not heard of the GPA or its secret meetings were caught off-guard, and panicked. The chairman of the Metropolitan Police Association (a presumed ally) attempted to discredit the very concept of such an association (Burke, 1993). Furthermore, leaders in the gay community expressed doubts that police culture could ever foster a supportive environment for lesbian and gay officers.

The initial panic and opposition did not last, however. This is not to say that lesbian and gay officers were immediately embraced by police agencies, other associations, or police unions. But the acknowledgment of the presence of a lesbian and gay association did not result in large-scale antigay campaigns, witch hunts within policing, or community backlash. No doubt this was due, in part, to the prior establishment of other identity-based associations, such as the British Association for Women in Policing (established in 1987), and in part to evolving notions about sexual orientation and the recommendations regarding diversity made in the Macpherson Report.

Efforts to oppose the GPA began to blow over in late 1991, when the largest police agency in the United Kingdom, London's Metropolitan Police, moved to alter its equal opportunity employment policies to prohibit discrimination against lesbian and gay people. Although two other police agencies had already changed their equal opportunity policies, the size and influence of the Met made its action more significant (Mullins, 1991). At the time, the Met had 28,000 uniformed officers and 16,500 civilian staff. While the first policy revision covered only civilian employees, the Met pledged to revise its policy for police officers too.

By 1995 the GPA was fully engaged in advancing its mission. In that year, the Sussex Police became the first UK agency to advertise for new police recruits in a gay newspaper (Braid and Bennetto, 1995). In that same year, the monthly magazine *Gay Times* celebrated its 200th issue with a photograph of GPA members in uniform, with the permission of Scotland Yard. Perhaps the most significant achievement of the year was the Home Office's approval and funding of the association as part of an effort to increase measurable support for lesbian and gay officers. At the time, the Home Office noted: "Funding was granted because LAGPA were able to show that they are contributing to the Home Secretary's aims for the police service" (Burrell, 2002). The funding meant that, like the British Association for Women in Policing and the National Black Police Association, the GPA would have money to reach out to lesbian and gay officers, offer them support, build its formal structure, and actively engage the police service from within in order to improve the working environment for lesbian and gay police and staff. The GPA's first funded priorities were a campaign for pension rights for same-sex partners and an outreach program to lesbian and gay officers around the country.

Despite formal support from the Home Office and Scotland Yard, however, the GPA's relationship with the police service has not always been amicable. One point of contention has been whether or not police officers should be allowed to march in uniform in gay pride parades.[6] As early as 2000, police agencies were establishing a presence at gay pride events in order to recruit lesbian and gay people. While officers were welcome to attend such parades and associated events, they were not allowed to wear their uniforms. Some in the police service argued that there was no history of uniformed police appearing as participants at political protests. Others expressed fear that community members might confuse police officers in the parades with officers assigned to patrol the events, which could cause problems in an emergency. GPA members and supporters argued that the visible presence of officers in uniform and marching in the parade would improve police relations with the community and would help recruitment efforts. Furthermore, other members suggested that sexual prejudice was the root cause of the ban on uniformed marching (Herek, 2000).

In 2003 the Met changed its policy to allow lesbian and gay officers to march in uniform in London's National Pride parade. At the time, at least eleven police agencies refused to allow their officers to participate in uniform.[7] In 2005 the GPA and the organizers of the parade invited chief constables to join the march in uniform. The GPA argued that its high-profile presence would send a valuable message of support to lesbian and gay officers and staff as well as to the LGBT community. Not many chief constables were convinced by the GPA's case for participation, however.

Today, all UK police agencies allow officers to march in uniform in gay pride parades. It is unclear whether this change is due to a simple lack of resistance to policy revision, to demographic shifts among chief constables, or to pressure from the Home Office, Scotland Yard, or the GPA, though it is likely that all these factors have had some influence. Although chief constables still retain the authority to decide whether members of their forces will be allowed to participate in gay pride parades in uniform, and although such decisions are subject to yearly review (and revision) by chief constables, no chief has denied participation in recent years. Nowadays, lesbian and gay police officers marching in gay pride parades are often joined by members of other emergency services and by uniformed members of the British military.

In 2006 a controversy erupted over a paid advertisement that the GPA placed in *The Independent* newspaper. The ad showed a Bible lying next to a pool of blood; the text read: "In the last 12 months, the Gay Police Association has recorded a 74 percent increase in homophobic incidents, where the sole or primary motivating factor was the religious belief of the perpetrator" (Shoffman, 2006). The advertisement, which appeared in the newspaper's Diversity Supplement (whose publication coincided with EuroPride festivities), was challenged by the Christian Police Association and a number of other faith-based organizations, including Christian Watch, the Trinitarian Bible Society, and the Fellowship of the Independent Evangelical Churches (Advertising Standards Authority, 2006). At the core of their objection was the implied link between Christianity and the alleged rise in hate crimes against lesbian and gay people. The GPA claimed that the data used to back this claim were based on 250 calls that the association received via its national helpline.

The more than 500 complaints filed about the advertisement led the Advertising Standards Authority to review the ad, ban the GPA from using it again, and order the GPA not to use statistics that could not be supported. Specifically, the Advertising Standards Authority (2006) found that the GPA had failed to provide evidence backing up its claim of increased attacks, had given the impression through the depiction of spilled blood that all of the attacks were physical, and had falsely implied that Christians were the perpetrators of the attacks.

Although the Advertising Standards Authority ruled against the GPA, the GPA stood by its advertisement and supporting statistics. The GPA also garnered support from other lesbian and gay community organizations. Within the police service, the controversy exposed a debate over the role of police associations, with some individuals and organizations calling for the disbandment of all such associations. Despite this incident, however, the lesbian and gay police officers who participated in my focus-group research now report amicable and professional working relationships with members of the religion-based associations.

In two decades, the GPA has gone from being an informal gathering of lesbian and gay police officers to an official police association with members in all fifty-two of the United Kingdom's police agencies. In 1990 the GPA was estimated to have 80 members; today it boasts over 5,000 members and supporters (Gay Police Association, 2009). As in the United States, the support that lesbian and gay officers receive in the United Kingdom varies from agency to agency. As noted in Chapter 4, lesbian and gay officers still face numerous difficulties on the job, from homophobic talk to physical violence. These data reaffirm the continuing need for associations like the GPA in improving the work lives of lesbian and gay people in law enforcement.

The Roles of Lesbian and Gay Professional Associations

Lesbian and gay professional associations play many different roles in police agencies as well as in communities. In both the United States and the United Kingdom, such associations primarily serve as bridges between police agencies and lesbian and gay communities, with an emphasis on collaboration. These associations are also semiautonomous, in that their work with police agencies is unnofficial.[8] Lesbian and gay police associations and police agencies have worked together closely in a number of areas, including advice and support to lesbian and gay officers on the force. Of course, some chiefs and agencies are less gay-

Voices from the Field

Name: Janice Kim
Police agency: Hampshire Constabulary
Rank: Police officer
Length of service: Twenty years

On the first lesbian and gay liaison officers in Hampshire:
"We had a lot [of] officers who actually weren't gay who wanted to be [GLOs], because it was a diverse strand that they'd never been involved in, and they wanted that understanding and they wanted that development. But we also had a group of people who were, quite clearly, gay officers, and I have to be honest, even probably in '96, '97, it still was a little difficult for gay officers within Hampshire, and we were still trying to find our feet and we were still trying to be accepted in our own right, let alone putting ourselves up for a position where we were quite clearly going to be identified, and having to create a situation for ourselves of acceptability within our own communities anyway."

On being openly gay in the 1990s:
"As far as I was concerned, it was my life. That was my personal lifestyle and it was absolutely nothing to do with anybody else in the job, and it was nothing I ever shared. And when we did, we got a hard time even as women, we got a hard time. The guys got it even harder. . . . They just didn't want to be associated [with GLOs] at that time."

On the GLO role becoming more formalized:
"You started to have a level of coordination which was the difference, which we hadn't had before, because it was so diluted, if you like, because individuals were doing it because of individual interest on individual divisions. And we had no central focus. And then as the community safety unit started operations up at headquarters, we started to get some central coordination, which made a big difference, because also those of us that were on division, knew who our senior managers were that we could trust and that we could go to and that we could speak to."

On hate crime victims:
"When they're not comfortable being out themselves, they're more likely to say 'it's not a hate crime' . . . or 'it's just an incident.' However, . . . you may get an officer that's a [GLO], that's been appointed to that job, that'll speak to the victim, and they'll say 'well actually, yes it was homophobic but I didn't want to say it at the time when it was reported,' so then oftentimes it was a hate crime."

friendly than others, and so revealing one's sexual orientation at work is not always a good idea. Police associations also play a vital role in supporting officers in ways that police agencies do not. For example, associations might raise money to help police officers (such as to pay legal fees or medical bills) or connect the officers to resources that are gay-related or gay-friendly.

More recently, lesbian and gay professional associations have also been active in developing training modules for police officers and staff, including training for new recruits, training for current officers, and specialized training for lesbian and gay liaison officers. For new recruits, training takes place at the academy, and therefore may present recruits with their first exposure to the LGBT community. These modules complement the training that new officers receive in diversity, hate crimes, profiling, and intimate-partner violence. For officers who have completed academy training, the associations have fought hard to ensure that certificate trainings and advancement standards include sufficient understanding of the lesbian and gay community and its unique challenges. Finally, for lesbian and gay liaison officers training must account for the fact that some liaisons are not themselves lesbian or gay and may therefore have less experience with the LGBT community. The modules developed for this sector of the police population were originally ad hoc but have become formalized over time as trainers discover what types of information police officers already know and what types of information need to be emphasized. Smaller agencies with limited resources often borrow such modules from larger agencies.

Lesbian and gay associations have also exerted influence in the areas of personnel administration and employment development. In both the United States and the United Kingdom, lesbian and gay associations have worked with public-sector entities, unions, and other organizations to assess personnel policies and to identify possible disparities faced by lesbian and gay workers. Such assessments usually extend beyond personnel issues and can include more general evaluations of harassment, discrimination, or unfair treatment. For example, in New York City, GOAL has been working with the city government and the state pension board to develop a process that allows partners of lesbian and gay officers to access their pension benefits.

Of course, these associations have also been very active in recruiting lesbian and gay police officers and in helping develop recruitment strategies. For instance, an association may use its membership to provide outreach to friends, family, and acquaintances who may have an interest in policing but have never talked to an openly lesbian or gay officer. Associations' recruiting efforts also include coordinating outreach at gay-related events and networking with other organizations that serve the lesbian and gay community. For example, both GOAL in the United States and the GPA in the United Kingdom conduct annual outreach at gay pride events.

Whether developing policies or conducting outreach, lesbian and gay associations provide a critical connection between police agencies and lesbian and gay officers. The collective knowledge and expertise of such associations can help improve the work lives of police and staff, and the collective efforts of these associations can force police agencies to become more gay-friendly and supportive. This was certainly the case in GOAL's relationship with the NYPD. In more than one seemingly unresolvable situation (such as when gay officers were forbidden to march in New York's gay pride parade in uniform), GOAL sued the NYPD to force it into compliance.

But the positive impact of lesbian and gay police associations has not been limited to their influence on police institutions. Their presence has been an important component of improved community policing as well, helping bridge the gap between lesbian and gay communities and police agencies. While many police agencies have lesbian and gay liaisons to facilitate community relations and policing, the professional associations are seen as having greater authenticity because they are external to police agencies. This autonomy allows an association to work more closely with individuals and institutions in the community and to help the community realize its policing goals. For example, in the United Kingdom, the GPA has worked closely with community organizations to encourage the reporting of bias crimes and incidents. To facilitate reporting, police constabularies, community groups, and the police associations have each established separate hotlines for incident reporting. Community members can thus make reports to whichever venue they feel most comfortable with and be assured that the information will be routed to the appropriate constabulary. This kind of cooperative working relationship also has implications for how often and how swiftly crimes are solved. In the United Kingdom, more accurate data are being collected about the number and types of crimes occurring in the LGBT community, giving police agencies a better knowledge base for resource deployment.

Conclusion

Lesbian and gay police associations have had a profound effect on police agencies, lesbian and gay communities, and individual officers. Forming groups and advocating en masse have served other police groups well, so it makes sense that these strategies have also proven useful for lesbian and gay officers. The external nature of these organizations has given lesbian and gay officers a place outside the chain of command where they can gain support and share information. This external nature has also given these associations the ability to force change through external pressure and influence. As Marc Burke (1993) noted, in the United Kingdom the Home Office had no idea about the size or influence of the Gay Police Association. It did not know whether the GPA represented 10 officers or 1,000 or 10,000. This led to significant victories in reforming the police to become more inclusive. The emergence of lesbian and gay police associations meshes nicely with the trend of individual officers identifying themselves as lesbian or gay and with the growing insistence by lesbian and gay communities that they be policed more equitably and effectively.

From establishing police associations, to bringing lawsuits to lift bans on marching in uniform in parades, to developing training for officers, the efforts and dedication of lesbian and gay officers have resulted in great strides for diversity in policing. However, in order to replicate such efforts, more sexual-minority officers are needed. Ultimately, this means improving recruitment, selection, and retention of officers. The next chapter discusses best practices for ensuring a place in law enforcement for the most qualified lesbian and gay officers.

Notes

1. Brotherhood-in-Action disbanded and reincorporated as the Corporation of Police Societies, and gave up the right to hold meetings during working hours, rather than admit GOAL.

2. There is a paucity of data and information about the GSPO's early days. According to Marc Burke, the original six goals of the GSPO were "to promote fellowship among its members and to provide resources for exchange of information within the Association and other associations; to foster educational opportunities for the Association through a variety of means, including conferences, workshops and seminars; to engage in charitable activities which benefit the gay and lesbian community; to network with similar organizations that have similar interests and objectives; to provide a forum for planning and implementation of activities and programs for the benefit of the Association; and to publish a regular newsletter" (1993, p. 208).

3. International lesbian and gay professional police organizations can be found in Australia, Austria, Canada, Denmark, Germany, Italy, the Netherlands, New Zealand, Switzerland, and the United Kingdom (Eurocops, 2010; GOAL Chicago, 2010). US states with lesbian and gay professional police organiza-

tions include Arizona, Florida, Illinois, Maryland, Minnesota, New Jersey, New York, Ohio, Oregon, Texas, Virginia, and Washington; the District of Columbia also has such an organization (Jirak, 2001).

4. LAGPA officially changed its name in 2001. For clarity and simplicity, I use the current acronym, GPA, throughout this discussion.

5. Given law enforcement's history of abusing and mistreating the LGBT community, many community members and organizations were as distrustful of the GPA as they were of the policing community.

6. Lesbian and gay police officers in the United States faced similar bans on marching in uniform in gay pride parades. In New York City, the uniform ban was in place until 1996, when GOAL filed a federal discrimination complaint against the NYPD. Given that police officers were allowed to march in uniform in other affiliation parades, for example the St. Patrick's Day parade and the Puerto Rican Pride parade, the NYPD dropped its gay pride–related ban in short order.

7. The Association for Chief Police Officers advocated for the "devolved" policy approach to this issue, with individual chief constables empowered to make the decision for their local constabularies.

8. The ideal of these associations as semiautonomous groups applies more to the United Kingdom than to the United States, as the British associations receive funding from the Home Office to help carry out their missions.

8

Best Practices for Recruitment and Human Resources

In studying lesbian and gay officer inclusion and diversity within police agencies, I make a number of assumptions. The first assumption is that diversity of the work force is good for any organization, but is especially important for public service organizations like police agencies. If community policing is to be the cornerstone of contemporary policing, agencies will need to know and understand the communities they serve. And one way to improve police agencies' community and cultural competence is through employment diversity.

In this sense, employment diversity in police agencies creates a strong case for inclusion of openly lesbian and gay officers. Police agencies that embrace diversity and create environments where all officers are treated professionally and fairly will reap the individual as well as organizational rewards. At the individual level, lesbian and gay officers who serve openly are less susceptible to corruptive forces that haunt police agencies. For example, they are less likely to become victims of blackmail, less likely to succumb to bribery, and may be less likely to use excessive force due to stress.

At the organizational level, a diverse police force will enhance an agency's understanding of the lesbian, gay, bisexual, and transgender (LGBT) community, and of the challenges of policing within this community. A police agency can more effectively respond to issues like intimate-partner violence, public sex environments, transgender prostitution, hate and bias crimes, bullying, and gay youth homelessness when openly lesbian and gay officers are integrated into policing. This is not to suggest that only lesbian and gay officers can respond to these issues, or that they are better at policing these types of issues. Is does suggest, however, that a diverse police agency that includes openly lesbian and gay officers is more likely to have sexual minority–oriented training, more likely to have both a lesbian and gay police association and an LGBT resource group, and more likely to have useful contacts within the LGBT community who can help with investigations and provide information critical to solving cases. Such collaboration is the ideal for community policing.

Throughout the book, we have seen both the advantages and the disadvantages that openly lesbian and gay police officers experience. No doubt, the environment for these officers has dramatically improved over the past two decades. Yet these improvements are uneven and inconsistent across policing agencies. An openly lesbian or gay person may find full acceptance and integration in one agency, but homophobic harassment and discrimination in another.

In order to improve the working conditions for lesbian and gay police officers, and enhance the functional performance of police agencies, organizational changes are needed. Based on the data presented in this book, there are at least four major components (and multiple subcomponents) to creating a diverse police force that is inclusive of lesbian and gay people: leadership, planned change, recruitment, and retention.

Leadership

There are many definitions of leadership and discussions about its importance in policing. The first characteristic of leadership, as highlighted by Derek Rollison, Aysen Broadfield, and David Edwards (1998), is that it is noncoercive; it guides followers toward a specific goal. The second characteristic is that it requires the willingness of followers to allow guidance, suggesting that leadership is a two-way process. With mutual consent, leaders lead, and followers follow. At first glance, this definition contradicts the way most people think about police agencies. The police agency is commonly understood as a "top-down" hierarchical organization, with authority vested in management. For the most part, police agencies still conform to this organizational structure; however, leadership need not reside solely in the agency management. Leadership, especially as it relates to diversity, can reside throughout the organization and include all levels of personnel.

Of course, any effort to change the attitudes, values, and beliefs— not to mention the policies and practices—of an organization needs vision, support, and guidance from the top. This was the case in

Washington, D.C., when the chief of the Metropolitan Police Department (MPD), Charles Ramsey, decided, in 1992, to formally create the MPD's Gay and Lesbian Liaison Unit (GLLU). This was also the case in Hampshire in the United Kingdom when Police Constable Paul Kernaghan approved, in 2001, police and staff efforts to get the constabulary listed in Stonewall's index of gay-friendly workplaces. In both instances, leadership from the top of the organization was needed to provide resources and legitimacy.

Although leadership from the top of an organization is critical, leadership from the lower levels is essential as well. In the case of community policing, the need for leadership can be devolved all the way down to the officer on the street. An officer responding to an incident might find him- or herself dealing with a sensitive situation. It is up to that officer to apply the correct police policy or practice, while understanding the unique nature of the situation. Such equitable application—both apparent and actual—can enhance community trust and improve policing outcomes. This was the situation when lesbian police officers in the MPD began to informally reach out to the gay and lesbian community to solve the Gallaudet murder case (see Chapter 1). In addition to solving the case, they engaged the community in a positive manner, thus fostering trust. This was also the case when lesbian and gay officers in the Hampshire Constabulary realized the recruiting potential of creating a gay-friendly workplace. In the latter case, the morale of lesbian and gay officers improved, and the community had tangible proof that the police agency was committed to an inclusive environment. In both cases, leadership traits were exhibited by street-level officers committed to improved policing (in the case of the MPD) and a more diverse workplace (in the case of the Hampshire Constabulary).

Whether exhibited from the top of the police agency or from within, there are several characteristics associated with leadership regarding diversity. John Grieve (2008) notes several characteristics of leaders committed to diversity. First, a leader must create a vision. The vision should inspire people (inside and outside policing) to imagine policing without harassment, discrimination, or unfairness. Such a vision has the potential to enhance community relations and ensure that police personnel understand and embrace the values embedded in the vision. Second, leadership in diversity requires communication. This means communication with and between colleagues and communities. Envisioning, planning, and implementing an agenda for a more diverse workplace can cause uncertainty among stakeholders, but competent communication skills can help to ameliorate negative perceptions and assumptions.

Third, leadership requires competence. Grieve notes that this includes both competence in behavior and competence in understanding diversity and its value to the police agency. Good leaders embrace diversity in their actions, and articulate these actions to different stakeholders. Fourth, leaders must care about others. At the end of the day, policing, whether community or problem-oriented policing, is about understanding people and their needs. The fifth characteristic is the ability to confront individuals and issues. As mentioned, work force diversification can create uncertainty, which can manifest in the form of negative attitudes and behaviors. A leader must be willing to confront individuals and to directly address issues raised. The sixth characteristic is a commitment to the business, in this case to policing and policing diversity. Grieve notes that good leaders understand and lead on the idea that good policing is built on fairness and justice, just like work force diversity. Finally, leadership requires charisma. Leaders who are secure in their values and in policing will be able to work confidently with fellow officers and communities to create a diverse work environment.

We have few examples of individuals who embody all of these leadership traits. Certainly, Police Chief Ramsey of the MPD in Washington, D.C., possessed many of these traits. It was during his tenure (1998–2006) that the MPD established a foundation for community policing, including the community-based GLLU as well as liaison units for Latino, Asian, and deaf communities. It was under Chief Ramsey that the MPD also began active recruitment of lesbian and gay officers. Ramsey's efforts included training to teach officers and staff about diversity and its importance in policing; working with various communities (especially the LGBT community) to demonstrate commitment to creating a police agency that would be representative of the Washington, D.C., population; speaking out to subordinates and superiors about the importance of innovation and diversity in policing; and ensuring follow-up with various stakeholders to address concerns directly. For example, Ramsey was often asked to explain why the MPD did not have a specialized unit for the black American community, given that it had specialized units for other minority groups (Metropolitan Police Department, 2011b).[1]

Leadership is the first and essential element for any police agency interested in diversity, especially inclusion of lesbian and gay officers. Ideally, this leadership will come from the top and include commitment of resources. Alternatively, leaders can emerge from anywhere within the organization, as long as they have the needed characteristics. Even a beat officer can be an effective and charismatic leader and inspire fairness and justice through work force diversity.

Planned Change

Efforts to move a police agency in a particular direction—change that involves individuals, groups, and organizational structures and processes—require a systematic and specific plan. This planned change often stems from declining resources (fewer staff, less money, less capacity, etc.), increased demand for accountability, or the expansion of knowledge and technology (Jiao and Kocher, 2000). Under these circumstances, the drive to increase work force diversity can be a beneficial catalyst in pushing an agency to adapt to its changing environment. Diversity can help a police agency to respond more efficiently and effectively to declining resources, to increase accountability (both among officers and within communities), and to expand its knowledge base about community-policing issues. Efforts to become more inclusive and diverse are more likely to be achieved when a strategic process like planned change is followed.

Strategic planning establishes a vision, a mission, goals, strategies, and criteria for and means of evaluation. A strategic plan is essentially a roadmap that guides an organization in moving in a particular direction. In terms of diversity in policing, this involves long-term changes to organizational structures and process.

Vision

A vision answers questions like, "Where does the organization want to go?" and "What will success look like?" It serves as the anchor to the strategic plan, in contrast to long-range planning, by depicting a new, idealized image of what the organization can become in the future. Although leadership is important throughout an entire police agency, the creation of a vision for the organization is the responsibility of the top leadership, who are positioned to initiate, fund, evaluate, and sustain change. Effective vision statements are comprehensive yet detailed, such that they inspire and compel action from all levels of the police agency (Lim, 2008).

The term *diversity* has evolved over decades to refer to an array of attributes—from the traditional categories of race and ethnicity, gender, age, religion, disability, and national origin, to other categories such as sexual orientation, language, talent, experience, paradigm, and even personality (Stockdale and Crosby, 2004). Some of these attributes are ascribed, while others can be achieved.

The dynamics of diversity span the spectrum as well. Some consider representation to be a measure of diversity in the workplace or a response to equal employment opportunity issues (Powell, 1993), while others value differences, managing diversity and inclusion as a new institutional paradigm (Golembiewski, 1995; Thomas, 1996; Gilbert, Stead, and Ivancevich, 1999).

For police agencies that embrace community policing and planned change with a focus on diversity, moving beyond the traditional ideas associated with equal opportunity is imperative. From this perspective, the vision for a diverse work force should be as inclusive and dynamic as possible. As Roosevelt Thomas noted, "diversity refers to the differences, similarities, and related tensions that exist in any mixture. Note especially that the term includes differences and similarities. Diversity is not limited to issues of race and gender, nor is it confined to the workforce" (2006, p. xi). This is not to say that a police agency should abandon legally mandated and voluntary efforts to recruit and retain people of color and women; instead it acknowledges that sexual orientation (and other differences) can be of value to the organization. For Thomas, "diversity is not solely—or even primarily—about improving racial and ethnic relations in the midst of pluralism. Diversity refers to any set of differences and similarities in any setting" (p. xiii).

The processes and outcomes of diversity efforts can vary greatly, depending on the vision of diversity that a police agency chooses to adopt. Without a common vision of diversity and agreement on approaches to diversity management, a strategic plan can fail due to different interpretations of the issues involved.

Mission

A mission articulates the identity of an organization, its reason for being (Goodstein, Nolan, and Pfeiffer, 1993). For members of the organization, it serves as a unifying thread that ties their day-to-day work to the organization's purpose and role in society.

Developing a mission statement can be a critical step for police agencies. In the past, police agencies confined diversity initiatives to human resource or personnel units. Within the strategic planning process, the mission for the larger police agency should be aligned to mesh with the newly developed vision. While human resource or personnel agencies can be assigned communication, implementation, and other responsibilities, the goal of increased diversity should be organization-wide as formulated in the mission statement (Lim, 2008).

There are many examples of police agencies that have embraced diversity as part of their mission; one is the Metropolitan Police

Department of Washington, D.C. The MPD's mission statement on employment reads: "fulfilling the mission of the Metropolitan Police Department requires a variety of individuals who are not only interested in serving D.C. communities, but who also have unique skills, perspectives and strengths to apply to the work they do. *By maintaining a workforce that is diverse and all-inclusive, MPD will continue to provide the District with the best possible response to community issues"* (2011a, emphasis added).

Another example is the British Transport Police (BTP). Its mission statement reads: "Our values promote equal opportunities by: treating everyone fairly, with respect and dignity; eliminating all forms of harassment, bullying and victimization; and *providing an inclusive, supportive work environment, taking positive action where necessary, so staff of all backgrounds can achieve"* (2011, emphasis added).

Goals

Once the mission is set, it can be translated into goals. Goals articulate the accomplishments needed to realize the mission and bring the strategic plan closer to implementation (Lim, 2008). Goals help bridge the gap between planning and implementation by actively engaging the rest of the organization with tangible efforts (Goodstein, Nolan, and Pfeiffer, 1993; McNamara and Bromiley, 1997).

If the vision of the police agency embraces a broad definition of diversity, one goal may be to simultaneously improve representation along several dimensions, including race/ethnicity, gender, religion, sexual orientation, discipline, geographic location, experience, and structural characteristics. An example of this can be seen in the Wiltshire Constabulary's mission statement on recruitment: "Wiltshire Police has a strong ethos of equality and diversity both within the organization and to the service we provide. We are committed to creating a police service that is representative of the communities we serve, and believe that in this way the force will be better able to reach the aim to have: trained and motivated staff who . . . think, deliver and promote equality and fairness to the public and to each other. . . . [I]t is therefore our continuing intention to: *identify environments where 'under representation' exists; set appropriate targets;* review policy, processes and perceptions in order to dismantle barriers; develop initiatives that promote equality and fairness both 'internally' and 'externally,' that further the Police Recruitment, Retention and Progression Strategy" (2010, emphasis added).

Strategies

Strategies give shape to implementation of the strategic plan and provide a roadmap for achieving established goals. A strategy can be defined as a specific policy deriving from a formulation process (Goodstein, Nolan, and Pfeiffer, 1993). Put differently, a policy is a strategy if it is deliberate and is associated with a bigger picture of where the organization is headed.

According to Nelson Lim (2008), there are two broad categories of diversity strategies: those that concern the processes affecting diversity outcomes (process strategies), and those that enable and facilitate movement toward the diversity vision (enabling strategies). Process strategies are related to operational elements—for example, training, career assignments, promotion, and retention. Enabling strategies involve functions that are more ambiguous—for example, leadership, accountability, and culture.

Traditionally, police agencies have focused on process strategies, especially when recruiting women and racial minorities. By manipulating the personnel process, the police agency effects the diversity outcome. For example, considering women and recruitment, efforts like advertising on job websites dedicated to women, or participating in e-mail listservs dedicated to women, are examples of traditional changes in process strategies.

Enabling strategies involve more substantial and typically longer-term efforts to effect diversity. Police agencies have used enabling strategies in this regard, but with much less consistency compared to process strategies. One example is the London Metropolitan Police (Met). In an effort to recruit women into its elite Special Firearms Command (roughly equivalent to a SWAT team in the United States), the Met established a women's development program. For this unit, the program sends potential applicants into residential neighborhoods to explain the day-to-day realities of the job, during which time they are mentored by female officers serving in the Special Firearms Command. This exposure and mentoring help prepare women for assignment to the specialized unit.

Evaluation

The strategic planning process does not end once the strategies have been identified. It continues with a plan for monitoring and evaluating the implementation of diversity efforts (Lim, 2008). The guiding question for police agencies is: "How will you know if you have achieved your goal?"

Because lack of empirical evidence about the effectiveness of diversity efforts often leads to early cancellation or defunding, program evaluations can help compare diversity efforts to determine which are the most successful. These evaluations can also provide information about the value of diversity efforts. As Lim (2008) notes, this information about returns on investment can be helpful in future resource allocation. Program evaluations can be the basis for motivation and accountability, as well as the rationale for mobilizing additional resources and support.

According to Thomas Kochan and colleagues (2003), quantifying the results of diversity programs is difficult, because relevant data are usually not collected, and because data on existing human resources do not capture the processes that lead to results. This assertion is especially relevant for organizations that use a broad definition of diversity. While certain attributes, such as race or gender, can be easily observed, sexual orientation is more difficult to measure.

While difficult, proper data collection on sexual orientation in police agencies is not impossible. In the United Kingdom, the Staffordshire Police Authority introduced sexual orientation monitoring throughout its human resource functions in 2001, including its employee opinion survey (Staffordshire Police, 2011). The results of this ongoing monitoring have been incorporated into the organization's diversity strategies and action plans. For example, based on its data collection about sexual orientation, Staffordshire has been able to track its efforts to recruit lesbian and gay police officers. With proper data collection, police agencies will be able to adjust programs based on the measured effects of such efforts.

* * *

With committed leadership and planned change, police agencies can prepare their forces for a more diverse and inclusive environment—an environment in which acceptance of lesbian and gay officers is increasingly widening. But this requires that diversity and inclusion be seen as positive values throughout the organization. This is an important first step, because cultural change in most police agencies is a long-term process, and because efforts to cultivate a more diverse and inclusive work force will fail if old cultural norms remain. We can see this in the fact that openly lesbian and gay officers report homophobic talk in the workplace in the same way that women have reported sexually inappropriate talk and people of color have reported racist talk. Beyond hateful speech, we can also see this in the challenges presented by performance evaluations and promotion among women, people of color, and openly lesbian and gay people. In this context of continuing challenges for minorities in policing, the question remains: What can police agencies do to increase diversity with respect to lesbian and gay officers? There are several recruitment and retention efforts that have proven successful in increasing lesbian and gay representation in police agencies.

Recruitment

Establish a Network or Resource Group

There are many ways to create support for lesbian and gay police officers. One of the most common is the establishment of a network or resource group. A network group is a formal mechanism for enabling lesbian and gay employees to come together to share information and support (Cowan, 2005). Such groups are supported by the organization, and work to enhance a positive climate in the workplace and to help group members to more effectively contribute to the mission of the organization. Resource groups operate in the same way, but usually include outside community members.

Not only does an effective network or resource group serve as a central hub in developing and implementing lesbian and gay–friendly efforts, but it can also have beneficial effects for the organization, lesbian and gay employees, and the community (Cowan, 2005). From the organization's perspective, the group promotes diversity. The existence of such a group in a police agency is a reminder that differences exist among officers and that this is a positive attribute for policing. The existence of the group will be an indicator to both homosexual and non-homosexual applicants that the police agency is serious about inclusion and diversity. Thus lesbian and gay people might be more likely to apply for a position knowing that an employer-sponsored support group is already in place.

Police agencies as employers and organizations might also benefit from the newly formed communication channel with lesbian and gay officers. In this case, the network or resource group can be used to determine whether current openly lesbian and gay officers are experiencing particular challenges in the agency. This knowledge can be helpful as the agency embarks on lesbian and gay–focused police recruitment planning and development.

The group can also act as a valued asset for diversity training and policymaking. For example, in Hampshire, the resource group worked closely with the training team to develop lesbian and gay–specific police scenarios for officers who had little or no practical experience working with the lesbian and gay community.

Within the organization, lesbian and gay officers of course also benefit from network and resource groups. Beyond enhancing communication and collaboration with police management, these groups provide lesbian and gay police officers with peer support that can directly counter antigay bias and its resultant feelings of isolation and tokenism (being selected as a single minority to stave off claims of discrimination). This peer support helps build confidence and employment satisfaction among officers.

Finally, the served community can benefit from networks and resource groups. In sending a message of common experience to the community, resource groups can improve community relations. Additionally, if leaders from the lesbian and gay community are part of the resource group, they will have a direct and open channel of communication to police management.

In both the United States and the United Kingdom, network and resource groups are essential for active recruitment and retention of lesbian and gay officers. These groups vary in size, shape, aim, mission, and activities, which can include developing recruitment strategies and diversity training modules, developing model nondiscrimination language and policies, maintaining support and advocacy systems for officers, providing lesbian and gay police officers for events, building relations with other network and resource groups, and promoting the police agency as a leader in diversity and inclusion. From New York to Boston, and from Wiltshire to London, network and resource groups are a central part of strategic diversity efforts in policing.

Develop Lesbian and Gay–Specific Strategies

In order to increase the number of openly lesbian and gay officers, police agencies will need to increase the number of openly lesbian and gay individuals in their recruitment pools. Agencies should develop lesbian and gay–focused recruitment strategies that are based on segmenting the recruitment field and targeting particular groups (Milgram, 2002). Although this approach is not new, it is not commonly used in the public sector, and even less commonly so in law enforcement, as policing is viewed as a calling rather than a career choice. However, by applying population-specific strategies, police agencies can diversify their recruitment pools. In terms of sexual orientation, these strategies include featuring lesbian and gay people on agency recruitment websites, creating advertisements and outreach notices on websites dedicated to lesbian and gay people, participating in e-mail listservs dedicated to lesbian and gay people, collaborating with lesbian and gay organizations during pride and outreach events, and developing long-term recruitment efforts with lesbian and gay–friendly youth and minority groups.

Website recruitment featuring lesbian and gay people is one of the easiest and least-expensive approaches to diversifying the recruitment pool. The police agency can relay important information about the changing nature of policing while focusing on diversity and inclusion. In the United Kingdom, the Wiltshire Constabulary's website included lesbian and gay–related symbols, like the rainbow flag, and allowed lesbian and gay liaison officers to wear small pins on their uniforms that identified them as such in their website photographs. Both efforts signaled to lesbian and gay people that the constabulary valued diversity. The Hampshire Constabulary's website included the logo of Stonewall and announced its success as a "diversity champion."

Creating advertisements and outreach notices on websites dedicated to lesbian and gay people is also an increasing popular approach to recruitment. As online job hunting becomes more common, the usefulness of this approach becomes more effective. Advertisements can reach numerous individuals from around the world who might be interested in a particular local community. Two of the largest networks together report reaching over 6 million users per month. Police agencies advertising with these networks reach individuals worldwide across 290 popular lesbian and gay–related websites, blogs, and social networks (www.gayadnetwork.com and lesbianadnetwork.com).

Participation in e-mail listservs dedicated to lesbian and gay people is a useful mechanism for staying connected with this community over time. Organizations like the National Gay and Lesbian Taskforce and the Human Rights Campaign operate such e-mail listservs that focus on workplace equality. The Human Rights Campaign (2011a) reports a membership of over 750,000. In Washington, D.C., the Metropolitan Police Department works closely with the DC Center for the LGBT Community and uses its listservs to reach out to members of the LGBT community who might be interested in police service.

Voices from the Field

Name: Michael Johnston
Police agency: Metropolitan Police Department (Washington, D.C.)
Rank: Sergeant
Length of service: Seventeen years

On measuring the success of the department's Gay and Lesbian Liaison Unit (GLLU):

"To me there are three big indicators. One: number of hate crimes being reported. As long as they keep increasing, we're doing a good job. It seems counter-intuitive, but it makes sense to me. Number two: how many officers are coming out on our police department? How many openly gay officers do we have working for us? I can't even count the numbers now. There are so many. I get calls every couple of weeks from somebody new that pops up out of the wood-work. "Hey, I'm thinking about joining your agency. I hear it's a great place to be a gay cop." That says a lot about where we are as [an] agency. . . . So it's the hate crimes, number of openly gay and lesbian officers, and then the third, to me, quite honestly is the intangible kind of temperature out there in the community on how they feel about us, and when you hear them crying and screaming about fucking with the Gay and Lesbian Liaison Unit and possibly changing its structure and how many people are there, that tells me it's very well-received, or they're being successful, because if they weren't . . . nobody would notice."

On the visibility of lesbian and gay liaison officers in the community, and the decision not to wear visible GLLU insignia:

"The unit was careful. I do remember this—the unit was careful. We actually had a discussion about whether or not to put the 'Gay and Lesbian Liaison Unit' in big letters out front, whether to put that on the cruisers, and we realized that there's a segment of the community that's on the down-low. They don't want you pulling up in front of their house—you may drop someone off at their house [but] you have to be very quiet about it. And so, there is that whole conflict between trying to be an outgoing, outreach-oriented unit but still maintaining a certain sense of confidentiality and staying quiet. . . . My rationalization when that decision had to be made, was: I do not want to potentially out somebody. It's bad enough, if I come on the scene, everyone knows it's a gay-related crime. That's just their assumption. The media knows, if I show up, it's going to be a gay homicide or it's some type of hate crime."

Collaboration and outreach with lesbian and gay organizations and events provides police agencies with an opportunity to recruit lesbian and gay people in the field. Opportunities for such collaboration and outreach are many. For example, police agencies can collaborate with local community and political organizations. For the New York Police Department, this has meant working with organizations like Stonewall NYC and the Audre Lorde Project to reach out to lesbian and gay New Yorkers who might not otherwise have thought about a career in policing. The most common among these collaboration and outreach efforts, however, take place during gay pride events. In most lesbian and gay communities, gay pride events provide an opportunity for law enforcement to meet with potential applicants, display state-of-the-art equipment, and support the community through physical presence. Pride events, depending on the community, can draw from tens of thousands to hundreds of thousands of participants, many of whom may never have considered police agencies as diverse and inclusive organizations.

Developing long-term recruitment efforts with youth groups is another way to build recruitment among lesbian and gay individuals. By establishing relationships with these youth groups, police agencies can create opportunities for young people to learn about policing. As a result, lesbian and gay youth grow up accustomed to working with police instead of viewing them with suspicion. Lesbian and gay youth will also be more likely to participate in police cadet programs and other police-sponsored activities. These youth organizations need not be exclusively lesbian and gay, but should have a track record of diversity and inclusion. For an agency like the MPD in Washington, D.C., such youth groups might include the United Way, the National Youth Advocacy Coalition, and the Gay, Lesbian, and Straight Education Network. For an agency like the Hampshire Constabulary in the United Kingdom, such groups might include Breakout and the Baseline Youth Inclusion Project.

Many of these efforts to increase diversity and inclusion could be applied to any group of individuals who are underrepresented in the recruitment pool, not just lesbian and gay people. Regardless, efforts to recruit any minority group into policing require both short- and long-term strategies. In some cases, these strategies are designed to reverse decades of maltreatment and neglect of a minority group. In other cases, these strategies are designed to establish new relationships with individuals and organizations that have no prior history with police agencies. In any case, these efforts will prove beneficial to the police agency, to its minority officers, and to the many communities served by the agency.

Retention

Recruitment is only one half of the challenge when developing a diverse and inclusive police force. Once lesbian and gay officers have joined the agency, concerted efforts will be needed to retain them. Retention efforts can take many forms, and may be monetary or nonmonetary in form. For example, officers might be offered additional training, choice schedules, or a parking spot near the office. In terms of monetary efforts, competitive salaries, retention bonuses, and education support have all been used by organizations. Retaining quality employees is a challenge for all organizations. For police agencies, the costs to replace officers who have been recruited, tested, vetted, selected, and trained make retention especially important. When officers, including lesbian and gay officers, prematurely leave policing, both the agency and the community are disadvantaged. With systematic efforts to retain quality officers, police agencies can reduce costs and institutional loss.

Compensation

Though there are many approaches that have helped to improve retention among officers, improved compensation is among the most important. David Yearwood and Stephanie Freeman (2004) found that nearly half of North Carolina police agencies attributed at least 70 percent of their attrition to compensation issues that drove officers to other agencies or professions. Compensation includes salary and benefits, but equally important for retention are viable career ladders, exciting training, the newest equipment, and the perception that a career in policing will afford a good life (Wilson, 2010). Improving the benefits and other perks that police officers receive increases the likelihood that they will remain in policing. Leigh Branham (2005) noted that inadequate compensation can contribute to feelings of devaluation and drive employees to leave an organization. While compensation and benefits were not considered barriers to equal opportunity for the lesbian and gay officers surveyed for my research, poor compensation and benefits can certainly add stress to the policing environment.

Since most compensation and benefits for careers in law enforcement are determined by the political and administrative bodies of a jurisdiction, police agencies need to lobby for valuable benefits that demonstrate appreciation of officers as employees. Such innovative benefits might include quality training, up-to-date equipment, tuition reimbursement, specialized perks, and multiple career options.

Training and Educational Advancement

Quality training is another proven tool for increasing retention among police officers, especially lesbian and gay police officers. Officers who do not receive the benefit of proper training can become discouraged or lose confidence (Orrick, 2008). Employees in most organizations expect frequent training opportunities to improve their knowledge, skills, and abilities. While basic and field training are essential to the development and enculturation of police officers, quality in-service or continuing education can make the difference between a low- and a high-performing officer. Continuing education varies from agency to agency, but usually consists of sessions on new laws, emerging technology, and newer techniques, including community and problem-oriented policing, dealing with youth gangs, and combating new types of illegal drugs (Jones et al., 2005). The most innovative police agencies offer continuing education in a multitude of areas, including communication skills, leadership development, and human resource management. Additionally, well-developed programs provide competitive training for specialized police work, including training in homicide investigation, SWAT, and emergency management. These innovative and specialized training modules are key to retention. When employees have access to such training, motivation and satisfaction increase, resulting in improved policing in the community. For lesbian and gay officers, selection is often competitive and represents an investment in the police officer and in the idea of a diverse police force.

Continuing education offers benefits beyond those that accrue to the police officers who participate in the training. In some cases, lesbian and gay officers are recruited as trainers, especially for courses focused on diversity, inclusion, and community policing within the lesbian and gay community. By recruiting lesbian and gay officers as trainers, police agencies can acknowledge and embrace their unique contributions.

Tuition reimbursement can provide police officers with the opportunity to obtain, maintain, or improve job-related capabilities through participation in courses of study at accredited colleges and universities. Many police agencies in the United States require new applicants to have completed at least two years of college, although some agencies require only a high school diploma. In the United Kingdom, there are no formal educational requirements for entry into the police service. Recruitment and selection procedures are managed by police services at the local level, although a nationally agreed competency-based framework is applied (Montgomery, 2010). In both countries, there is a shared belief that additional education and training for officers has a positive effect on policing. Scott Smith and Michael Aamodt (1997) noted that improved performance of police officers was correlated with higher education. Officer performance was measured by supervisor evaluations of overall performance, communication skills, public relations skills, report-writing skills, response to new training, decisionmaking ability, and commitment to policing. The only variables that did not prove to be significantly related to education were objective measures of volume of arrests, number of disciplinary measures, and number of accidents.

For lesbian and gay police officers, tuition reimbursement and educational advancement can have doubly positive effects. On the tuition reimbursement side, lesbian and gay officers get to take advantage of a benefit that will increase their competitiveness in the agency and the broader employment field. Like other benefits, tuition reimbursement helps to create loyalty among officers. In addition to personal enrichment, lesbian and gay officers will benefit from a better-educated police agency. Gregory Herek (2004) noted that higher education is positively correlated with less homophobic attitudes. In other words, better-educated officers are more accepting of lesbian and gay people.

Perks and Incentives

Perks or additional incentives can also help retain police officers. These types of benefits are not legally mandated and are usually offered optionally. Just as educational incentives can increase job satisfaction, so too can perks (Holtom, Mitchell, and Lee, 2006). Common employment perks or incentives that might be of interest to police officers include on-site childcare, fitness facilities, flexible shifts, and take-home vehicles (cars, bikes, motorcycles, etc.). Perks or incentives of particular interest to lesbian and gay officers might include second-parent paternity or maternity leave, health benefits for same-sex partners, family leave, family assistance services, hardship transfers, and relocation expenses. Employee perceptions of these perks might be more directly related to positive organizational culture than to the actual benefits received. Thus lesbian and gay police officers might be more inclined to stay with a force just because perks and incentives are offered, even if they don't access them. The offering itself sends a signal of support from the police agency.

Career Laddering

Another important factor affecting retention is career laddering, which shows police officers their pathways to organizational success. Career ladders provide for vertical advancement in an organization through established promotion opportunities, testing for open positions, and certification. Career laddering can allow officers greater access to higher levels of promotion (Prince, 2003) through cross-training, professional development, management and leadership training, and, less commonly, affirmative or positive action benchmarking.

The existence of multiple career ladders—like perks—can have symbolic meaning. Offering multiple routes to success in the agency can foster loyalty through visible opportunity for advancement and achievement of career ambitions (Staiger, Auerbach, and Buerhaus, 2000). This is especially important for lesbian and gay officers. Police agencies have a long history of exclusion and cronyism regarding promotions, and lesbian and gay officers report a lack of promotional opportunities as a barrier to equal opportunity in policing. By having transparent and open processes for promotions, police agencies can counter the notion that only officers assigned to select units (like homicide or narcotics) are promoted.

Mentoring

Mentoring is usually a formal or informal relationship between two people—a senior mentor and a junior mentee. Typically, a mentor is outside of the mentee's chain of supervision. Mentoring is an important organizational tool that can be used to increase morale, satisfaction and productivity, and professional development (US Office of Personnel Management, 2008). More specifically, mentoring can be used to help new recruits, trainees, or graduates settle into the organization; enhance skills; cement professional identity; identify opportunities for career development; reinforce education; implement planned change; enhance customer service; improve recruitment and retention; and aid knowledge transfer. In a mentoring relationship, the mentor can be described as a coach or guide tasked with supporting junior employees to help ensure their success in the organization.

Although the importance of mentoring has been well established in the literature, little data or information exists about mentoring in policing. Available research in other areas shows that mentoring can be highly successful (Wilson, 2010). Scott Seibert (1999) conducted an informal experiment on the effectiveness of mentoring in a Fortune 100 corporation and found that employees who participated in a mentoring program had significantly higher levels of job satisfaction compared to the nonmentored control group. Similarly, Thomas Smith and Richard

Ingersoll (2004) found that new teachers who were mentored by other teachers in the same subject field were less likely to move to other schools or to leave the teaching profession after their first year. Finally, Ellen Ensher and Susan Murphy (1997) found that race was a factor in the mentoring relationship, specifically in mentee perceptions of career support and in perceived likeability of mentees by their mentors.

Traditionally, police agencies have focused on field training as a form of mentoring. Though critical to police training, field training does not involve the support and professional development components of mentoring. Instead, it focuses on applying the specific knowledge, skills, and abilities associated with being a police officer.

In order to establish a successful mentoring program, police agencies should connect mentoring to organizational goals and community policing efforts. For example, mentoring schemes intended to produce more qualified applicants for promotion to leadership roles will look vastly different than those intended to improve knowledge transfer within a division and agency.

Connecting lesbian and gay officers to lesbian and gay leadership can both improve the image of the leadership and enhance the retention of the officers. Additionally, new lesbian and gay officers might feel more comfortable candidly discussing issues with other lesbian or gay officers. Empathy and guidance from senior lesbian and gay officers can reduce cognitive dissonance (I am doing the job, but I do not belong here) and increase comfort (I do belong here).

Retention of good officers can be further enhanced through same–sexual orientation mentoring. Like training and networking, connecting with senior officers helps new officers to visualize various career paths within the police agency. Over time, as more openly lesbian and gay officers begin serving throughout the agency, more routes to success will be identified. And as diversity and inclusiveness increase, lesbian and gay officers (as well as heterosexual officers) will feel more comfortable working within the agency.

Officer Associations

Unlike network groups or mentors, lesbian and gay officer associations can exist completely outside of the police agency structure. As noted in Chapter 7, these associations provided an early sense of community for lesbian and gay officers in the late 1980s and early 1990s. They provided a safe place for officers to seek support, mentoring, and counsel on the universe of issues associated with policing. This was especially important for younger officers, who were less likely to be open about their sexual orientation at work. These associations also played a critical role in pressuring agencies to recognize lesbian and gay officers as a part of the policing world. This effort included revising nondiscrimination policies, developing and improving training materials, ensuring equal benefits for lesbian and gay officers and their same-sex partners, and developing policies to address harassment and discrimination in the workplace.

Today, these officer associations also act as liaisons between the lesbian and gay community and police agencies. From the perspective of lesbian and gay officers, these associations provide a voice for engaging agency management. From the perspective of police agencies, these associations yield positive community support, partnership for diversity and inclusion efforts, and connection to members of the broader community (and within the policing community). One example is the Bedfordshire Gay Police Association, a local branch of the United Kingdom's national gay police association that was established with the support of the local chief constable. The chief constable noted that he "saw the group as a valuable tool for furthering the force's diversity work" (Cowan, 2005). Because he recognized the potential benefits for both the constabulary and the wider community, he allocated resources to develop the local gay police association. With this senior support, the association has been able to conduct proactive outreach work with the lesbian and gay community in Bedfordshire.

Career Development

Unlike mentoring and career laddering, career development is a concerted and strategic effort to increase officer retention through increased opportunities vertically and horizontally in the police agency (Dick, 2007). Career development is about making sure that each police officer has what he or she needs to develop both personally and professionally within the organization. For a police agency, the range of career development goods and services may vary depending on available resources and the particular needs of the officers. For example, developing career opportunities for lesbian and gay police officers can range from simply providing officers with information about forthcoming opportunities available to them, to providing targeted training opportunities to help develop skills.

According to Sam Dick (2007), there are six observable benefits associated with career development for lesbian and gay employees. The first benefit is that employees feel more confident and valued. As we know, police officers who feel confident and valued are less likely to engage in corrupt behavior. Second, career development helps employees identify all available opportunities and enables them to reach their full potential. Such opportunities need not result in high levels of participation by all employees, but when a lesbian or gay officer is ready, the information and support will be in place. Another benefit to lesbian and gay officers is improved levels of job satisfaction. Officers who are satisfied will be less likely to succumb to corruption and other negative forces. And as the thinking goes, increased satisfaction translates into increased motivation—the fourth benefit of career development—which in turn translates into increased productivity. For police officers, motivation has direct implications for the communities served, because it can influence the relationship between the police and the people. The fifth benefit of career development is its capacity to enhance the attractiveness of an agency in the eyes of potential recruits. If a police agency has a reputation for supporting and promoting officers, its reputation as a good employer will be widespread in the community. This is especially the case for officers from minority communities. Particular groups and communities of people often seek out particular employers or particular fields based on reputation. Good career development is one way to achieve that reputation. Finally, career development can help an organization to become more diverse and inclusive. This is often accomplished by setting organizational goals or benchmarks and using career planning and development to achieve those goals. For example, a police agency might decide that it would like to increase the percentage of female inspectors. By working with women on the force and helping to develop viable career paths, the agency increases the likelihood of meeting its goals.

Of course the benefits of career development are not limited to lesbian and gay police officers; all employees benefit from this effort. However, like other minority groups who have been historically shunned in policing, lesbian and gay people face particular challenges in policing and career development. First, discriminatory attitudes from supervisors and management have been used in the past to deny career development opportunities to lesbian and gay officers. Survey results in both the United States and the United Kingdom revealed the perception that promotion-related opportunities were limited for lesbian and gay officers.

Without proper career development planning, lesbian and gay officers might also be reluctant to move to different posts within the agency in order to avoid situations where they must again reveal their sexual orientation or risk working with others who may be homophobic.

Finally, lesbian and gay officers might be hesitant to commit to working in a police agency because of scrutiny at the higher levels of the organization. Lesbian and gay police officers may be anxious about aspects of their private life being made public and also about the effects this may have on relations with various communities and public bodies. These officers may fear that lesbians and gay people can only rise so far in an organization before being knocked down. In this sense, the glass ceiling for lesbian and gay officers can only be broken with strategic career development.

To counter these barriers, police agencies should tailor training for lesbian and gay police officers. This includes providing information about agency nondiscrimination policies and how to seek redress if needed. Training should also prepare lesbian and gay police officers to deal with homophobic language and behaviors in the police agency. This should include interpersonal communication and negotiation skills.

In addition to specialized training for lesbian and gay officers, police agencies should also promote general diversity training for other officers and management. This training will prepare heterosexual officers to work within a diverse police agency and inform them about the consequences for violating nondiscrimination policies.

Perhaps the most important effort for increasing diversity is the promotion and celebration of openly lesbian and gay police officers and agency leaders. As the axiom goes, actions speak louder than words. Police agencies should ensure that openly lesbian and gay officers are visible and embraced within the organization—the ultimate goal of strategic and career planning. When openly lesbian and gay officers are promoted—and celebrated—the inclusive nature of the agency is seen by all police officers as well as the communities served.

Engagement

Police agencies can increase retention of lesbian and gay people through greater employee engagement—strategies to help employees balance work and career (Cartwright and Holmes, 2006; Jamrog, 2004). These engagement strategies often emphasize empowering employees with autonomy and responsibility over work-related issues. In many organizations this includes greater input for employees in the evaluation process, and cross-training in job responsibilities. At its core, engagement requires flexibility if police agencies are to meet specialized needs of officers as individuals, instead of officers as a collective group. For lesbian and gay officers, specialized employee engagement should consist of liaison training and service opportunities, multiple evaluation and feedback opportunities, job shadowing, rotational assignments, cross-training, and intervention for those officers who are at risk of departure.

Lesbian and gay liaison training and service is a proven opportunity to actively engage police officers. Though the roles and responsibilities of liaisons vary from agency to agency, they usually include community outreach at a minimum, and usually involve training for the post. Lesbian and gay liaison officers (GLOs) in both the United States and the United Kingdom report satisfaction in being able to engage the larger lesbian and gay community directly. For agencies that have more established liaison units, lesbian and gay officers are able to participate in investigative work that is connected to the lesbian and gay community. Of course, not all lesbian and gay officers want to participate in this aspect of policing, nor should they be required to. However, for interested officers, this is an effective way to bring together two important aspects of their lives: gay identity and police identity.

Liaison engagement is not limited to the officers who participate. The presence of lesbian and gay liaison officers is often seen as a visible and tangible effort to engage in community policing as well as to promote diversity and inclusion. As one police officer in Wiltshire noted:

> [As] far as the community is concerned, by announcing a GLO, by promoting it, by being acknowledged as [a GLO], it raises the profile . . . and the Wiltshire Constabulary is well recognized now as being one of the leading agencies—it is recognized as not being homophobic or as not as . . . homophobic as it perhaps once was . . . [as] being more understanding of difference, where, in fact, before [homophobic behavior] was just considered traditional and entrenched. (personal communication, 2009)

Whether GLOs are providing training to other officers, providing support to victims of hate crimes, or investigating crimes within the lesbian and gay community, their work engages them on both professional and personal levels, which increases participation, satisfaction, and motivation for police work.

In the traditional process of evaluation and feedback, police officers are given periodic reviews of their performance. These typically annual events are fraught with problems. One problem is the error of "central tendency," in which the supervisor appraises all officers around the middle point of the rating scale and avoids rating any of them higher or lower. Supervisors—in this situation—often follow this "play it safe" policy because of accountability to management or lack of knowledge about the individuals being evaluated. Other problems include supervisor bias (a supervisor dislikes or likes the officer without regard to the work performed), and "halo and horn" effects (over- or underrating an officer in all aspects of the evaluation based on a single incident that occurred early in the period under review, and nothing the officer has done subsequently will change the initial rating). In short, the traditional performance appraisal process can be one-sided and unreliable (Berman et al., 2009). In most cases, more frequent appraisals, and opportunities for employer and employee feedback, create dialogue and engage employees in improving their performance over time. This form of incremental feedback is especially valuable for new police officers. When officers see that feedback is designed to help them become better officers (as opposed to penalizing or embarrassing them), they will be more likely to address issues and challenges before they become intractable.

Job shadowing, rotational assignments, and cross-training all have tremendous potential for police agencies and officers. Job shadowing involves spending time with an expert and observing their work (Schmidt, 2007). Shadowing can expose an officer to different divisions and units within the agency. For a lesbian or gay police officer, this might be an opportunity for exposure to areas of police work beyond the traditional assignments of training and liaison posts. This is also an effective way to expose officers to divisions and units that have traditionally lacked diversity.

A rotational assignment is a way to offer an employee a short-term assignment away from their regular position (Engle, 2004). These assignments require a longer commitment than does job shadowing, as they typically range from three to six months and rarely exceed a year. The purpose is to provide employees the opportunity to gain knowledge, broaden skills, and enhance professional growth. In the case of policing, an officer might be given a temporary assignment in another part of the agency in order to experience the daily requirements of working in a different unit. For lesbian and gay officers, such day-to-day interaction gives them a more realistic impression of the unit compared to job shadowing. Rotations expose officers to unique work environments without requiring them to fully commit or transfer.

Cross-training allows an employee to learn how to perform different work in an organization (Brown, Reich, and Stern, 1992). Cross-training often occurs with teams of employees, with each member learning to perform the tasks of one or more other members. This effort helps employees develop their skill-sets beyond the requirements of their current job. For police officers, cross-training can be both internal and external—for example, officers might train as investigators within specialized units, or as firefighters in a hazardous-materials responder capacity.

Fundamental to job shadowing, rotational assignments, and cross-training is the belief that employees want to be challenged in the work environment and exposed to tasks that will enhance their knowledge, skills, and abilities. In this sense, lesbian and gay police officers are just like their heterosexual counterparts—they want opportunities to advance and learn within their chosen career of law enforcement. Since policing has traditionally tended to route minority officers into administrative areas (analysis, liaison, and training), and to direct nonminority officers into high-skill and high-promotion areas (usually homicide and narcotics), opportunities for cross-exposure are critical for retaining officers. In addition to increased retention, agencies will benefit from greater job satisfaction and a better-trained police force.

At-risk officers are those who are likely to leave the agency for any number of life transitions, including the birth of a child, children graduating from high school or college, divorce, separation, or family illness. At-risk officers are also those who are contemplating leaving due to organizational issues, like frustration with a peer or supervisor, being passed over for promotion, or an unfulfilling assignment or patrol. In fact, supervisory issues are among the leading factors for police attrition. As Dwayne Orrick notes, "people don't quit jobs, they quit bosses" (2008, p. 159). Among supervisory behaviors that contribute to officer attrition are setting poor examples, indecisiveness, unfairness, being overly critical, not sharing credit for work, and poor communication. In addition to these factors, minority officers report leaving the police agencies due to cultural issues, including tokenism and feelings of isolation (Bolton, 2003). Furthermore, lesbian and gay police officers report homophobic talk, being "outed," and personal property damage as reasons for leaving. Intervention can help prevent loss of officers who need minimal support to stay in the agency.

In order to intervene with at-risk officers, supervisors need to be attuned to the words and actions of the officers under their command, and seek opportunities to meet the needs of officers. For example, increased use of sick leave might be an indication that something negative is happening in an officer's home life. Additionally, officers who schedule meetings to review their record or discuss retirement options are likely considering an exit from policing. In both cases, loss of the officer may be averted with supervisor support and intervention. The supervisor can take the lead to make sure the officer has what he or she needs through human resources. The supervisor may also help the officer address whatever issues are causing consternation, including mediation, transfer, time off, flexibility schedules, and training and development.

The ideal for police agencies should be to develop a dynamic understanding of their work forces by conducting regular surveys about job satisfaction and organizational commitment. These results can assist in improving short-term retention and long-term commitment to the agency. The surveys should attempt to differentiate among groups, including women, minorities, ranks, generations, new employees, and near-retirees (Dick, 2007). Knowing employees and their individual needs intimately is a hallmark of a proactive human resource–centered agency and can lead to targeted problem solving when retention becomes issue a concern (Haggerty, 2009).

Conclusion

Creating a diverse police agency that is inclusive of lesbian and gay officers is not a passive endeavor. Agencies must actively engage their officers and the communities they serve, and embrace planned change. But planned change cannot happen without leadership throughout the organization. The police chief or chief constable must lead diversity efforts if they are to be successful. Additionally, officers and staff need opportunities to demonstrate leadership, as well as the autonomy and flexibility necessary for creatively addressing and solving problems.

Beyond demonstrating leadership and embracing planned change, diverse and inclusive police agencies must actively and directly engage in recruitment and retention. Lesbian and gay people are not likely to be drawn to policing in great numbers unless the agency has made visible efforts to promote an inclusive workplace, and to reverse perceptions of exclusivity. Police agencies do this by actively seeking openly lesbian and gay applicants through networks, groups, and community organizations. They also do this by creating lesbian and gay–specific incentives, benefits, and opportunities.

Agencies that are reflective of the communities they serve will achieve better results with community policing, including more effective policing, as communities become vested in the effort; more efficient use of resources, as officers become better trained, more motivated, and less likely to leave; and more equitable service delivery, as all members of the community become connected to the policing mission.

Note

1. Chief Ramsey often noted that while numerous problems existed between the black community and the police, the MPD was trying to address them, through both court-imposed and voluntary efforts. Additionally, Ramsey argued that Washington's black community had a number of political and legal outlets for enforcing fairness and justice, while other minority communities, namely Asians, Latinos, the deaf, and especially lesbian and gay people, did not.

9

Roadmap
for the Future

This book is an attempt to better understand the work lives of lesbian and gay police officers. The survey information of US and UK officers presented here represents the most comprehensive dataset ever collected. Given the characteristics of this population and the cultural environment in which lesbian and gay officers work, collecting larger and more systematic datasets could be problematic. But the research presented here, despite its limitations, allows us to draw some valuable conclusions. Additionally, it highlights the need for more research into the lives of lesbian and gay police officers and their contributions to the field. Both police agencies and lesbian and gay officers have made incredible progress, and many additional opportunities for exploration remain.

Like most people who enter public service, lesbian and gay police officers do so for specific reasons. Good career opportunities and job security, as well as the desire to perform a civic duty, are central to their decisions to join the police. While efforts to diversify and professionalize police agencies have met with varying degrees of success, integration of lesbian and gay officers has followed much the same pattern as for integration of racial minorities and women. As with people of color and women, lesbian and gay officers report bias mostly in areas where supervisory discretion is highest.

These manifestations of bias are not surprising, given how gay and lesbian officers see themselves within police agencies. The majority report being subjected to social isolation and homophobic talk. In cases where an officer's sexual orientation is not widely known, homophobic talk is more likely to occur. Because other officers are more willing to speak in an openly antigay way if they think that no gay or lesbian people are present, social isolation becomes prevalent.

Attitudinal and employment barriers have adverse effects on both lesbian and gay officers and law enforcement organizations. For the individual officers, stunted opportunities for promotion and advancement may adversely affect job satisfaction and motivation, prompting these officers to seek other employment opportunities. For an organization as a whole, the barriers faced by lesbian and gay officers may compromise the agency's ability to meet its mission. A compromised mission—a form of organizational failure—may result from factors such as structural failure, oversight failure, cultural deviation, and institutionalization.

Structural failures include processes and procedures that create barriers to success. For example, higher-ranking officers might abuse their discretionary authority in assignment, evaluation, and promotion, which can disparately affect lesbian and gay officers. Oversight failures occur when accountability mechanisms are not functioning properly. Oversight agencies may not recognize their function to prevent and deter discrimination in the workplace—for example, an internal investigations unit would not normally consider antigay activity as a form of corruption or as contributing to organizational failure.

Cultural deviation appears to be one of the strongest explanations for organizational failure. Many scholars have noted how the unique nature of law enforcement contributes to unusually strong bonding and socialization (Belkin and McNichol, 2002; Bolton, 2003; Miller, Forest, and Jurik, 2003; O'Hara, 2005). It is easy to imagine supervisors and other decisionmakers discriminating or retaliating against any officer (whether homosexual or heterosexual) who does not conform to the dominant culture or is perceived as anything other than a typical officer.

Finally, institutionalization occurs when police agencies put the needs of some officers above those of others or above the mission of the organization. The experiences of lesbian and gay officers seem to suggest that despite efforts to diversify police agencies and to create representative bureaucracies, institutional mechanisms sometimes override these new values.

While the data suggest that lesbian and gay officers experience both barriers and access points in the law enforcement environment, barriers are more often reported. The root causes of these barriers are not clearly known. These burdens could stem from a number of sources, including the aforementioned structural and oversight failures, cultural deviation, and institutionalization. Given the different treatment that lesbian and gay officers report, cultural deviation seems to be the dominant factor: casual homophobic talk does not fall within the arena of structural and oversight failures, and also seems removed from the idea of institutionalization.

Where lesbian and gay officers serve openly, employment success is more likely—in fact, some agencies are even using these officers to help recruit other lesbian and gay people. In this respect, integration of openly lesbian and gay officers seems to be improving. We can attribute this achievement to the willingness of individual officers to disclose their sexual orientation, to the work of lesbian and gay professional associations, and, since timing is important, to the simultaneous emergence of the community policing model. Without such a model, achieving inclusion and diversity would be much more difficult. The community policing model has been helpful in maintaining productivity while improving communication and coordination with constituents.

These positive trends notwithstanding, police agencies are still in need of additional policies and procedures that ensure equal employment opportunities for all qualified applicants and officers. Most sorely needed are policy initiatives that affect those human resource areas where managerial discretion is most important—assignment, evaluation, and promotion. In contrast, the research presented in this book suggests that human resource areas that are not so closely bound to managerial discretion—areas such as hiring and firing, and salary and benefits—have been equalized among all categories of police officers.

Efforts to address attitudinal bias should also be vigorously pursued. Since there is an emerging shared perception, at least among some lesbian and gay officers, that being open about sexual orientation on the force carries some actual benefits, efforts to increase this shared perception could help to reduce attitudinal bias. While access points are less commonly experienced than barriers, the fact that lesbian and gay officers do report some special access points suggests that attitudinal change is possible in law enforcement.

By examining the shared perceptions of lesbian and gay officers, this research has enhanced our understanding of both lesbian and gay officers and the law enforcement agencies they work for. It has helped us identify opportunities for organizational improvement. Future research endeavors might analyze differences among the experiences of lesbian and gay officers at different levels of visibility within law enforcement—including fully revealed and fully hidden sexual orientation. Research into the timing of revealed sexual orientation—at the academy, on the force, or after retirement—would also provide insights into officer perceptions. Too, given the broadened acceptance of homosexuality—in police agencies as in society at large—additional research is needed to better understand both the barriers faced by openly lesbian and gay officers and any special access they enjoy.

In the end, police agencies, like all public service delivery organizations, must embrace the idea of representative service delivery. This simply means having an organization that reflects the community it serves. Broadly diversifying the organization is the most effective and efficient approach to representative service delivery. By recruiting and retaining lesbian and gay police officers today, police agencies also create a climate that ensures that they will constantly evolve to meet the changing needs of the community. With the introduction of lesbian and gay officers, agencies increase the cultural capacity of the entire organization. This increased capacity improves the effectiveness of policing because police officers are better equipped to engage all community members, and it improves the lives of members of the community because members know that the police agency is part of the community and the people they know are on the force. In other words, community policing can only work if the community, including the lesbian and gay community, is involved in policing.

References

Adler, F. (1999). "Sisters in Crime." In F. T. Cullen and R. Agnew (eds.), *Criminological Theory: Past to Present Essential Readings* (pp. 347–354). Los Angeles: Roxbury.

Advertising Standards Authority (ASA) (2006). "Adjudication on Gay Police Association." October 18. Retrieved July 1, 2010, from www.asa.org.uk /Complaints-and-ASA-action/Adjudications/2006/10/Gay-Police -Association/TF_ADJ_41843.aspx.

Alderson, K. (2003). "The Corporate Closet: Career Challenges of Gay and Lesbian Individuals." Paper presented at the National Consultation on Career Development Convention, Ottawa, January.

Alex, N. (1969). *Black in Blue*. New York: Meredith.

Alpert, G., Flynn, D., and Piquero, A. (2001). "Effective Community Policing Performance Measures." *Justice Research and Policy* 3 (2): 79.

Amnesty International USA (2005). "Stonewalled: Police Abuse and Misconduct Against Lesbian, Gay, Bisexual, and Transgender People in the U.S.—New York, NY." Retrieved July 1, 2010, from www.amnestyusa.org/lgbt-human -rights/stonewalled-a-report/page.do?id=1106610.

Anastas, J. (2001). "Economic Rights, Economic Myths, and Economic Realities." In M. E. Swigonski, R. S. Mama, and K. Ward (eds.), *From Hate Crimes to Human Rights: A Tribute to Matthew Shepard* (pp. 99–116). New York: Haworth Press.

Association of Chief Police Officers (ACPO) (2000). *Hate Crime: Delivering a Quality Service*. London: ACPO Race and Diversity Working Group.

Badgett, M. (1995). "The Wage Effects of Sexual Orientation Discrimination." *Industrial and Labor Relations Review* 48 (4): 726–739.

———— (2007). "Discrimination Based on Sexual Orientation: A Review of the Literature in Economics and Beyond." In M. Badgett and J. Frank (eds.), *Sexual Orientation Discrimination: An International Perspective* (pp. 19–43). London: Routledge.

Bardwick, J., and Douvan, E. (1972). "Ambivalence: The Socialization of Women." In Judith M. Bardwick (ed.), *Readings on the Psychology of Women* (pp. 225–241). New York: Harper and Row.

Belkin, A., and McNichol, J. (2002). "Pink and Blue: Outcomes Associated with the Integration of Open Gay and Lesbian Personnel in the San Diego Police Department." *Police Quarterly* 5 (1): 63–95.

Bell, D. (1982). "Policewomen: Myths and Realities." *Journal of Police Science and Administration* 10: 112–120.

Berman, E., Bowman, J., West, J., and Van Wart, M. (2009). *Human Resource Management in Public Service: Paradoxes, Processes, and Problems.* 3rd ed. Thousand Oaks, CA: Sage.

Bernstein, M., and Kostelac, C. (2002). "Lavender and Blue: Attitudes About Homosexuality and Behavior Toward Lesbians and Gay Men Among Police Officers." *Journal of Contemporary Criminal Justice* 18 (3): 302–328.

"*The Bill* Is Slashed to One Episode a Week: Police Drama Will Be Screened After Watershed to Allow for Grittier Storylines" (2009). *Daily Mail Online,* January 23. Retrieved March 23, 2011, from www.dailymail.co.uk/tvshowbiz/article -1126913.

"*The Bill* Will Be Cut Back to One Episode per Week" (2009). *STV,* January 23. Retrieved March 23, 2011, from http://entertainment.stv.tv/tv/71652-the-bill -will-be-cutback-to-one-episode-per-week.

Birkland, T. (1997). *After Disaster: Agenda Setting, Public Policy, and Focusing Events.* Washington, DC: Georgetown University Press.

Boin, A. (2001). *Leadership in Two Prison Systems.* Boulder: Lynne Rienner.

Bolton, K. (2003). "Shared Perceptions: Black Officers Discuss Continuing Barriers in Policing." *Policing: An International Journal of Policing Strategies and Management* 26 (3): 386–399.

Bowling, B., and Phillips, C. (2007). "Ethnicities, Racism, Crime, and Criminal Justice." In M. Maguire, R. Morgan, and R. Reinert (eds.), *Handbook of Criminology* (pp. 421–460). Oxford: Oxford University Press.

Braid, M., and Bennetto, J. (1995). "Gay Police in Pink over First Job Advert." *The Independent,* May 18. Retrieved July 1, 2010, from www.faqs.org /abstracts/Retail-industry/Why-police-show-a-red-card-to-this-hooligans-book -Rising-tide-of-crime-swaps-S-African-police.html.

Branham, L. (2005). *The 7 Hidden Reasons Employees Leave: How to Recognize the Subtle Signs and Act Before It's Too Late.* Saratoga Springs, NY: American Management Association.

British Transport Police (BTP) (2011). "Vision, Mission, and Values." Retrieved March 23, 2011, from www.btp.police.uk/about_us/vision,_mission_and _values.aspx.

Brown, C., Reich, M., and Stern, D. (1992). "Becoming a High-Performance Work Organization: The Role of Security, Employee Involvement, and Training." Berkeley: University of California, Institute for Research on Labor and Employment. Retrieved March 23, 2011, from http://escholarship.org/uc /item/0pj25436.

Brown, J., and Heidensohn, F. (2000). *Gender and Policing.* New York, NY: Palgrave Macmillan.

Buhrke, R. (1996). *A Matter of Justice: Lesbians and Gay Men in Law Enforcement.* New York: Routledge.

Burke, M. (1993). *Coming Out of the Blue: British Police Officers Talk About Their Lives in "The Job" as Lesbians, Gays, and Bisexuals.* New York: Cassell Publishing.

―――― (1994). "Homosexuality as Deviance: The Case of the Gay Police Officer." *British Journal of Criminology* 34 (2): 192–203.

Burrell, I. (2002). "Blunkett Approves Funding for Gay Police Association." *The Independent,* May 27. Retrieved July 1, 2010, from www.independent.co.uk /news/uk/politics/blunkett-approves-funding-for-gay-police-association-652408.html.

Button, J., Rienzo, B., and Wald, K. (1995). "Where Local Laws Prohibit Discrimination Based on Sexual Orientation." *Public Management* 77 (4): 9–14.

―――― (1997). *Private Lives, Public Conflicts: Battles over Gay Rights in American Communities.* Washington, DC: Congressional Quarterly Press.

Button, S. (2001). "Organizational Efforts to Affirm Sexual Diversity: A Cross-Level Examination." *Journal of Applied Psychology* 86 (1): 17–28.

―――― (2004). "Identity Management Strategies Utilized by Lesbian and Gay Employees." *Group and Organization Management* 29 (5): 470–494.

Cartwright, S., and Holmes, N. (2006). "The Meaning of Work: The Challenge of Regaining Employee Engagement and Reducing Cynicism." *Human Resource Management Review* 16 (2): 199–208.

Cathcart, B. (1999). *The Case of Stephen Lawrence.* London: Viking.

Chaiken, M. (2001). "COPS: Innovations in Policing in American Heartlands." Washington, DC: National Institute of Justice, September. Retrieved July 1, 2010, from www.ncjrs.gov/pdffiles1/nij/grants/194604.pdf.

Cherney, A. (1999). "Gay and Lesbian Issues in Policing." *Current Issues in Criminal Justice* 11 (1): 35–52.

Chojnacki, J., and Gelberg, S. (1994). "Toward a Conceptualization of Career Counseling with Gay/Lesbian/Bisexual Persons." *Journal of Career Development* 21: 3–10.

Chrobot-Mason, D., and Quiñones, M. (2001). "Training for a Diverse Workplace." In K. Kraiger (ed.), *Creating, Implementing, and Managing Effective Training and Development* (pp. 117–159). San Francisco: Jossey-Bass.

Chung, B. (2001). "Work Discrimination and Coping Strategies: Conceptual Frameworks for Counseling Lesbian, Gay, and Bisexual Clients." *Career Development Quarterly* 50 (1): 33–44.

Clair, J., Beatty, J., and MacLean, T. (2005). "Out of Sight but Not Out of Mind: Managing Invisible Social Identities in the Workplace." *Academy of Management Review* 30: 78–95.

Clements, P. (2008). *Policing a Diverse Society.* 2nd ed. London: Oxford University Press.

Cohen, R., O'Byrne, S., and Maxwell, P. (1999). "Employment Discrimination Based on Sexual Orientation: The American, Canadian, and U.K. Responses." *Law and Inequity* 17 (1): 1–20.

Colvin, R. (2000). "Improving State Policies That Prohibit Public Employment Discrimination Based on Sexual Orientation." *Review of Public Personnel Administration (ROPPA)* 20 (2): 5–19.

———— (2004). "Policy Brief: The Extent of Sexual Orientation Discrimination in Topeka, KS." Washington, DC: The National Gay and Lesbian Task Force.

———— (2007). "The Rise of Transgender-Inclusive Laws: How Well Are Municipalities Implementing Supportive Nondiscrimination Public Employment Policies?" *Review of Public Personnel Administration (ROPPA)* 27 (4): 336–360.

———— (2008). "Innovations in Antidiscrimination Laws: Research on Transgender-Inclusive Cities." *Journal of Public Management and Social Policy* 14 (1): 19–34.

———— (2009). "Shared Perceptions Among Lesbian and Gay Police Officers: Barriers and Opportunities in the Law Enforcement Work Environment." *Police Quarterly* 12 (1): 86–101.

Colvin, R., and Riccucci, N. (2002). "Employment Nondiscrimination Policies: Assessing Implementation and Measuring Effectiveness." *International Journal of Public Administration* 25 (1): 95–108.

Community Safety Partnership (2008). "Swindon's Crime and Drugs Reduction Strategy, 2005–2008." Retrieved August 1, 2010, from www.swindon.gov.uk /print/swindon_crime_and_drug_reduction_strategy.pdf.

Comstock, G. (1989). "Victims of Anti-Gay/Lesbian Violence." *Journal of Interpersonal Violence* 4 (1): 101–106.

Connell, R. (1985). "Theorizing Gender." *Sociology* 19 (2) (May): 260–272.

Cowan, K. (2005). *Network Groups: Setting Up Networks for Lesbian, Gay, and Bisexual Employees.* Stonewall, UK: Stonewall Workplace Guides.

Croteau, J. (1996). "Research on the Work Experiences of Lesbian, Gay, and Bisexual People: An Integrative Review of Methodology and Findings." *Journal of Vocational Behavior* 48 (2): 195–209.

Croteau, J., Anderson, M., and VanderWal, B. (2008). "Models of Workplace Sexual Identity Disclosure and Management: Reviewing and Extending Concepts." *Group and Organization Management* 33 (5): 532–565.

Croteau, J., and Bieschke, K. (1996). "Beyond Pioneering: An Introduction to the Special Issue on the Vocational Issues of Lesbian Women and Gay Men." *Journal of Vocational Behavior* 48 (2): 119–124.

Croteau, J., and Lark, J. (1995). "On Being Lesbian, Gay, or Bisexual in Student Affairs: A National Survey of Experiences on the Job." *NASPA Journal* 32 (1): 223–239.

Davis, J. (1992). "Identifying Acute Post-Traumatic Stress Disorder (PTSD) in Disaster Victims and Emergency Responders." Disaster Management Training Seminar, San Diego, May.

Degges-White, S., and Shoffner, M. (2002). "Career Counseling with Lesbian Clients: Using the Theory of Work Adjustment as a Framework." *Career Development Quarterly* 51 (1): 87–96.

D'Emilio, J. (1991). *Sexual Politics, Sexual Communities: The Making of a Homosexual Minority in the United States, 1940–1970.* Chicago: University of Chicago Press.

Diamond, D., and Weiss, D. (2009). "Community Policing: Looking to Tomorrow." Washington, DC: US Department of Justice, Office of Community-Oriented Police Services. Retrieved July 1, 2010, from www.ncjrs.gov/app/publications /abstract.aspx?ID=249606.

Dick, S. (2007). *Career Development: How to Support Your Lesbian and Gay Employees.* Stonewall, UK: Stonewall Workplace Guides.

Dresang, D. (2009). *Public Personnel Management and Public Policy.* 5th ed. New York: Longman.

Duberman, M. (1994). *Stonewall.* New York: Plume.

Eck, J., and Rosenbaum, D. (1994). "The New Police Order: Effectiveness, Equity, and Efficiency in Community Policing." In D. Rosenbaum (ed.), *The Challenge of Community Policing: Testing the Promise* (pp. 3–23). Thousand Oaks, CA: Sage.

El-Ghobashy, T. (2011). "Minorities Gain in NYPD Ranks." *Wall Street Journal,* January 7. Retrieved March 23, 2011, from http://online.wsj.com/article/SB10001424052748704415104576066302323002420.html.

Engle, A. (2004). "Transnational Roles, Transnational Rewards: Global Integration in Compensation." *Employee Relations* 26 (6): 613–625.

Ensher, E., and Murphy, S. (1997). "Effects of Race, Gender, Perceived Similarity, and Contact on Mentor Relationships." *Journal of Vocational Behavior* 50 (3): 460–481.

Entman, R. (1989). *Democracy Without Citizens: Media and the Decay of American Politics.* London: Oxford University Press.

Equal Employment Opportunity Commission (EEOC) (2007). "Laws and Guidance." Retrieved July 1, 2010, from www.eeoc.gov/laws/index.cfm.

Equality and Human Rights Commission (2010). "Triennial Review 2010: How Fair Is Britain? Equality, Human Rights, and Good Relations in 2010." Retrieved September 21, 2011, from www.equalityhumanrights.com/key-projects/how-fair-is-britain.

Ermer, V. (1978). "Recruitment of Female Police Officers in New York City." *Journal of Criminal Justice* 6 (4): 233–246.

Essed, P. (1991). *Understanding Everyday Racism: An Interdisciplinary Approach.* Newbury Park, CA: Sage.

Eurocops (2010). "Eurocops Members." Retrieved August 1, 2010, from www.eurocop.org/index.php?id=41.

Evans, M. (1970). "The 'Gay' People Demand Their Rights." *New York Times,* July 5.

Fernandez, M., and Leonnig, C. (2000). "Gallaudet Students Turn to Each Other; School's Size May Help Solve Slaying." *Washington Post,* October 2.

Fielding, N., and Innes, M. (2006). "Reassurance Policing, Community Policing, and Measuring Police Performance." *Policing and Society* 16 (2): 127–145.

Fillichio, C. (2006). "The New Beat: The Washington Metropolitan Police Department's Gay and Lesbian Liaison Unit Is Transforming Law Enforcement and Redefining the Concept of 'Community' Policing." *Public Manager* 35 (3): 56–60.

Fine, T. (1992). "The Impact of Issue Framing on Public Opinion Toward Affirmative Action Programs." *Social Science Journal* 29 (3): 323–334.

Fretz, B. (1975). "Assessing Attitudes Toward Sexual Behaviors." *Counseling Psychologist* 5 (1): 100–106.

Gallup (2010a). "Americans' Opposition to Gay Marriage Eases Slightly." May 24. Retrieved July 1, 2010, from www.gallup.com/poll/128291/Americans-Opposition-Gay-Marriage-Eases-Slightly.aspx.

——— (2010b). "In U.S., Broad, Steady Support for Openly Gay Service Members." May 10. Retrieved July 1, 2010, from www.gallup.com/poll /127904/Broad-Steady-Support-Openly-Gay-Service-Members.aspx.

Garcia, V. (2003). "Difference in the Police Department: Women, Policing, and Doing Gender." *Journal of Contemporary Criminal Justice* 19 (3): 330–344.

Gash, N. (1984). *Mr. Secretary Peel: The Life of Sir Robert Peel to 1830*. London: Longman.

Gay and Lesbian Activists Alliance (GLAA) (1998). "GLAA on Public Safety." Retrieved July 1, 2010, from www.glaa.org/projects/safety.shtml.

Gay and Lesbian Liaison Unit (GLLU) (2008). "GLLU Hate Crime Factsheet." Washington, DC: Metropolitan Police Department. Retrieved July 1, 2010, from www.gllu.org/PDFs/facts_hate.pdf.

Gay Men and Lesbians Opposing Violence (GLOV). "GLOV 1998 Annual Statistical Report." Retrieved November 7, 2011, from http://www.glaa.org/glov.

Gay Officers Action League. (2006). "The History of GOAL." Retrieved March 1, 2009, from http://www.goalny.org/Home.html.

Gay Peace Officers Association of Southern California (GPOA) (2010). "About Us." Retrieved July 1, 2010, from www.gpoasc.org.

Gay Police Association (GPA) (2004). "Gay Police Association." Retrieved July 1, 2010, from www.gay.police.uk/index.html.

——— (2009). "National Executive Committee." Retrieved July 1, 2010, from www .gay.police.uk/NEC%20Candidate%20Information%20Brochure.pdf.

Gedro, J. (2009). "LGBT Career Development." *Advances in Developing Human Resources* 11 (1): 54–66.

Gilbert, J., Stead, B., and Ivancevich, J. (1999). "Diversity Management: A New Organizational Paradigm." *Journal of Business Ethics* 21 (1): 61–76.

Gillespie, W. (2008). "Thirty-Five Years After Stonewall: An Exploratory Study of Satisfaction with Police Among Gay, Lesbian, and Bisexual Persons at the 34th Annual Atlanta Pride Festival." *Journal of Homosexuality* 55 (4): 619–647.

Githens, R., and Aragon, S. (2009). "LGBT Employee Groups: Goals and Organizational Structures." *Advances in Developing Human Resources* 11 (1): 121–135.

GOAL Chicago (Chicago Gay Officers Action League) (2010). "Links." Retrieved August 1, 2010, from www.goalchicago.info/?page_id=27.

Goldstein, H. (2001). "Center for Problem-Oriented Policing." Retrieved July 1, 2010, from www.popcenter.org/about/?p=whatiscpop.

Golembiewski, R. (1995). *Managing Diversity in Organizations*. Tuscaloosa: University of Alabama Press.

Goodstein, L., Nolan, T., and Pfeiffer, W. (1993). *Applied Strategic Planning: A Comprehensive Guide*. New York: McGraw-Hill.

Government Office for the South West (GOSW) (United Kingdom) (2010). "Community Safety." Retrieved July 1, 2010, from http://webarchive.national archives.gov.uk/20100528142817/www.gos.gov.uk/gosw/commsafety/?a=42496.

Greene, J. (2000). *Community Policing in America: Changing the Nature, Structure, and Function of the Police*. Washington, DC: US Department of Justice, National Institute of Justice.

Grieve, J. (2008). "Seven Cs of Leadership." In Phil Clements, *Policing for a Diverse Society,* 2nd ed. (p. 131). Oxford: Oxford University Press.

Grieve, J., Hall, N., and Savage, S. (eds.) (2009). *Policing and the Legacy of Lawrence.* Cullompton, Devon, UK: Willan.

Haggerty, C. (2009). "From the Field Experiences." Santa Monica, CA: Rand. Retrieved June 24, 2010, from www.rand.org/ise/centers/quality_policing/cops/resources/field_experiences.catherine_haggerty.html.

Hampshire Constabulary (2010). "Policing with the Lesbian, Gay, Bisexual and Transgender Communities." Retrieved July 1, 2010, from www.hampshire.police.uk/Internet/advice/lgbtpolicing.htm.

Hartocollis, A. (2007). "Claiming Constant Harassment: Gay Police Officer in City Files Suit." *New York Times,* September 29. Retrieved March 23, 2011, from www.nytimes.com/2007/09/29/nyregion/29gay.html.

Harvard University Kennedy School of Government (2006). "Gay and Lesbian Liaison Unit: 2006 Winner; 2005 Finalist." Retrieved July 1, 2010, from www.innovations.harvard.edu/awards.html?id=48931.

Hassell, K., and Brandl, S. (2009). "An Examination of the Workplace Experiences of Police Patrol Officers: The Role of Race, Sex, and Sexual Orientation." *Police Quarterly* 12 (4): 408–430.

Heaton, R. (2000). "The Prospects for Intelligence-Led Policing: Some Historical and Quantitative Considerations." *Policing and Society* 9 (4): 337–356.

Herek, G. (1998). *Stigma and Sexual Orientation: Understanding Prejudice Against Lesbians, Gay Men, and Bisexuals.* Thousand Oaks, CA: Sage.

―――― (2000). "The Psychology of Sexual Prejudice." *Current Directions in Psychological Science* 9 (1): 19–22.

―――― (2003). "Evaluating Interventions to Alter Sexual Orientation: Methodological and Ethical Considerations." *Archives of Sexual Behavior* 32 (5): 438–439.

―――― (2004). "Beyond 'Homophobia': Thinking About Sexual Stigma and Prejudice in the Twenty-First Century." *Sexuality Research and Social Policy* 1 (2): 6–24.

Herek, G., Jobe, J., and Carney, R. (1996). *Out in Force: Sexual Orientation and the Military.* Chicago: University of Chicago Press.

Holdaway, S., and O'Neill, M. (2007). "Where Has All the Racism Gone? Views of Racism Within Constabularies After Macpherson." *Ethnic and Racial Studies* 30 (3): 397–415.

Holder, K., Nee, C., and Ellis, T. (1999). "Triple Jeopardy? Black and Asian Women Police Officers' Experiences of Discrimination." *International Journal of Police Science and Management* 3 (1): 68–87.

Holtom, B., Mitchell, T., and Lee, T. (2006). "Increasing Human and Social Capital by Applying Job Embeddedness Theory." *Organizational Dynamics* 35 (4): 316–331.

Home Office (United Kingdom) (1999). *The Stephen Lawrence Inquiry: Report of an Inquiry.* London: Stationery Office.

―――― (2005). "Police Service Strength." *Home Office Statistical Bulletin,* December. Retrieved July 1, 2010, from http://rds.homeoffice.gov.uk/rds/pdfs05/hosb1205.pdf.

House of Commons (United Kingdom) (2009). "Fifth Report of Session 2009–10." London: Home Affairs Committee on Police Service Strength. Retrieved August 1, 2010, from www.publications.parliament.uk/pa/cm200910/cmselect /cmhaff/50/50.pdf.

———— (2010). *Digest Journal*. London: National Policing Improvement Agency. Retrieved March 23, 2011, from www.nypolfed.org.uk/assets/uploads/PDFs /digest_sep_2009.pdf.

Human Rights Campaign (2010). "Issue: Workplace." Retrieved July 1, 2010, from www.hrc.org/issues/workplace/equal_opportunity/equal_opportunity_laws.asp.

———— (2011a). "About Us." Retrieved March 23, 2011, from www.hrc.org/about _us/index1.html.

———— (2011b). "Census Bureau Releases New Estimates of Married Same-Sex Couples." Retrieved November 13, 2011, from http://www.hrc.org/blog/entry /census-bureau-releases-new-estimates-of-married-same-sex-couples.

Jamrog, J. (2004). "The Perfect Storm: The Future of Retention and Engagement." *Human Resource Planning* 27 (3): 26–33.

Jensen, M. (2009). "Exclusive: NBC's New Drama 'Southland' Includes an Arresting Gay Character." *AfterElton,* March 24. Retrieved July 1, 2010, from www.afterelton.com/TV/2009/3/southlandsgaycharacter.

Jiao, A., and Kocher, C. (2000). "Auditing and Altering the Police: The Emerging Model of Planned Change." *Police Practice and Research: An International Journal* 1 (4): 527–558.

Jirak, D. (2001). "Gay and Lesbian Law Enforcement Groups Fend for Their Rights." *Diversity Factor* 9 (4): 34–37.

Jones, S., Wilson, J., Rathmell, A., and Riley, K. (2005). *Establishing Law and Order After Conflict*. Santa Monica, CA: RAND. Retrieved March 23, 2011, from www.rand.org/pubs/monographs/MG374.

Judd, T. (2005). "Bitter Lesson Learnt from Stephen Lawrence Murder." *The Independent,* August 1. Retrieved March 23, 2011, from www.independent.co .uk/news/uk/crime/bitter-lesson-learnt-from-stephen-lawrence-murder -500993.html.

Kanter, R. (1977). *Men and Women of the Corporation*. New York: Basic.

Kerley, K., and Benson, M. (2000). "Does Community-Oriented Policing Help Build Stronger Communities?" *Police Quarterly* 3 (1): 46–69.

King, E., Reilly, C., and Hebl, M. (2008). "The Best and Worst of Times: Dual Perspectives of Coming Out in the Workplace." *Group and Organization Management* 33 (5): 566–601.

Kingdon, J. (1995). *Agendas, Alternatives, and Public Policies*. 2nd ed. New York: HarperCollins College.

Kirby, D., Barth, R., Leland, N., and Fetro, J. (1991). "Reducing the Risk: Impact of a New Curriculum on Sexual Risk-Taking." *Family Planning Perspectives* 23 (6): 253–263.

Kochan, T., Bezrukova, K., Ely, R., Jackson, S., Joshi, A., Jehn, K., Leonard, J., Levine, D., and Thomas, D. (2003). "The Effects of Diversity on Business Performance: Report of the Diversity Research Network." *Human Resource Management* 42 (1): 3–21.

Koegel, P. (1996). "Lessons Learned from the Experiences of Domestic Police and Fire Department." In G. Herek, J. Jibe, and R. Carney (eds.), *Out in Force* (pp. 131–153). Chicago: University of Chicago Press.

Korczynski, M. (2003). "Communities of Coping: Collective Emotional Labor in Service Work." *Organization* 10 (1): 55–79.

Kuehnle, K., and Sullivan, A. (2001). "Patterns of Anti-Gay Violence: An Analysis of Incident Characteristics and Victim Reporting." *Journal of Interpersonal Violence* 16 (9): 928–943.

—— (2003). "Gay and Lesbian Victimization: Reporting Factors in Domestic Violence and Bias Incidents." *Criminal Justice and Behavior* 30 (1): 85–96.

Kurki, L. (2000). "Restorative and Community Justice in the United States." *Crime and Justice: A Review of Research* 27: 235–303.

Langworthy, R., and Travis, L. (1999). *Policing in America: A Balance of Forces.* Upper Saddle River, NJ: Prentice Hall.

Leinen, S. (1984). *Black Police, White Society.* New York: New York University Press.

—— (1993). *Gay Cops.* New Brunswick, NJ: Rutgers University Press.

Leo, R. (1998). *The Miranda Debate: Law, Justice, and Policing.* York, PA: Maple.

Lester, D. (1983). "Why Do People Become Police Officers? A Study of Reasons and Their Predictions of Success." *Journal of Police Science and Administration* 11 (2): 170–174.

Levine, M. (1989). "The Status of Gay Men in the Workplace." In M. Kimmel and M. Messer (eds.), *Men's Lives* (pp. 251–266). New York: Macmillan.

Lewis, G. (2006). "Who Knows Gay People and What Impact Does It Have on Attitudes Toward Homosexuality and Gay Rights?" Paper presented at the annual meeting of the American Political Science Association, Philadelphia, September.

Lewis, G., and Rogers, M. (2000). "Does the Public Support Equal Employment Rights for Gays and Lesbians?" In E. Riddles (ed.), *Gays and Lesbians in the Democratic Process* (pp. 118–145). New York: Columbia University Press.

Lim, N. (2008). *Planning for Diversity: Options and Recommendations for DOD Leaders.* Santa Monica, CA: RAND, National Defense Research Institute.

Lo, M. (2005). "Law and Order Treats Gay Men Fairly." *AfterElton,* June 13. Retrieved March 23, 2011, from www.afterelton.com/archive/elton/TV/2005/6/lawandorder.html.

Loftus, B. (2008). "Dominant Culture Interrupted: Recognition, Resentment, and the Politics of Change in an English Police Force." *British Journal of Criminology* 48 (6): 756–777.

Lombardo, R., Olson, D., and Staton, M. (2010) "The Chicago Alternative Policing Strategy: A Reassessment of the CAPS Program." *Policing: An International Journal of Police Strategies and Management* 33 (4): 586–606.

Lonsway, K., Freeman, L., Cortina, L., Magley, V., and Fitzgerald, L. (2002). "Understanding the Judicial Role in Addressing Gender Bias: A View from the Eighth Circuit Federal Court System." *Law and Social Inquiry* 27 (2): 205–233.

Lyons, P., DeValve, M., and Garner, R. (2008). "Texas Police Chiefs' Attitudes Toward Gay and Lesbian Police Officers." *Police Quarterly* 11 (1): 102–117.

Lyons, W. (2002). "Partnerships, Information, and Public Safety: Community Policing in a Time of Terror." *Policing* 25 (3): 530–542.

Martin, S. (1994). "Outsider Within" the Station House: The Impact of Race and Gender on Black Women Police." *Social Problems* 4 (3): 383–400.

Martin, S., and Jurik, N. (2007). *Doing Justice, Doing Gender.* 2nd ed. Thousand Oaks, CA: Sage.

McCluskey, C. (2004). "Diversity in Policing." *Journal of Ethnicity in Criminal Justice* 2 (3): 67–81.

McManus, J. (2006). "Gay and Christian Police in Row." *BBC News,* July 21. Retrieved July 1, 2010, from http://news.bbc.co.uk/2/hi/uk_news/england /5200962.stm.

McNamara, G., and Bromiley, P. (1997). "Decision Making in an Organizational Setting: Cognitive and Organizational Influences on Risk Assessment in Commercial Lending." *Academy of Management Journal* 40 (4): 1063–1088.

Melloy, K. (2009). "Tampa, Fla. Gets Lesbian Police Chief." *The Edge,* September 18. Retrieved July 1, 2010, from www.edgeboston.com/index.php?ch=news&sc =&sc2=news&sc3=&id=96449.

Menashe, C., and Siegel, M. (1998). "The Power of a Frame: An Analysis of Newspaper Coverage of Tobacco Issues." *Journal of Health Communication* 3 (4): 307–326.

Metropolitan Police (London) (2010). "Diversity." Retrieved July 1, 2010, from www.met.police.uk/dcf/diversity_s.htm.

——— (2011). "History of the Metropolitan Police." Retrieved March 23, 2011, from www.met.police.uk/history/index.htm.

Metropolitan Police Department (MPD) (Washington, D.C.) (2011a). "About the Mission." Retrieved Mach 23, 2011, from http://mpdc.dc.gov/mpdc/cwp/view,a ,1230,Q,537757,mpdcNav_GID,1529,mpdcNav,%7C,.asp.

——— (2011b). "Charles H. Ramsey." Retrieved March 23, 2011, from http://mpdc .dc.gov/mpdc/cwp/view,a,1230,q,537799,mpdcNav_GID,1529,mpdcNav,%7C.asp.

Milgram, D. (2002). "Recruiting Women to Policing: Practical Strategies That Work." *Police Chief* 69 (4): 23–29.

Miller, S. (1999). *Gender and Community Policing: Walking the Talk.* Boston: Northeastern University Press.

Miller, S., Forest, K., and Jurik, N. (2003). "Diversity in Blue: Lesbian and Gay Police Officers in a Masculine Operation." *Men and Masculinities* 5 (4): 355–385.

Mitchell, D. (1992). "Contemporary Police Practices in Domestic Violence Cases: Arresting the Abuser—Is It Enough?" *Journal of Criminal Law and Criminology* 83 (1): 241–249.

Monkkonen, E. (2002). *Crime, Justice, History.* Columbus: Ohio State University Press.

——— (2004). *Police in Urban America, 1860–1920.* New York: Cambridge University Press.

Montgomery, J. (2010). "Police Officer Entry Requirements." Retrieved March 23, 2011, from http://ww2.prospects.ac.uk/p/types_of_job/police_officer_entry _requirements.jsp.

Moon, B., and Hwang, E. (2004). "The Reasons for Choosing a Career in Policing Among South Korean Police Cadets." *Journal of Criminal Justice* 32 (3): 223–229.

Moore, M., Trojanowicz, R., and Kelling, G. (2000). "Crime and Policing." In W. Oliver (ed.), *Community Policing: Classical Readings* (pp. 41–59). Upper Saddle River, NJ: Prentice Hall.

Mullins, W. (1991). "A Predictive Model for the Psychological Selection of Police Officers." Conference paper delivered at the Society of Police and Criminal Psychology, October, Richmond, VA.

Myers, K., Forest, K., and Miller, S. (2004). "Officer Friendly and the Tough Cop: Gays and Lesbians Navigate Homophobia and Policing." *Journal of Homosexuality* 47 (1): 17–37.

National Gay and Lesbian Task Force (2009). "State Nondiscrimination Laws in the U.S." Retrieved September 3, 2007, from www.thetaskforce.org/downloads /reports/issue_maps/non_discrimination_7_08.pdf.

Nelson, T., Clawson, R., and Oxley, Z. (1997). "Media Framing of a Civil Liberties Conflict and Its Effect on Tolerance." *American Political Science Review* 91 (3): 567–583.

New York City Gay Officers Action League (GOAL NY) (2006). "The History of GOAL." Retrieved November 14, 2007, from www.goalny.org/Historyofgoal.pdf.

Niederhoffer, A. (1967). *Behind the Shield.* New York: Doubleday.

Noe, D. (2011). "The Importance of Quality Customer Service." *Helium,* February 3. Retrieved March 23, 2011, from www.helium.com/items/2082797-the-importance-of-quality-customer-service.

Nottinghamshire Police (2010). "Lesbian, Gay, Bisexual and Transgender IAG (LGBT)." Retrieved July 1, 2010, from www.nottinghamshire.police.uk /about/organisation/diversity_in_policing/lgbt.

"Obituary: Lord Scarman" (2004). *The Economist,* December 24. Retrieved March 23, 2011, from www.economist.com/node/3518597?story_id=3518597.

Office for National Statistics (United Kingdom) (2007). "Police Resources: Record Number of Police Officers in 2006." Retrieved March 23, 2011, from www.statistics.gov.uk/cci/nugget.asp?id=1767.

———— (2010). "Population Estimates for U.K., England and Wales, Scotland and Northern Ireland." Retrieved August 10, 2010, from www.statistics.gov.uk /statbase/Product.asp?vlnk=601.

O'Hara, P. (2005). *Why Law Enforcement Organizations Fail: Mapping the Organizational Fault Lines in Policing.* Durham, NC: Carolina Academic Press.

Orrick, D. (2008). *Recruitment, Retention, and Turnover of Police Personnel: Reliable, Practical, and Effective Solutions.* Springfield, IL: Charles C. Thomas.

Paterson, N. (2010). "History of the Metropolitan Police." Retrieved March 23, 2011, from www.met.police.uk/history/index.htm.

Phillips, C. (2007). "The Re-emergence of the 'Black Spectre': Minority Professional Associations in the Post-Macpherson Era." *Ethnic and Racial Studies* 30 (3): 375–396.

Powell, G. (1993). "Promoting Equal Opportunity and Valuing Cultural Diversity." In Gary N. Powell (ed.), *Women and Men in Management* (pp. 225–252). Thousand Oaks, CA: Sage.

Pressman, J., and Wildavsky, A. (1978). *Implementation.* 3rd ed. Los Angeles: University of California Press.

Pride Agenda (2001). "Anti-Gay/Lesbian Discrimination in New York State." Retrieved July 1, 2010, from www.prideagenda.org/portals/0/pdfs/survey.pdf.

Pride Behind the Badge (PBB) (2010). "Pride Behind the Badge." Retrieved July 1, 2010, from http://pbtb.14.forumer.com.

Prince, H. (2003). *Retention and Advancement in the Retail Industry: A Career Ladder Approach.* Boston: Jobs for the Future. Retrieved June 24, 2010, from www.jff.org/publications/workforce/retention-and-advancement-retailindustr/310.

Princeton Survey Research Associates International (2008). *Newsweek* poll, December 3–4. Retrieved July 1, 2010, from www.pollingreport.com/civil.htm.

Purdum, T. (1987). "Homosexuals to Help Police to Recruit Officers." *New York Times,* May 4. Retrieved July 1, 2010, from www.nytimes.com.

"Q&A: Stephen Lawrence Murder" (2004). *BBC News,* May 5. Retrieved March 23, 2011, from http://news.bbc.co.uk/2/hi/uk_news/3685733.stm.

Quindlen, A. (1981). "A Tough Month in the New Life of a Policeman." *New York Times,* December 5. Retrieved July 1, 2010, from www.nytimes.com.

Rabe-Hemp, C. (2008). "Female Officers and the Ethic of Care: Does Officer Gender Impact Police Behaviors?" *Journal of Criminal Justice* 36 (5): 426–443.

Radford, K., Betts, J., and Ostermeyer, M. (2006). *Policing, Accountability, and the Lesbian, Gay, and Bisexual Community in Northern Ireland.* Belfast: Institute for Conflict Research.

Ratcliffe, J. (2008). "Intelligence-Led Policing." Cullompton, Devon, UK: Willan. Retrieved September 21, 2011, from http://jratcliffe.net/research/ilp.htm.

Reiner, R. (1992). *The Politics of Police.* 2nd ed. Toronto: University of Toronto Press.

Riccucci, N., and Gossett, C. (1996). "Employment Discrimination in State and Local Government: The Lesbian and Gay Male Experience." *American Review of Public Administration* 26 (2): 175–200.

Riley, J. (2002). "Minority Recruitment in Criminal Justice." *Criminology and Criminal Justice* 2 (3): 257–276.

Roberg, R., Crank, J., and Kuykendall, J. (2000). *Police and Society.* 2nd ed. Los Angeles: Roxbury.

Rollinson, D., Broadfield, A., and Edwards, D. (1998). *Organizational Behavior and Analysis.* Essex: Longman.

Rowe, M. (2007). *Policing Beyond Macpherson: Issues in Policing, Race, and Society.* Portland, OR: Wilan.

Ruggiero, K., Mitchell, J., Krieger, N., Marx, D., and Lorenzo, M. (2000). "Now You See It, Now You Don't: Explicit Versus Implicit Measures of the Personal/Group Discrimination Discrepancy." *Psychological Science* 11 (6): 511–514.

Rumens, N. (2008). "The Complexities of Friendship: Exploring How Gay Men Make Sense of Their Workplace Friendships with Straight Women." *Culture and Organization* 14 (1): 79–95.

Schmidt, S. (2007). "The Relationship Between Satisfaction with Workplace Training and Overall Job Satisfaction." *Human Resource Development Quarterly* 18 (4): 481–498.

Schneider, A., and Ingram, H. (1993). "Social Construction of Target Populations." *American Political Science Review* 87 (2): 334–347.

Scott, J., Duffee, D., and Renauer, B. (2003). "Measuring Police-Community Coproduction: The Utility of Community Policing Case Studies." *Police Quarterly* 6 (4): 410–439.

Seibert, S. (1999). "The Effectiveness of Facilitated Mentoring: A Longitudinal Quasi-Experiment." *Journal of Vocational Behavior* 54 (3): 483–502.

Seklecki, R., and Paynich, R. (2007). "A National Survey of Female Police Officers: An Overview of Findings." *Police Practice and Research* 8 (1): 17–30.

"Sergeant Craig Gilmore" (2010). *The Bill Biographies*. Retrieved March 23, 2011, from http://thebillbios.co.uk/gilmore.htm.

Shallenberg, D. (1994). "Professional and Openly Gay: A Narrative Study of the Experience." *Journal of Management Inquiry* 3 (2): 119–142.

Sheehan, K. (2001). "E-Mail Survey Response Rates: A Review." *Journal of Computer-Mediated Communication* 6 (2). Retrieved November 7, 2011, from http://jcmc.indiana.edu/vol6/issue2/sheehan.html.

Shoffman, M. (2006). "Gay Community Faces 'Police Liaison Lottery.'" *Pink News,* December 27. Retrieved July 1, 2007. from www.eurogaycops.com/index2php ?option#com_content&task#view&id#39&p.

Simon, H., and Daly, E. (1992). "Sexual Orientation and Workplace Rights: A Potential Land Mine for Employers?" *Employee Relations Law Journal* 18 (1): 29–60.

Sklansky, D. (2006). "Not Your Father's Police Department: Making Sense of the New Demographics of Law Enforcement." *Journal of Criminal Law and Criminology* 96 (3): 1209–1243.

Smith, S., and Aamodt, M. (1997). "The Relationship Between Education, Experience, and Police Performance." *Journal of Police and Criminal Psychology* 12 (2): 7–14.

Smith, T., and Ingersoll, R. (2004). "What Are the Effects of Induction and Mentoring on Beginning Teacher Turnover?" *American Educational Research Journal* 41 (3): 681–714.

Southern Poverty Law Center (2003). "Disposable People." *Intelligence Report* no. 112 (Winter). Retrieved July 1, 2010, from www.splcenter.org/get -informed/intelligence-report/browse-all-issues/2003/winter/disposable -people?page=0,2.

Staffordshire Police (2011). "Equality and Diversity Monitoring Report, 2009–2010." Retrieved March 23, 2011, from www.staffordshire.police.uk/media/10810 /annual_reports/pdf/Equality_and_Diversity_0910.pdf.

Staiger, D., Auerbach, D., and Buerhaus, P. (2000). "Implications of a Rapidly Aging Registered Nurse Workforce." *Journal of the American Medical Association* 283 (22): 2948–2954.

Stiffler, S. (2010). "Police LGBT Liaison Units: How Effective Are They?" *The Edge,* February 16. Retrieved July 1, 2010, from www.edgeboston.com /index.php?ch=news&sc=&sc2=news&sc3=&id=102392.

Stockdale, M., and Crosby, F. (2004). *The Psychology and Management of Workplace Diversity.* Malden, MA: Blackwell.

Stolberg, G. (2010). "After Fall of 'Don't Ask,' Pushing for 'I Do.'" *New York Times,* December 20. Retrieved March 23, 2011, from www.nytimes.com /2010/12/21/us/politics/21rights.html.

Stonewall (2010). "Workplace Equality Index 2010." Retrieved July 1, 2010, from www.stonewall.org.uk/workplace.

"Stonewall Rebellion" (2009). *New York Times,* April 10. Retrieved March 23, 2011, from http://topics.nytimes.com/topics/reference/timestopics/subjects/s /stonewall_rebellion/index.html.

Storry, M., and Childs, P. (2002). *British Cultural Identities.* London: Routledge.

Sudetic, C. (1996). "Gay and Lesbian Officers Suing the Police for Bias." *New York Times,* April 4. Retrieved July 1, 2010, from www.nytimes.com/1996 /04/04/nyregion/gay-and-lesbian-officers-suing-the-police-for-bias.html.

Sun, I., and Triplett, R. (2008). "Differential Perceptions of Neighborhood Problems by the Police and Residents: The Impact of Neighborhood-Level Characteristics." *Policing: An International Journal of Police Strategies and Management* 31 (3): 435–455.

Tatchell, P. (2010). "The Gay Liberation Front's Social Revolution." *The Guardian,* October 12. Retrieved March 23, 2011, from www.guardian.co.uk/comment isfree/2010/oct/12/gay-liberation-front-social-revolution.

Taylor, D., et al. (1990). "The Personal/Group Discrimination Discrepancy: Perceiving My Group, but Not Myself, to Be a Target for Discrimination." *Personality and Social Psychology Bulletin* 16 (2): 254–262.

Taylor, F. (1911). *The Principles of Scientific Management.* New York: Harper and Brothers.

Taylor, V., and Raeburn, N. (1995). "Identity Politics as High-Risk Activism: Career Consequences for Lesbian, Gay, and Bisexual Sociologists." *Social Problems* 42: 252–273.

Thomas, R. (1996). *Redefining Diversity.* New York: AMACOM.

——— (2006). *Building on the Promise of Diversity.* New York: AMACOM.

Travis. L., and Langworthy, R. (2007). *Policing in America: A Balance of Forces.* 4th edition. Prentice Hall: Upper Saddle River, NJ.

Trojanowicz, R., Kappeler, V., Gaines, L., Bucqueroux, B., and Sluder, R. (1998). *Community Policing: A Contemporary Perspective.* 2nd ed. National Criminal Justice Reference Service. Retrieved September 21, 2011, from www.ncjrs.gov/App/Publications/abstract.aspx?ID=174124.

Truckenbrodt, Y. (2000). "The Relationship Between Leader-Member Exchange and Commitment and Organizational Citizenship Behavior." *Acquisition Review Quarterly* (Summer): 233–244.

"UK: When Soaps Go Gay: A 'Briefish' History of Gay Storylines" (2010). Actup.org. October 22. Retrieved March 23, 2011, from www.actup.org/forum /content/uk-when-soaps-go-gay-briefish-history-gay-storylines-2264.

US Bureau of Labor Statistics (2009). "Highlights of Women's Earnings in 2009." Report no. 1025. Retrieved March 23, 2011, from www.bls.gov/cps /cpswom2009.pdf.

US Census Bureau (2010). "2010 Census Data." Retrieved November 7, 2011, from http://2010.census.gov/2010census/data/index.php.

US Conference of Mayors (2000). "The Influence of Community Policing in City Governments: A 282-City Survey." Washington, DC.

US Department of Commerce (2010). "Occupational Safety and Health (OSH) Program." Retrieved July 1, 2010, from http://hr.commerce.gov/s/groups/public /@doc/@cfoasa/@ohrm/documents/content/dev01_006463.pdf.

US Department of Justice (2010). "About Crime in the U.S. (CIUS)." Retrieved November 7, 2011, from www2.fbi.gov/ucr/cius2010/data/table_74.html.

―――― (2011). "FY 2012 Performance Budget." Office of Community Oriented Policing Services. Retrieved November 13, 2011, from http://bjs.ojp.usdoj.gov /content/pub/pdf/tle08.pdf.

US Government Accountability Office (1997, 2000, 2002). "Sexual Orientation–Based Employment Discrimination: States' Experience with Statutory Prohibitions." Report nos. OGC-98-7R (1997), OGC-00-27R (2000), 02-878R (2002). Washington, DC.

US Office of Personnel Management (2008). "Best Practices: Mentoring." Retrieved March 23, 2011, from www.opm.gov/hrd/lead/BestPractices-Mentoring.pdf.

Van Hoye, G., and Lievens, F. (2003). "The Effects of Sexual Orientation on Hirability Ratings: An Experimental Study." *Journal of Business and Psychology* 18 (1): 15–30.

Vaughan, E., and Seifert, M. (1992). "Variability in the Framing of Risk Issues." *Journal of Social Issues* 48: 119–135.

Wagenaar, A., and Streff, F. (1990). "Public Opinion on Alcohol Policies." *Journal of Public Health Policy* 11: 189–205.

Wainewright, W. (2011). "Born Again Brixton." *The Times.* Retrieved November 6, 2011, from http://willwainewright.files.wordpress.com/2011/06/tim041 gt081.pdf.

Walker, S. (1977). *A Critical History of Police Reform: The Emergence of Professionalism.* Lexington, MA: Lexington Books.

―――― (1985). "Racial Minorities and Female Employment in Policing: The Implication of 'Glacial Change.'" *Crime and Delinquency* 31: 555–572.

―――― (1992). "Public Solidly Favors Mixed Police/Civilian Review Boards." *Law Enforcement News* 8: 19–49.

―――― (1999). *The Police in America.* 3rd ed. Boston: McGraw-Hill College.

Warn, S. (2004). "Fall 2004 TV Preview." *AfterEllen,* September. Retrieved March 23, 2011, from www.afterellen.com/archive/ellen/TV/92004/fall.html.

Weatherburn, P., Reid, D., Hammond, G., and Stephens, M. (2005). "Risk and Reflexion: Findings from the United Kingdom Gay Men's Sex Survey, 2004." London: Sigma Research. Retrieved July 1, 2010, from www.sigmaresearch.org .uk/downloads/report05c.pdf.

White, M. (2008). "The Political Life of Brian." *The Guardian,* January 14. Accessed on July 27, 2010, at www.guardian.co.uk/commentisfree/2008/jan/14 /thepoliticallifeofbrian.

White, R., and Perrone, S. (2005). *Crime and Social Control.* London: Oxford University Press.

Wickberg, D. (2000). "Homophobia: On the Cultural History of an Idea." *Critical Inquiry* 27 (1): 42–57.

Wilkins, V., and Williams, B. (2005). "Black or Blue: Racial Profiling and Representative Bureaucracy." Presentation at the Eighth Public Management Research Conference, Los Angeles, September 29–October 2.

Williams, M., and Robinson, A. (2004). "Problems and Prospects with Policing the Lesbian, Gay, and Bisexual Community in Wales." *Policing and Society: An International Journal of Research and Policy* 14 (3): 213–232.

Willis, P. (1977). *Learning to Labor.* New York: Columbia University Press.

Wilson, J. (2010). *Police Recruitment and Retention for the New Millennium: The State of Knowledge.* Santa Monica, CA: RAND.

Wilson, J., and Kelling, G. (1982). "Broken Windows." *Atlantic Monthly,* March. Retrieved July 1, 2010, from www.sog.unc.edu/programs/mcap/pdfs /LawEnforcement.pdf.

Wilson, O. (1950). *Police Administration.* New York: McGraw-Hill.

Wiltshire Constabulary (2005). "Policy Statement on Homophobic and Transphobic Incidents." Retrieved July 1, 2010, from http://wiltshire.police.uk/index.php ?option=com_docman&task=doc_download&gid=95&Itemid=390.

——— (2010). "About Us" Retrieved July 1, 2010, from www.wiltshire.police.uk /index.php?option=com_content&view=article&id=202&Itemid=381.

Yang, A. (1999). *From Wrongs to Rights, 1973 to 1999: Public Opinion on Gay and Lesbian Americans Moves Toward Equality.* New York: National Gay and Lesbian Task Force.

Yearwood, D., and Freeman, S. (2004). "Analyzing Concerns Among Police Administrators: Recruitment and Retention of Police Officers in North Carolina." *Police Chief* 71 (3): 43–49.

Younglove, J., Kerr, M., and Vitello, C. (2002). "Law Enforcement Officers' Perceptions of Same-Sex Domestic Violence: Reason for Cautious Optimism." *Journal of Interpersonal Violence* 17 (7): 760–772.

Index

About the Book

Roddrick Colvin assesses the impact of lesbian and gay police officers on law enforcement in the United States and the United Kingdom, as well as the policies that enable a diverse work environment.

Colvin tracks the evolution of police agencies toward being more gay-friendly both as employers and as service providers. He also provides insights into the day-to-day barriers and opportunities that lesbian and gay officers experience working within organizations that traditionally have been hostile to them. Integrating quantitative and qualitative research, he offers a compelling demonstration that police agencies can best fulfill their missions when they are representative of the communities they serve.

Roddrick Colvin is associate professor of public administration in the department of public management at John Jay College of Criminal Justice, City University of New York.